War, Peace, and
Prosperity in the
Name of God

War, Peace, and Prosperity in the Name of God

The Ottoman Role in Europe's Socioeconomic Evolution

MURAT IYIGUN

The University of Chicago Press   Chicago and London

MURAT IYIGUN is professor of economics at the University of Colorado Boulder.

The University of Chicago Press, Chicago 60637
The University of Chicago Press, Ltd., London

Printed in the United States of America

24 23 22 21 20 19 18 17 16 15   1 2 3 4 5

ISBN-13: 978-0-226-38843-4 (cloth)
ISBN-13: 978-0-226-23228-7 (e-book)

DOI: 10.7208/chicago/9780226232287.001.0001

Library of Congress Cataloging-in-Publication Data

Iyigun, Murat, author.
    War, peace, and prosperity in the name of God : the Ottoman
role in Europe's socioeconomic evolution / Murat Iyigun.
        pages cm
    Includes bibliographical references and index.
    ISBN 978-0-226-38843-4 (cloth : alkaline paper)
    ISBN 978-0-226-23228-7 (e-book)
        1. Economics—Religious aspects—History.   2. Monotheism—
Influence.   3. Religion and politics—History.   I. Title.

    HB72.I95 2015
    201'.73—dc23 ' 2014031883

♾ This paper meets the requirements of ANSI/NISO Z39.48-1992 (Permanence of Paper).

Mustafa Kemal'in ve Anadolu'nun
örnek evladı Şemsi İyigün'ün anısına . . .

Contents

Preface

Human rationality and enlightenment might have well bequeathed modern economic prosperity and hitherto unprecedented standards of living in some parts of the world today. But it is hard to deny that religious beliefs have had a profound impact on how societies and polities evolved historically. Differences in those beliefs have also produced some of the nastiest confrontations in human history, especially among the adherents of the big three monotheisms: Judaism, Christianity, and Islam. As we painfully continue to observe in the twenty-first century, differences of faith and religion are often still enough to evoke political tension and seemingly unresolvable conflict. And, time and again, the One God/One True Faith duality inherent in monotheisms in particular continues to provide an essential backdrop against which some societies and groups view the world.

To sociologists, political scientists, and philosophers, this has been all too obvious, with each field having a long and cherished tradition of exploring the role of religion in sociopolitical and economic change. For development economists and economic historians, however, religion has more or less remained a *sacred* topic. To be sure, none other than Adam Smith weighed in on this topic in *The Wealth of Nations* ([1776] 2001). It is also true that there exists a small but nascent economics strand that has taken religion seriously. Those exceptions notwithstanding, it is fair to say that the economics literature on religion's role in conflict, economic history, and development still remains thin.

In this day and age, when faith and religion delineate societies along political, social, and economic fissures and provide a backdrop for some pivotal global confrontations, I believe it is incumbent upon the economics profession to make more headway in the nexus of faith, conflict, and economic development.

I have penned this book with such an objective and as an attempt to *identify* and *quantify* the historical role of religion in sociopolitics and economics. My obvious hope in this venture is that the literatures I invoke, the tools I utilize, and the evidence I offer stand on their own merit. Nonetheless, with socially delicate and risky, third-rail ventures such as this, I believe it is requisite to clarify at the outset the modus operandi. Mine was simple: in all that follows, I adopted a *functionalist* view in that my perspective was driven by the social, political, and economic functions of religion—nothing more and, hopefully, nothing less.

Moreover, while this subject matter involves some grandiose, contentious, and often sensitive topics, the book is also intended to have a narrow and simple focus. As such, it is my scholarly imperative to impart what the book is really *not* about.

For starters, this book is not a statement on the contemporaneous status of "underdevelopment" of Muslim countries vis-à-vis the West. To be sure, there is some cursory material below devoted to the sociopolitical and economic differences between the West and the Near East from a comparative perspective. I have included this material mainly for contextual purposes and not so much because what lies ahead can satisfactorily speak to the issue of why the West took off with the Industrial Revolution and Dar al-Islam stagnated in a comparative sense. Instead, to the extent that the themes throughout involve religion, conflict, and sociopolitical as well as economic change, the first-order goal is to identify the role of faith-based effects in the historical evolutions of societies, sociopolitically and economically. There might very well have been manifold mechanisms and channels through which those first-order effects persisted to underlie the existing economic and sociopolitical differences between the West and Near East, and some later sections of the book do address them in some superficial fashion.

Implicit in this claim is the fact that the book is also not about the narrowly defined contemporary measures of economic well-being, such as incomes per capita, literacy, life expectancy, infant mortality, or health. As the topic dictates, the time frame of analysis throughout typically covers from four and a half millennia ago to the late seventeenth and early eighteenth centuries, a time interval for which such data are hard if not impossible to come by. The upshot of all this is that most if not all the ideas I espouse in this book have well-articulated historical precedents in the writings of historians, philosophers, and theologians, some of whom deliberated the functional aspects of faith and religion in the broader terms of political, social, economic stability and strength. It is partly on this basis that, when matters revolve around economic development in this book, they typically and unabashedly emphasize the sociopolitical stability, endurance, and geographic size of ancient civilizations, in addition to the degree to which internal peace was sustained among and within social groups and polities.

This book may well have a simple and narrow-minded focus. Still, it is not meant to be a tomb of monocausal explanations. It is my obvious hope that there are some clear and interesting issues on which this book can shed some light, but I neither believe nor mean to convey that ramifications and manifestations of faith and religious identity were the most important, let alone the sole, determinant of the sociopolitical and economic developments discussed here.

In essence, this book is about three critical questions that blend the functionalist aspects of religion with the evolution of human societies: Why and how did political power and organized religion become so swiftly and successfully intertwined? What has been the role of religion in conflict historically? And what were some of the sociopolitical, demographic, and economic effects of religiously motivated conflicts?

Faith and religion have played a pivotal role in societies historically, but the era between 800 BCE and 600 CE has been particularly prolific in the advent of new faiths and spiritual belief systems. All three Abrahamic monotheist religions—Judaism, Christianity, and Islam—were born during this period, which the German philosopher Karl Jaspers labeled the *Axial Age*. What is remarkable is the extent to which organized religion—especially Christianity and Islam and, to a lesser extent, Judaism—spread among the polities in the Old World within a relatively short course of time. This might have been quite possibly a manifestation of some of the comparative advantages inherent to monotheistic faiths.

Nevertheless, many if not most monotheistic faiths are about One True God, and they are pillared, at least implicitly, on One True Religion, too. Take these mutually exclusive claims in tandem with a potent and compelling creed and, sooner or later, you have adherent masses of the faithful contending with each other. The facts available illustrate that, once monotheisms were pitted against one another as a consequence, *differences among* them were strong enough to typically trump and relegate *disagreements within* them. And, insofar as Europe and the Middle East are concerned, I will verify that such dynamics did have some serious and lasting repercussions for the organization of societies as well as their polities.

The book is divided into four parts. The preliminary one covers the stand-alone chapter 1, which sets the background with a comprehensive discussion of the literature on the role of religion in sociopolitical organization and centralized government. Sociologists, in particular, had much to say about the role of religion and whether moral as well as ethical considerations associated with faith serve as a *foundation for social stability*. A strand within sociology, in fact, has promoted the notion that monotheism was particularly effective in serving this function. Political scientists, on the other hand, homed in on the extent to which ecclesiastical and political power complemented each other in influencing the efficacy of centralized government. They also extensively documented the degree to which religious rivalries or affinities, especially those involving the three major Abrahamic, monotheistic faiths, produced and sustained violent conflicts throughout history.

Part 2 contains two chapters, which deal with how political authority and organized religions interacted historically, conferring societies some sociopolitical advantages. Chapter 2 begins by establishing the extent and speed with which Abrahamic monotheisms spread around the globe between the eighth and fifteenth centuries CE. The chapter then documents how monotheist societies—in particular, those that adhered to Christianity and Islam—flourished and prospered, perhaps on the back of various sociopolitical, functionalist advantages of monotheism.

Chapter 3 documents and discusses the chronologies of Judaism, Christianity, and Islam, subsequent to their births. While these religions shared a lot in common, there were salient differences among them as well, especially in how they evolved in medieval societies. But one common trait has consistently been their adherents' zeal and motivation for actively promoting the teachings of One True God. And the success of monotheisms in spreading and generating stability and durability for sociopolitical systems meant that, sooner or later, civilizations associated with Judaism, Christianity, and Islam would be in direct confrontation.

Part 3 includes four chapters that explore the association between cooperation, conflict, and religion. Collectively they document the extent to which monotheisms intensified and prolonged interfaith conflicts among their adherents. As a corollary, they also show that interfaith conflicts often subdued and relegated intrareligious feuds.

In order to provide an analytical foundation for the discussions that follow, chapter 4 introduces a simple conceptual framework that emphasizes the role of cultural affiliation—in particular, that of religious affinity—in cooperation and conflict. The framework is intended to identify the conditions under which external threats encourage within-group cooperation instead of intensifying existing domestic conflicts.

The rivalry of the Ottoman Turks with European secular and ecclesiastical authorities during the fifteenth and sixteenth centuries is the epitome of such conflicts. In no small part due to that religious and geopolitical rivalry did the Ottoman Empire have a profound and lasting impact in Europe, the Middle East, and North Africa, especially during the apogee of its power between the fifteenth and seventeenth centuries. Chapter 5 reviews the rise of the Ottoman Empire in the fourteenth century and documents the extent to which it became a serious threat to Europe. As we will see, differences of faith had a lot to do with how Ottomans and Europeans viewed each other. This manifested in the main imperial objectives of the early Ottoman rulers and had its earlier precursors in the Holy Crusades the Europeans organized against the Muslims between the eleventh and thirteenth centuries.

In their early heydays, the Ottomans ignored Europe as a cultural and economic backwater, but they began to reluctantly yet sluggishly emulate it starting in the eighteenth century, when the social, economic, and political gap between their empire and European societies started to become undeniable. This much is common knowledge. What is less obvious is the extent to which the Ottomans influenced some key developments in Europe. And while social scientists have, for the most part, been intrigued by the extent to which religion influences conflict and cooperation, there is a broader and equally relevant issue for economists: if religious affiliation helps sustain cooperation in the face of existential threats, were there historical instances in which religiously distinct threats drove internal coexistence and supported sociopolitical and economic change?

To that end, it is important to acknowledge that there were various challenges to the ecclesiastical monopoly of the Roman Catholic Church in the fourteenth and fifteenth centuries, but neither of those movements got off the ground. In contrast, the birth, survival, and growth of Protestantism in the sixteenth century and subsequently of its various offshoots, such as Zwinglianism, Calvinism, and Anabaptism, came to represent a watershed in European history. But how did Lutheranism and its offshoots proliferate, whereas previous reform attempts failed?

The conventional historiography attributes Lutheranism's rise and spread to the invention of the printing press some sixty years prior to the appearance of Martin Luther at the doorsteps of the castle church in Wittenberg in 1517. Accordingly, there may not have been a reformation without the printing press—at least, not the one sparked off by Martin

Luther. Nevertheless, some historians challenge this monocausal view and claim that the Muslim Ottomans' military prowess and its European conquests also aided and abetted the survival and spread of the Protestant Reformation in Europe. Chapter 6 discusses the ways in which the Ottomans might have aided the Protestants. Some authors, for instance, have emphasized that Ottomans' European moves factored in the bargaining between the German Protestant leaders, on the one hand, and the Holy Roman emperor, the king of the Hapsburgs, and the Catholic pope, on the other. Some others have noted that the Ottomans' lopsided victories against the Hapsburgs in the early sixteenth century turned into a bargaining chip for the budding Protestants, who were more than eager to exploit and capitalize on it. All this was playing out when none other than Martin Luther himself announced that the brutal Ottoman Turks pounding away on Europe's eastern frontiers were nothing but Christians' divine punishment for straying from the true faith and the divine path.

Chapter 6 proceeds with an analysis of the extent to which Ottomans' European conquests influenced intra-European violent confrontations and, in particular, those between the Protestant reformers and the Catholic counterreformers. As we will see, the intensity of military engagements between the Protestant reformers and the Counter-Reformation forces did depend negatively on Ottomans' military activities in Europe. There is some solid statistical evidence that the Ottomans' military conquests influenced the length of intra-European feuds as well. Moreover, the impact of the Ottomans' ventures in Europe seems not to have weakened and persisted with distance from the Ottoman frontier, although the influence of Ottomans on intra-European conflicts was waning over time, and it dissipated completely around the late sixteenth century or the early seventeenth century.

Religious and ethnic identities colored Ottoman-European political discourse and interactions in other, subtler ways, too. Chapter 7 explores the Ottomans' unique imperial history to examine the influence of state ideologies versus that of ethno-religious ties in perpetuating or diverting conflicts and war. Ottoman history is relevant for this quest because its ideology of *holy war* in the name of Islam against the West is often put forward as the reason the Ottomans initiated more conflicts in the West. And another—not necessarily mutually exclusive—hypothesis claims that the imperial harem wielded considerable political power in Ottoman affairs. Moreover, within a fairly swift period of time following its foundation, the empire became a multiethnic and multireligious civilization, with many important posts within the military, administrative, and palace hierarchies routinely being held by converts to Islam from the Balkans, the Mediterranean, and the Black Sea.

In this light, it is most germane that, of the thirty-one sultans who ruled the empire between 1400 CE and 1909 CE, all but six had non-Turkish or non-Islamic matrilineal backgrounds. For a powerful empire whose early motives might have included holy war, this ethnic diversity can be put to good use to explore the relationship between religious identity and persistence of conflict. Doing so reveals that Ottomans' imperial objectives, as exemplified by Gaza, were important for conquests and wars but they were not sufficient. What also mattered almost as much were the sultans' ethno-religious identities, with the reign of a sultan with a European and Christian maternal background being enough to offset most of the empire's western orientation in imperial expansion.

In culmination, part 4 accounts for the longer-term ramifications of religiously motivated conflicts and cooperation on demographic, socio-political, and economic organization. For example, religious and ethnic fractionalizations play prominent roles in the empirical growth and development literature and have been repeatedly shown to have a wide array of effects. In various studies, ethnolinguistic differences have been identified as having detrimental effects on sociopolitical cohesion, the quality of political institutions, and long-run economic growth. Despite the importance of social fractionalization on various economic and political outcomes, we know very little about how and why societies became fractionalized in the first place. Chapter 8 documents that religious fractionalization is, at least in part, an artifact of the history of conflicts, with countries in which more Christian on Muslim wars unfolded historically between 1400 CE and 1900 CE reflecting more religious homogeneity today. Chapter 9 then establishes that the longer-term history and patterns of conflict also came to bear on political borders in the modern world.

Chapters 10 and 11 then turn to a review of how religious identity and rivalry affected developments in Europe and the Middle East from a comparative perspective. As a matter of fact, while conflict and violent struggles were sustained between Islamic and Christian powers of Europe, the Middle East, and North Africa, religious coexistence and acceptance spread within Europe. Thus religious pluralism within Christianity accompanied European political fragmentation and competition, and it preceded the run-up to the continent's economic takeoff, whereas, as covered in the final chapter of the book, interfaith differences were an important factor in the various reactions of the Islamic world to Europe's economic rise.

The organization of the book is such that some chapters, such as 2, 4, and 6 through 9, are fundamentally based on quantitative and statistical analyses. However, in order to make the book more widely accessible, I have relegated all such technical material to online appendices and referred the readers to these sources as well as the relevant articles published in peer-reviewed professional outlets and working papers.

As the book progresses, the readers will also notice that the emphasis varies a great deal, with a more general treatment of Judaism, Christianity, and Islam in the early portion giving way to documentation and analysis predominantly of the relationship between Christianity and Islam. This evolution, in part, mirrors the historical record and the fact that the pivotal confrontations of faith or those involving it between the fifteenth and the eighteenth centuries often took place between Islamic and Christian societies.

This project got off the ground, matured, and culminated with the support, encouragement, and guidance of a lot of people. In this regard, I am truly indebted to the University of Chicago Press and my senior editors, David Pervin and Joe Jackson. Their patience and optimism, as well as efforts to keep me honest and coherent, were instrumental for seeing this venture through.

My true introduction to economics was at Brown University as a graduate student in the mid-1990s. The late Herschel Grossman was my advisor at Brown and some of the conceptual material throughout draws on his contributions to the field of political economy. I learned from Herschel the value of unusual insight and a passion for and a devotion to all things economics and politics.

Joel Mokyr of Northwestern University and Avner Greif of Stanford set the "gold standard" in economic history, and Timur Kuran of Duke has expanded our understanding of Islam and economics as no other scholar ever has. I am lucky and extremely grateful for their support and guidance, as well as their detailed but constructive critique of my earlier manuscript drafts. For their detailed feedback and comments, I also owe much intellectual gratitude to two anonymous reviewers; my colleagues at the University of Colorado, Lee Alston, Ann Carlos, Wolfgang Keller, and Carol Shiue; as well as Professor Emeritus of Sociology and Education at Brown University, John Modell. I could not have seen this ambitious undertaking through to its culmination without all their support and critical input.

Over the years, I have worked with a number of mentors, coauthors, colleagues, and students without whom my professional journey would have been neither complete nor rewarding. On this score, I thank Avner Greif at Stanford, Nathan Nunn at Harvard, Nancy Qian at Yale, Ann Owen at Hamilton College, Pinar Dogan at the Harvard Kennedy School, Andrew Levin at the Federal Reserve Board, Naci Mocan at Louisiana State, Oded Galor and David Weil at Brown, Galina An at Kenyon College, Maggie Chen at George Washington University, Dustin Frye, Tim Larsen at Colorado, and Erin Fletcher (with whom I collaborated to produce the material in chapters 8 and 9). I also thank Joshua Schabla for research support in the critical closing phases of this project, as well as Jillian Tsui at the University of Chicago Press for guiding me through the final editorial and production stages.

The foundations of this book are based on a research agenda that I have pursued on and off during the last decade. As part of that endeavor, I also produced a few academic papers, with which I received invaluable help from a number of friends and scholars. They include Ron Findlay at Columbia University; Rachel MacCleary and Robert Barro at Harvard University; Jared Rubin at Chapman University; Yadira de Gonzales de Lara at the European University Institute; Alan Olmstead, Peter Lindert, and Gregory Clark at the University of California at Davis; John Wallis at Maryland; and Philip Hoffman at Caltech. I am grateful for their input and suggestions for improvement.

Since 2003, I have had the good fortune of working with Pierre-Andre Chiappori of Columbia University and Yoram Weiss of the University of Tel Aviv. My collaboration with them focuses on family economics and has little to no overlap with the central themes of this book. Nonetheless, working with them has shown me what gifted minds, devotion to detail, and passion for work can do.

I have known Dani Rodrik of the Institute for Advanced Study in Princeton since 1998, although it wasn't until another five years before we reconnected and collaborated on a project. What makes Dani a special scholar is his effortless combination of a powerful intellect with an open-mindedness that is quite unique in our profession. I am indebted to him for many detailed suggestions and comments on various drafts of this book.

I am grateful to my sisters, Gülesin Pinar and Gülsevin Roberts, and my brothers-in-law, Halit Pinar and Tom Roberts, for their unwavering support and encouragement. I am married to my high school sweetheart, Oya Iyigun, who has been my guiding light for over a quarter century. I am indebted to her for editing and proofreading various versions of the book draft. Oya and I have been blessed with two extraordinary daughters, Erin and Dora Iyigun. Watching them grow up to become remarkable individuals has been my ultimate gift in life.

I will forever be grateful to my parents, Ayten and Şemsi İyigün, who, during their sixty-two years of marriage, set an example of happiness, integrity, and endless intellectual curiosity. This book is dedicated to my father, who passed away in November 2011.

PART ONE

The Preliminaries

ONE

Societies, Polities, and Religion

If the modern lexicon reflects a ubiquitous and prominent role for religion in social organization, it is somewhat evolved from its maiden precursors, which essentially emerged with the Enlightenment. Nowadays, we may debate whether "culture matters" for human progress or whether, in the post–Cold War world, geopolitics are defined on the basis of the fundamental cultural rifts that exist among "civilizations." But the essence of it all rests on a *functionalist perspective*, according to which the social scientist or the casual observer remains—pardon the early pun—agnostic with respect to everything else except the sociopolitical functions of cultures, ideologies, or religion.

This much is clear: a functionalist perspective on the matters of faith arrived neither naturally nor expeditiously in the West. Many key actors of the Enlightenment were nothing if not pious men. Still they lived in an era when seismic shifts in mentality were taking place, with inquiries on the ecclesiastical subjects becoming increasingly more tolerated. One has to put in this context the pursuits of the men of the Enlightenment to comprehend and tally the extent to which religious beliefs and adherence influenced the sociopolitical realm.

In this opening chapter, I will first set the necessary background by reviewing the relevant literature on the role of religion in sociopolitical organization and centralized government. As I will establish shortly, sociologists especially honed in on whether religious, moral, and ethical considerations associated with faith serve as a *foundation for social stability*. A strand within sociology, in particular, has promoted the notion that monotheism was particularly effective in serving this function. By contrast, political scientists have emphasized the extent to which ecclesiastical and political power complemented each other in influencing the efficacy of centralized government. They have also extensively documented the degree to which religious rivalries or affinities, especially those involving the three major Abrahamic, monotheistic faiths, produced and sustained violent conflicts throughout history. Following this lead, this chapter establishes some fundamental historical and statistical facts that will help put the rest of this book in comparative perspective.

1.1 Faith and Social Order

Progressive thinkers of the post-Enlightenment era, such as Émile Durkheim, Auguste Comte, and David Hume, were mostly of the view that spiritual faith and religion would experience an inevitable decline in the face of scientific and technological advances. Their presumed tradeoff between faith and education was later dubbed the *secularization hypothesis*. More important for the purposes of what lies ahead is the fact that such progressives also articulated in detail the social functions of faith and religion. According to Hume (1911), for example, benevolence and moral considerations associated with religion are the pillars of social harmony and stability. And Durkheim (1915) saw in group and social cohesion the manifestations of religious practices, norms, and rituals.

In the 1930s, the *structural-functionalist* school, led by Talcott Parsons, began to assert that the cohesion of societies depended on their members sharing a common purpose, conceptions of morality, and an identity. In this, they were adhering to Durkheim, who saw these social necessities in religion. Whether a shared religion or credence enhances social cohesion is debatable; "social cohesion" itself is an abstraction. For what it's worth, however, Stark (2001, p. 245) does point out that the United States, which is religiously tolerant and pluralistic, is also "socially cohesive" as well as quite nationalistic.

Nevertheless, one can think of less abstract functions of religious beliefs and adherence, such as the sustenance of social order via individual moral self-restraint. As Reinhold Niebuhr (1932, p. 20) eloquently puts it, for instance, societies' survival depends on their efficacy in eliminating—or, at the very least, holding in check—all forms of self-serving violence: "The problem which society faces is clearly one of reducing force by increasing the factors which make for a moral and rational adjustment of life to life: of bringing such force as is still necessary under responsibility of the whole society; of destroying the kind of power which cannot be made socially responsible (the power which resides in economic ownership for example); and of bringing forces of moral self-restraint to bear upon types of power which can never be brought completely under social control."

Human beings are genetically encoded to survive, which is manifested in their *will to live*. But, according to Niebuhr, that same survival instinct easily morphs into "will to power" because individuals recognize that social, political, and economic power can enhance survival. Since social stability requires the elimination of violence and anarchy and the abuse of various types of power, one way to attain that stability and equilibrium is through the moral self-restraint that religions offer:

Essentially religion is a sense of the absolute. When, as is usually the case, the absolute is imagined in terms of man's own highest ethical aspirations, a perspective is created from which all moral achievements are judged to be inadequate. Viewed from the relative perspectives of the historic scene, there is no human action which cannot be justified in terms of some historic purpose or approved in comparison with some less virtuous action. The absolute reference of religion eliminates these partial perspectives and premature justifications. . . . The history of religion is proof of the efficacy of religious insights in making men conscious of the sinfulness of their preoccupation with self. (Niebuhr, 1932, pp. 52, 55)

As Ekelund et al. (1996) and Ekelund and Tollison (2011) have argued, it is important to bear in mind that religious services involve metacredence goods. That is, they are in the class of products whose quality cannot be ascertained objectively and certainly even after purchase. And the long-term survival and success of belief systems depend on how easily they can establish credence.

What is clear is that religion is a collective consumption good with large network externalities—that is, individuals' satisfaction from its use depends on others' participation and adherence (Janeba, 2007). It is generally difficult to subsidize activities that generate these kinds of network externalities. In the language of economics, religion is a cultural good for which free riding could be an impediment for its growth and sustainability. Religions have typically overcome such problems by establishing norms and rituals that penalize or inhibit alternative uses of time and resources (Iannaccone, 1992, 1994; Berman, 2000; Berman and Laitin, 2008). The sustenance of such norms and rituals not only helps screen out the less committed free riders but also forms the cornerstone of a common social "culture." Such norms and rituals appear to be crucial for the Durkheimian argument. In this regard, all sociopolitical innovations that raise accountability and loyalty among the adherents help limit free-rider problems and bolster credence. And those belief systems whose credence is more effectively established among the populace would also be the ones with a comparative advantage in serving the sociopolitical stability function.

Wright (2009, pp. 55–57) even attributes the rise of religion to its social-stability, which began to evolve in the transition from hunter-gatherer societies, which were based on personal interaction, to settled agricultural societies, which were more impersonal:

[Laissez-faire] law enforcement is a shakier source of social order in chiefdoms than in hunter-gatherer societies. In a hunter-gatherer village, you know everyone and see them often and may someday need their help. So the costs of getting on someone's bad side are high and the temptation to offend them commensurately low. In a chiefdom, containing thousands or even tens of thousands of people, some of your neighbors are more remote, hence more inviting targets for exploitation. . . . In this phase of cultural evolution, a supplementary force of social control was called for. Religion seems to have responded to the call. . . . Whereas religion in hunter-gatherer societies didn't have much of a moral dimension, religion in the Polynesian chiefdoms did; it systematically discouraged anti-social behavior. . . . Believing that anyone you mistreat might haunt you from the grave could turn you into a pretty nice person.

1.2 Does Theistic Competition Matter?

There isn't much consensus on whether monotheistic faiths structurally differ in their functional impact on their adherent societies. Still there are some scholars who saw in monotheism certain advantages in establishing an ecclesiastical monopoly within societies. We'll get to that debate soon enough. Before we do, however, note that there is hardly a consensus among theology scholars even on the origins of monotheism.

The conventional literature on the topic assumed a linear progression from polytheistic faiths to monotheism during the socioeconomic and political evolution of human societies and held the view that Judaism was the first monotheistic faith. For example, Baring-Gould (1877, pp. 237, 258) observed, "Two facts arrest our attention at the outset—the prevalence of monotheism and the tendency of civilization towards it. . . . It is the glory of the Semitic race to have given to the world in a compact and luminous form that monotheism which the philosophers of Greece and Rome only vaguely apprehended, and which has become the heritage of the Christian and the [Muslim] alike."

But in the early twentieth century, two anthropologists, Andrew Lang and Wilhelm Schmidt, began to advance that monotheism predated polytheistic faiths, and the recent literature has begun to reflect the view that Judaism was probably not the first monotheistic religion in human history. In his book *One True God*, Rodney Stark (2001, p. 32) discusses Aten, who the residents of Egypt around 1000 BCE considered as their unique god, possessing omnipotence and unlimited scope. Karen Armstrong (1993, pp. 4–7) seconds Stark's opinion by noting that "there had been a primitive monotheism before men and women had started to worship a number of gods. Originally, they had acknowledged only one Supreme Deity, who had created the world and governed human affairs from afar. Belief in such a High God . . . is still a feature of the religious life in many indigenous African tribes."

In any case, what we do know is that spiritual belief systems in general began to proliferate in various different geographic regions of the world more or less simultaneously and independently during what was described by Karl Jaspers (1953) as the *Axial Age*, covering roughly between 800 BCE and 200 BCE. All three major monotheisms (Judaism, Christianity, and Islam) were born between 606 BCE and 622 CE in the Middle East. The subsequent diffusion of the One God faiths in North Africa, Asia, and Europe was not only rapid and remarkable but also accompanied by the rise of centralized government. In the words of Diamond (1997, pp. 266–67),

At the end of the last Ice Age, much of the world's population lived in [hunter-gatherer societies] and no people then lived in a much more complex society. As recently as 1500 [CE], less than 20 percent of the world's land area was marked off by boundaries into states run by bureaucrats and governed by laws. Today, all land except Antarctica's is so divided. Descendants of those societies that achieved *centralized government* and *organized religion* earliest ended up dominating the modern world. The combination of *government* and *religion* functioned, together with germs, writing, and technology, as one of the four main sets of proximate agents leading to history's broadest pattern.

In fact, by the year 2000, 161 countries subscribed predominantly to one or more of the three monotheistic faiths, representing 86 percent of the 188 countries and close to 3.3 billion people—roughly 55 percent of the world population (Iyigun, 2010).

7

While Judaism, Christianity, and Islam are not the only three monotheistic faiths that have emerged in history, they have had and continue to have the most adherents by far. These monotheisms have also been geographically dominant in the Middle East, Europe, and the Near East ever since their advent, and the spread of Christianity and Islam in particular in those regions has been quite extraordinary by historical standards (a topic discussed further in chapter 2).

Moreover, while other religious faiths have been classified as monotheist by some theologians, there have been long-running scholarly disputes about the theistic attribute of many of those. A case in point is Zoroastrianism. Founded by the Iranian reformer Zoroaster in the sixth century BCE, it involves a clear hierarchy among its various divine beings, with *Lord Mazda* as the supreme god, followed by seven other deities, *the Holy Immortals*. But precisely due to the fact that Lord Mazda's role in the detailed hierarchy is unambiguous, Zoroastrianism is accepted by some scholars as an early precursor of modern monotheisms (Armstrong, 2006, pp. 9–14).

The date when Judaism became unambiguously monotheist is also subject to debate. By some accounts, this did not occur until the early seventh century, in 606 BCE, although the birth of Judaism is traced back to the twelfth century BCE (Armstrong, 1993, p. 61; Stark, 2001, pp. 24–25).

We know very little if anything about why monotheisms spread as rapidly as they did and came to be so closely intertwined with governments and stable societies. The fact is, not only did many historical civilizations subscribe to and promote Judaism, Christianity, and Islam, but also the political elite in these societies often derived their temporal authority from their respective monotheist ecclesiastical institutions. In turn, the latter derived substantial financial and political benefits from being associated with One God. Thus the stability of preindustrial societies came to be linked with their respective ecclesiastical institutions. Stable polities, societies, and economies might not have been sufficient for ushering in human enlightenment, industrialization, and sustainable economic progress but seem to have been the precursors of all those (e.g., Diamond, 1997; North et al., 2006, 2008; Mokyr, 2010).

So if monotheistic faiths were especially adept at sustaining sociopolitical stability, what were their common features that mattered in this regard? Although they are not exclusive to the three main monotheisms, there are at least three salient traits of monotheistic faiths regarding their impact on the economic and sociopolitical realms.

1.2.1 Social Advantages of Economies of Scale

Judaism, Christianity, and Islam all acknowledge and promote the "one-ness" of God, and the barriers to entry in the religion market are substantially lower when there are many gods. By nature, this introduces monopoly power and elements of increasing returns to scale in the provision of religious services when entry barriers are high (as they are under One God).

Ekelund et al. (1996, 2002) and Barro and McCleary (2003, 2005) claim that the fixed setup costs of religion influence the equilibrium number of faiths that can be sustained by a society or state. Most germane to what I discuss here is the idea that a state religion is more likely to emerge when the cost of establishing a religion is high. Monotheisms entail relatively high costs of entry into the religion market. Ekelund et al. (1996, p. 28) elaborate, for instance, how, as an institution, the Roman Catholic Church benefited from its association with an omnipotent God:

As an extensive and pervasive monopolist in medieval society, the Church held a major advantage as producer of the credence good of salvation, which included intercession with God. The monopoly status of the Church, coupled with its great temporal power, reinforced the credibility of its claims concerning the quality of its nontestable product. The Church could convincingly maintain that its temporal position was testament to the veracity of its claims. Thus, aspiring entrants to the medieval religious market faced a daunting task: convincing their potential customers that the alternative product they offered was more reliable than that already available from an institution endorsed by an Omnipotent God.

In fact, Armstrong (1993, p. 49) identifies that monotheistic faiths were unique in their mutual exclusivity, especially with respect to the belief in One God. On the one hand, it is true that the effective monotheism of any particular One God faith is a matter of degree, as a single deity shares ecclesiastical power with angels, saints, prophets, and other holy people. On the other hand, however, the hierarchy between the one deity and other ecclesiastical actors is very clear. Along these lines, Stark (2001, pp. 19, 34) draws a critical distinction between individuals' relationship with One God under monotheism and that with multiple deities in polytheism, according to which competition between various divine beings played a role in shortening the interactions between the adherents and their gods.

Taken together, the One God/One Faith duality inherent in Abrahamic monotheisms made them mutually exclusive vis-à-vis other faiths. That mutual exclusivity, in turn, enabled monotheistic faiths to more than likely emerge as the socially dominant, or even state, religion once they gained traction within a society. A monotheistic state religion, then, involved fairly difficult to surmount entry barriers for other faiths, precisely due to the mutual exclusivity inherent in its creed and its association with and endorsement of state political authorities.

The view that synergies exist between political and ecclesiastical authorities has a long but varied history: "The Empire fell and the Church survived just because the Church gave leadership and enlisted loyalty whereas the Empire had long failed to do either to one or the other. Thus the Church, a survivor from the dying society, became the womb from which in due course the new [Empire] was born" (Toynbee, 1946, pp. 13–14).

Of course, it is one thing to point out the synergies between secular and ecclesiastical authorities but a whole different thing to assert that monotheisms were particularly potent in providing and sustaining them. As Niebuhr (1932, pp. 6–7) noted, the impact of One God religions could well extend into the sociopolitical realm: "The two most obvious types of power are the military and the economic, though in primitive society the power of the priest, partly because he dispenses supernatural benefits and partly because he establishes public order by methods less arduous than those of the soldier, vies with that of the soldier and the landlord."

Monotheisms differ from one another in the extent to which they are "clerical" or "congregational"; although, in this regard, the heterogeneity within Christianity is unique. In Islam, which by construction is congregationalist, the caliphate was heavily used to legitimize political authority. Naturally, the clerical system enabled more of a fusion between ecclesiastical authority and temporal political power. The extent to which the clergy had ecclesiastical authority often influenced the political sphere because the clergy could use their powers to bolster or undermine the legitimacy of secular authorities. As a particular example of such interactions between secular and ecclesiastical political power, some scholars have documented interdependence between political and religious authorities on Islamic sociopolitical and economic development (Rubin, 2008, 2010).

In this spirit, one could argue that the prolific variety of denominations within Christianity and, to a much lesser extent, Islam contradicts the argument that monotheisms are easier sustained as monopoly religions. However, as Ekelund et al. (1996) have shown, most of the denominational pluralism within Christianity occurred because the Roman Catholic Church began to operate as a heavily price-discriminating monopolist. That presumably left room for Lutheranism and its various offshoots to eventually enter the European religion market. In contrast, the Shi'a-Sunni split within Islam is an artifact of the disagreement over who was the legitimate successor of the prophet Mohammed.

These differences are real and fundamental, but they should not obscure the fact that many preindustrial civilizations were theocracies that sought and derived temporal authority from their respective monotheistic faiths. One has to view in this light the prominent monopoly roles of the Roman Catholic Church in western Europe during the common era, the Greek Orthodox Church in eastern Europe between the fourth and nineteenth centuries CE, as well as that of the caliphate in the Rashidun, the Umayyad and Abbasid dynasties between 600 CE and 900 CE, and the Ottoman Empire between 1517 and 1924.

1.2.2 Personalized Spiritual Exchange

Human spirituality is pillared on the desire to grasp the meaning of existence and rationalize, at least to an extent, natural phenomena that are incomprehensible to the human mind. With atheistic spiritual movements, explanations of such phenomena typically involve supernatural powers that do not have the conscious will required for personalized involvement and communication. In polytheistic faiths, there are multiple deities who rule various aspects of temporal life, but there exists none with the omnipotence to control all aspects of temporal and spiritual existence. In contrast, monotheistic faiths involve one omnipotent divine being who has not only control over the whole universe but also desires he wishes humans to fulfill, which he can communicate to them.

Stark (2001, pp. 15–19) provides a utilitarian analysis of the psychological and sociological effects of monotheism. He draws attention to the fact that individual accountability toward One God is a unique feature of monotheistic faiths and that, since the relationship between the deity and individual is personalized and extended into the afterlife, there is a strong element of beneficial exchange on the basis of personal commitment. A relevant assertion he makes is that, by personalizing spiritual exchange and reinforcing accountability, theology and faith provide a very effective means to deal with human wants and desires, such as survival, health, financial security, and so on, which are often fleeting and inherently in short supply.

By nature, otherworldly rewards are compensation for individuals' temporal deeds and, to an extent, they substitute for material necessities that are in short supply or entirely unavailable. As a consequence, they introduce an element of continuity and commitment to the exchange between the deity and the individual—two features that are entirely lacking in atheism and polytheism (Stark, 2001, p. 19).

1.2.3   Longer Time Horizons due to Afterlife

The belief in afterlife is not unique to monotheisms but, the Judgment Day, when individuals are held accountable for their deeds and are judged by God accordingly, is.

In Jewish liturgy, there is significant prayer and talk of a "book of life" that one is written into, indicating that God judges each person each year, even after death. This annual judgment occurs on *Rosh Hashanah*. In Christianity, the Last Judgment or *Day of the Lord* is the simultaneous judgment of every person when, after the resurrection of the dead, Christ will return to judge the living and the dead. Those positively judged will be saved and live in God's presence in heaven, and those who are negatively judged will be cast to eternal hell. In Islam, the *Day of Judgment* is described in the Qur'an and the Hadith. The Islamic Judgment Day starts thirty years before the end of the earth and sees the return of the prophet Jesus to the earth. The last thirty years on earth will involve a line of events that will see the resurrection of the deceased. This will be followed by Judgment Day beyond the universe, involving hell and heaven and the weighing of good and evil.

By contrast, religions that include reincarnation, such as Hinduism, lack a Judgment Day—the determination of how an individual is to be reborn being a particular judgment on the merit of the life just lived.

As Stark (2001, pp. 15–19) explains, the fact that individuals are held accountable by *one* god for their temporal deeds and that his rewards are often delayed until after death "is a major factor allowing Godly religions to generate the long-term levels of commitment necessary to sustain strong religious organizations."

1.3   Monotheisms Rule . . .

Insofar as monotheisms had a scale advantage in the religion markets, they were more likely to have attained monopoly status in the provision of religious goods within polities. By the same token, if monotheisms also promoted individual accountability, responsibility, and patience (to defer instant gratifications in exchange for spiritual gains in the afterlife) on the basis of otherworldly compensators, they ought to have produced a variety of positive social externalities that came to impart *domestic* as well as *external* effects.

There are various views on this issue, as scholars of theology, psychology, sociology, and, to some extent, economics have recognized the moral, ethical, and egalitarian aspects of religion, in general, and monotheist traditions, in particular (McCleary and Barro, 2006; Iyigun, 2010). For example, according to Armstrong (1993, p. 48), "It has to be said that this imaginative portrayal of God in human terms has inspired a social concern that has not been present in Hinduism. All three of the God-religions have shared the egalitarian and socialist ethic of Amos and Isaiah. The Jews would be the first people in the ancient world to establish a welfare system that was the admiration of their pagan neighbors."

If indeed there exist synergies between religious and temporal powers in government, there ought to have been important comparative advantages for both polities and ecclesiastical entities historically. As Stark (2001, pp. 15–19) notes, "An exclusive relationship with One God is also an *extended* relationship—usually lifelong. No longer are humans able to go 'God shopping' or to pit one God against another. This results in extremely strong organizations possessed of immense resources, consistent with a God of unlimited power and concern."

With respect to the impact of each monotheist religion on its adherent societies *domestically*, the economic history literature is fairly well developed with regard to the impact of various Christian denominations—in particular, those of the Protestant Reformation and its offshoots—on the European economic takeoff. As is well known, the impact of Protestantism on European sociopolitical and economic evolution has been extensively debated. The origins of this debate can be traced back to Weber, who articulated the view that Protestantism—particularly its offshoot Calvinism—had cultivated an intense devotion to one's work or "calling" in order to assure that one had in fact been selected for salvation. In his words, "the calling and the premium it placed upon ascetic conduct was bound directly to influence the development of a capitalistic way of life" (Weber, 1930, p. 111). Others have emphasized that perhaps the most important legacy of the recognition of Protestantism and its various offshoots by the Catholic Church in the sixteenth century was greater social cohabitation in Europe (see MacCulloch, 2003, p. 652).

In recent years, there has also emerged a fledgling body of work that has begun to focus on the link between faith-related institutions and economic development within Jewish, Christian, and Muslim societies. Botticini and Eckstein (2005, 2007, 2012) make this argument with respect to Judaism: the reading of the Torah and the Talmud became a requirement of Judaism following the burning of the Jewish Temple in Jerusalem in 64 CE, thereby leading to advanced literacy and a steep path of human capital accumulation in the Jewish communities of the Middle East between 64 CE and 200 CE.

One of the main thrusts of Martin Luther was his emphasis on the laity's responsibility to study and personally examine the scripture for themselves. As such, Protestantism had two discernible, long-term effects on the European society and its organization. First, it clearly empowered the individual and emphasized his personal responsibility as superior over ecclesiastical regulations and regimentations (see Hillerbrand, 1968, p. xxiv). Second, the Lutheran calls for individuals to study and read the Bible themselves spurred a greater emphasis on literacy as well as various interpretations of the scripture, with the translation and the printing of the Bible in the vernacular instead of its original Latin. In expounding on this idea, Hillerbrand (1968) notes that about one million copies of Luther's tracts had been published by 1523 and that the literature produced by the Reformation scholarship—led by the preeminent figures of the time such as Luther, Zwingli, and Calvin, as well as other minor reformers such as Bucer, Melanchthon, and Carlstadt—would not have been published had there not been sufficient demand. This point is verified by Becker and Woessmann (2009), who find empirical support for the idea that the Protestant reforms spurred human capital accumulation among the Protestants.

Armstrong (1993) and Lewis (2002) discuss various institutional features of Islam and their impact on ancient Arab civilizations, such as the Abbasids, Umayyads, and Mamluks. Kuran (2004a, 2004b) and Lewis (2002) elaborate on how Islam and its interactions with Christianity and Judaism influenced the institutions of the Ottoman Empire. For instance, Timur Kuran ascribes the early successes of Muslim societies to Islam's unique institutions, such as individually oriented contract law and a highly egalitarian system of inheritance laws. But he also notes that, although none of these Islamic institutions per se was a hindrance in a relatively static socioeconomic environment, such as the medieval era, these same institutions inadvertently began to stifle economic advancement in a world in which technological and economic change began to rule.

Along similar lines, Rubin (2008, 2010) articulates in detail how some distinct Islamic practices, such as the interest ban and printing prohibitions, were deliberately designed to promote sociopolitical cohesion and stability during the medieval era. He goes on to document that these same features might not have been flexible enough to foster economic growth in the more dynamic phase following the Industrial Revolution of eighteenth-century Europe.

The common thread among these works is that the Islamic culture helped promote stability in social, political, and economic realms, although, in the case of the Ottoman Empire, some of the very institutional traits that promoted stability in a static setting came at the cost of dynamic flexibility in the longer term.

1.4 . . . and Conflict

If indeed the advent of the three Abrahamic monotheistic faiths produced sociopolitical stability internally, it also provided the galvanizing elements for confronting external foes when they did not subscribe to the One True Faith. The short of it is that religious beliefs complemented and augmented military power in fighting external adversaries. Various scholars, in fact, articulated that monotheisms might have been uniquely potent in this regard.

Niebuhr (1932, pp. 65–66) accepts that stoking patriotic notions of identity was important for galvanizing a society in external conflicts, too. From his perspective, what made religion especially effective as a complementary component of national defense was the "absolute" nature of its claims, rewards, and punishments. Along these lines, Stark (2001, p. 35) ties this aspect of monotheism to its more benign forms, such as its adherents' extensive missionary zeal and desire to spread the word of the One True God.

Before I examine these hypotheses more systematically, I want to take a step back and examine the bigger picture. There are some distinct patterns of warfare historically, which Woods and Baltzly (1915) were among the first to examine. Analyzing data through the end of the nineteenth century, they identified that warfare was diminishing over time, with the eighteenth century representing the most peaceful era historically. But they also identified that the decline was not uniform from 1450 to 1900. Others who followed were also able to verify these general trends (Richardson, 1960; Wilkinson, 1980; Lagerlöf, 2010).

Figure 1.1 is based on data that I will extensively discuss and rely on for the book's main arguments. For the time being, however, they suffice to document that there was a sharp drop in conflict starting around the middle of the seventeenth century. The overall conflict propensity was lower throughout the next hundred years and, although there was a noticeable increase in international violence in the late nineteenth and

Figure 1.1 Number of conflicts over six centuries

twentieth centuries, the general trend in global conflicts over the last six centuries was one of a decline.

What is perhaps most striking is the extent to which these trends were driven by intra-European warfare. The dashed line in figure 1.1 shows how European conflicts remained steady and persistent through the onset of the Protestant Reformation around the 1530s to 1550s, followed by another wave of escalated warfare and conflict. That second wave begins to subside only in 1648 after the Peace of Westphalia, which marked the official recognition of the Protestant Reformation by the Roman Catholic Church. I return to these issues and confront them more thoroughly in part 3.

The general decline in conflict frequencies, especially starting in the seventeenth century and primarily driven by trends in intra-European confrontations, also coincides with violent confrontations getting shorter but more fatal. As shown in figure 1.2, for instance, whereas a typical conflict lasted more than five hundred days in the 1650s, it was resolved or terminated within less than fifty days by the 1950s.

As for fatalities, figure 1.3 excludes the enormous death tolls of thirty-seven million and fifty-six million individuals killed in the First and Second World Wars, respectively. Despite that, it lays bare the rising death toll of violent conflicts over time, with the average number of deaths that typically hovered around the one to five thousand threshold throughout

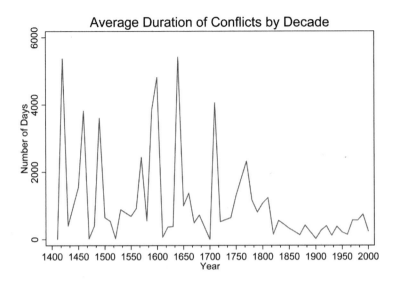

Figure 1.2 Average duration of conflicts over six centuries

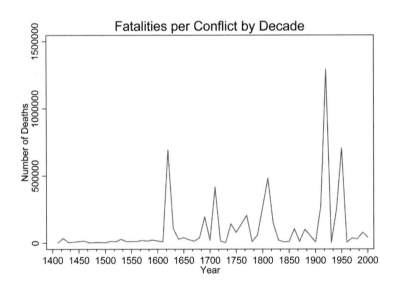

Figure 1.3 Fatalities per conflict over six centuries

the seventeenth century creeping up to the half-million mark by the nineteenth century.

Returning to the role of faith in violent conflicts, the rise and spread of the three main monotheistic religions—specifically those of Christianity and Islam—produced some of the most notable confrontations in history among their faithful. Alas, the remnants of these tensions define various pivotal international conflicts and confrontations today.

Judaism, Christianity, and Islam are all built on fundamental beliefs of One God and One Religion, a concept of duality labeled *particularism*. Various theologians, such as Rodney Stark (2001) and Karen Armstrong (1993, 2006), have suggested that this is an important reason why, as monotheisms spread and dislocated other faiths and belief systems in the Old World, faith-based conflicts and confrontations began to take hold in Europe, North Africa, Asia, and the Middle East. Along these lines, note that the clerical institutions of the three religions all earn rents from the beliefs they espouse. Thus the members of the ecclesiastical hierarchy stand willing to fight for their core beliefs, in part, because their income depends on the size of the flock that holds those views.

After compiling data on more than three hundred violent conflicts around the world between 1820 and 1949, Richardson (1960, pp. 239) was the first to reveal that differences of religion, especially those of Christianity and Islam, have been causes of wars and that, to a weaker extent, "Christians fought Christians more than would be expected from their population." Richardson's approach was straightforward but illuminating: Classify each of the three-hundred-plus conflicts by discerning which of the involved parties were coreligionists. Then categorize religious affiliation by whether it helped pacify or aggravate a conflict. He found that none of the observed conflicts arose because the two sides identified with the same religion; he also did not find any conflicts that were restrained because the involved parties adhered to different religions. Instead, conflicts arose and persisted due to religious differences, or they were subdued or eventually contained primarily because the actors involved coreligionists. Richardson also found that war alliances had subdued and prevented wars between former allies, although this influence faded with the passage of time since the alliance.

Figures 1.4 to 1.6 help put in context violent confrontations that were at least in part driven by religious motives vis-à-vis others. First, as can be seen in figure 1.4, while trends in conflicts of a religious nature track the broader patterns discussed previously, they also exhibit a lot more persistence over time, in general. Second, religious confrontations not only

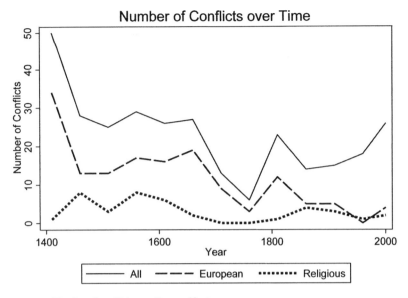

Figure 1.4 Number of conflicts over time and by type

lasted longer than nonreligious violent conflicts (as shown in figure 1.5) but also seem to have been typically more fatal (as shown in figure 1.6).

Such generalizations are useful, but they mask some distinct differences in the patterns of warfare for Christianity and Islam. In fact, while religious affiliation helped avoid or contain conflicts, the propensity for Christian groups to engage their coreligionists was a lot higher than it was within Islam, at least until the mid-sixteenth century. This observation is thanks to Wilkinson (1980, pp. 87–90), who identified that, of the 111 to 134 interreligious violent conflicts in Richardson's data set, 56 to 63 were Christians against Muslims. That corresponds to nearly half of all interreligious wars. An equally telling fact is that, of the 111 to 134 interreligious conflicts, only 5 to 7 involved neither a Muslim nor a Christian party, which is just about 5 percent of all interreligious wars. Interestingly, Wilkinson also documented that, of the 93 to 128 conflicts involving coreligionists, 87 to 119 involved Christian pairs, accounting for roughly 90 percent of all coreligionist wars. By comparison, only 4 to 8 of those represented Muslim on Muslim conflicts.

In terms of how the patterns of political evolution could have come into play in influencing these trends in violent conflict, continental Europe as a whole was typically very fragmented politically, although north central Europe—in particular, those areas under the domain of the Hanseatic League and the German Diets—during the medieval era was

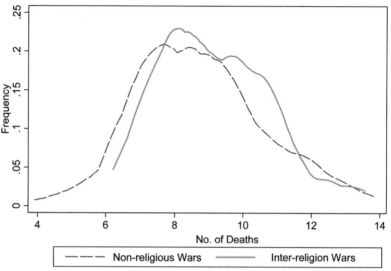

Figure 1.5   Conflict deaths by conflict type

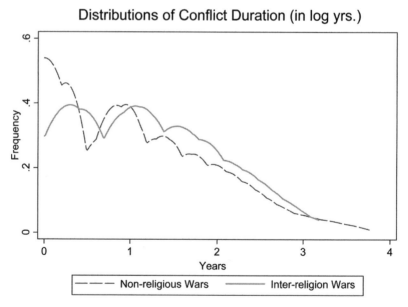

Figure 1.6   Conflict duration by conflict type

especially dominated by small city-states. A somewhat uneven trend of political consolidation existed over time. On the one hand, the continent was politically most fragmented in 1300 CE and most consolidated in 1900 CE. On the other hand, political consolidation occurred a lot earlier in eastern Europe, the Middle East, and North Africa than it did in continental Europe, due primarily to the Ottoman Empire's rise and expansion from the fourteenth through the seventeenth centuries. Moreover, the trend toward higher fragmentation that occurred in much of Europe during the latter part of the twentieth century took place about a century earlier in the Middle East, North Africa, and the Balkans, this time due to the dissolution of the Ottoman Empire starting in the early nineteenth century. For more on these and related themes, see Toynbee (1946, 1957), Kennedy (1987), and Tilly (1992).

These long-term military as well as political developments occurred against the backdrop of various innovations and refinements in military technology. First, as Parker elaborates, the invention of powerful siege guns can be traced back to 1405, when a single cannon fire sufficed for Scottish soldiers to surrender to the British at Berrick-upon-Tweed, and to 1449, when the canon "Mons Meg" was cast for the duke of Burgundy in 1449. The regular use of heavy firearms in eastern Europe and the Middle East did not occur until the Ottoman siege of Constantinople in 1453. And the widespread use of heavy firearms in western Europe had to wait until the French invasion of the Italian Peninsula in 1494. Nevertheless, it is imperative to recognize that the impact of heavy firearms on military conflict was highly contingent on geographic attributes. As Parker (1988, p. 7) states, "Weapons like these had a limited future in the West. In the first place, they were so huge and unwieldy that they could only be transported by water: they could strike only [in places] accessible by sea or river. Second, there were some fortifications against which, either because of natural defenses or skillful design, even the largest bombard was powerless."

The second critical military innovation came about a century later with the advent of the volley system. Its benefit lay in the fact that rifled guns required significant loading times, a disadvantage that could be mitigated by a logistical innovation of drawing up soldiers in a series of long lines, with "the first rank firing together and then retiring to reload and the following ranks coming forward and doing the same" (Parker, 1988, pp. 7, 19). As with the introduction of heavy firearms, it is plausible that the advent of the volley system also had effects on violent conflict that were contingent on geographic characteristics.

If differences in religious beliefs influenced the patterns of conflict and cooperation, did they also produce some lasting sociopolitical and economic effects?

That is the fundamental question to which I seek some answers in the last two sections of this book. Before I do that, however, I ought to investigate if and why the worlds collided and the cultures clashed. The gist of it all is that the major Abrahamic monotheistic faiths—in particular, Christianity and Islam—were remarkably adept at crowding out the ecclesiastical landscape in preindustrial Europe, the Middle East, North Africa, and the Near East. Nevertheless, if the social functions of monotheism did give societies a survival advantage and aided monotheistic societies to flourish, the One God/One True Faith duality inherent in monotheistic religions also produced some of the most pronounced confrontations in human history.

PART TWO

The Rise of Monotheism

If God does not exist, all is permitted.
IVAN IN FYODOR DOSTOYEVSKY'S *THE BROTHERS KARAMAZOV* (1880)

TWO

Empires Strike Back . . . under One God

How rapidly did the Abrahamic monotheistic creeds spread in the Old World, and how did their patterns of diffusion relate to societies and polities? These questions are not easy to answer. Aside from the fact that one would have to overcome serious data limitations for a topic that dictates reliable information from many millennia covering vast geographic domains, at a more elementary level, one would have to come to terms with definitional and categorical ambiguities that bear upon some key concepts: What kind of society qualifies as a "civilization"? Which attributes would one need to observe for a society to be labeled as such? And, along the same lines, how would one identify whether a civilization was predominantly monotheist?

There are many abstractions, ambiguities, and overlaps in these concepts and definitions. This is mostly why many alternative and acceptable conceptualizations could be employed. Hence, in order to lay the groundwork for the discussions and analyses to come, section 2.1 defines as clearly and consistently as possible the relevant concepts, terminologies, and classifications explored in this chapter.

In the rest of the chapter, I will then seek to unearth some statistical evidence that relates to the ideas reviewed in chapter 1—that is, whether moral as well as ethical considerations associated with monotheistic faiths did indeed serve as a *foundation for social stability* historically. And, in particular, I will examine if the extent to which human civilizations that cycled through the historical political landscape possessed some specific advantages aided by the extent to which ecclesiastical and political power complemented each other in influencing the efficacy of centralized government.

2.1 Some Definitions

Haywood (2005, pp. 8–10) notes in *The Penguin Historical Atlas of Ancient Civilizations* that all human civilizations exhibit some combination of standard features. These characteristics are defined as the *Childe-Redman criteria*, according to which the relevant traits are broken down into two categories.

The primary Childe-Redman characteristics involve various aspects of social organization, such as settlement in cities, labor specialization, concentration of surplus production, class structure, a state organization, and government. The secondary Childe-Redman features encompass aspects of material culture in the form of monumental public works, long-distance trade, artwork, writing, and scientific pursuits, such as those in arithmetic, geometry, and astronomy. The primary data sources that I will discuss shortly typically adhere to these criteria when screening human societies as historic civilizations and, in what follows, I will simply take as given their classifications.

But how should one go about classifying civilizations by their theistic attributes? For practical purposes, let a human civilization be defined as *monotheist* if it satisfied at least one of the three following criteria:

1. A majority of its citizens adhered to one of the three main monotheist religions.
2. Its government was ruled by or (to some degree) subject to religious authority.
3. Its government and political organizations promoted one of the three monotheist traditions through their social, economic, and military policies.

It goes without saying that these criteria are subjective and thus the designation *monotheist civilization*, in particular, suffers from a somewhat crude generalization. For one, it treats all individuals of a given society identically. In reality, there exists a great deal of variation and differences in the degree to which individuals adhere to and practice the state monotheism of their society (see, for example, Finke and Stark, 1992). History shows that, even in the case of forced conversions following conquests and subversive campaigns, there was no guarantee that the converts practiced the dictated state religion. A relevant example is the plight of the Jewish converts in al-Andalus prior and subsequent to the pogroms of 1391. The conversion of many Jews during this era in order to avoid massacre at the hands of Christians was not enough to quell suspicions that they were in fact "closet Jews," and those co-religionists who dared not convert were also promoting Judaism at the expense of Christianity.

Given the historical record, we have no hope of coming up with a measure of individuals' overall intensity of adherence to monotheism. On the one hand, we would be overstating the spread of monotheistic creeds over time and space, due to the fact that these data are based on aggregation up to the society level. On the other hand, we would be glossing over regional differences in adherence to monotheistic faiths—differences that would otherwise provide useful variations for our identification purposes. Thus the lack of religious adherence data aggregated up from the individual level would stand to complicate efforts to detect any systematic role of monotheisms in societies.

2.2 Sources and Data

Definitional and conceptual complications aside, we need a comprehensive data set on human civilizations that covers a wide enough historical time span enveloping the births of the three monotheistic faiths on both ends. With these constraints and demands in mind, I will focus on a 4,250-year period between 2500 BCE and 1750 CE. The start date of 2500 BCE is purely due to data limitations, as a systematic record of historical civilizations only dates this far back. And I'll cap the sample dates at 1750 CE in order to focus on the preindustrial era and prior to the prevalence of nation states.

There are a variety of alternative data sources to tally a historical record of civilizations, such as the Oxford *Atlas of World History* (2002), the Rand McNally *Historical Atlas of the World* (2005), the *Encyclopedia Britannica*, McEvedy (1992, 2002), Haywood (2005), Farrington (2002, 2006), and Anglin and Hamblin (1993). From these sources, I recorded various facts about these civilizations—the most important of which are their years of foundation and collapse (if they occurred before 1750 CE). For geographical information on land areas, I relied on the CIA's *World Factbook* (n.d.). For geographic classifications, I divided Europe, the Middle East, Africa, Asia, and America into thirty-three regions according to their historical significance and as classified by Anglin and Hamblin. Using these historical records and various sources, I was able to identify 277 civilizations that inhabited one of the five continents over a time span between 2500 BCE and 1750 CE.

Three clarifications are now in order: First, for all statistical analyses below, the final dates are capped at 1750 CE, and when a civilization terminated past that date, this cap was also binding. In other words, even if a civilization lasted long past 1750 CE, I only considered its duration up to that date. Doing so will help abstract from the roles of the Industrial Revolution and the rise of the nation states on duration and peak land mass attained. Still bear in mind that, since a state was more likely to have been predominantly monotheist later in time, capping the duration of societies that existed in the mid-eighteenth century artificially truncates the life span of what turns out to be mostly monotheistic societies.

Second, this list is far from complete and definitive of all civilizations past. Our exercise takes the information available in the main sources as the starting point. The data are intended to be as comprehensive as possible, but to the extent that I could not verify relevant crucial data on the foundation and extinction dates, peak land mass, and so on of these civilizations, there are some nonsystematic data omissions.

Third, along the same lines, this is meant to be a list of ancient, medieval, and preindustrial civilizations that had some *autonomy* and *scale*. This is the reason the data encompass kingdoms, dynasties, and empires, as well as early American civilizations about which we have less-specific information on government structure, state organization, and social life. This is also the reason the data exclude feudal principalities, medieval fiefdoms, suzeranities, the Anatolian derebeyliks, and various city-states. As I will explain in some detail below, this effectively yielded sovereigns that ruled over at least about 25,000 km².

Based on these criteria, I was able to identify another 110 civilizations that had to be omitted from our exercise for one or more of the reasons mentioned immediately above.

2.3 A Brief History

Based on the data set, the civilization that lasted longest was the Kingdom of Elam, a polytheist culture based in what is now a region of Iran. It is one of the oldest recorded civilizations that existed between 2200 BCE and 644 BCE. It endured for close to 1,600 years. The Christian Nubian kingdoms of Northeast Africa, which survived about 1,200 years; the Byzantine Empire, which survived 113 decades in Asia Minor, the Middle East, and the Balkans; and two civilizations of the Americas, Adena in the

Mississippi Delta and Olmecs in the Gulf of Mexico, which both lasted 1,100 years, were some of the other durable civilizations. It is noteworthy that among these most durable societies, only the Nubian kingdoms and the Byzantine Empire adhered to a form of monotheism.

In terms of the land mass achieved during the peak of empire, the Arab Umayyad Dynasty tops the list with about fourteen million km^2. That was followed by various Chinese dynasties, such as Xia, Qin, Han, and Song, as well as the Ottoman Empire, all of which spread as large as about six million km^2, and the Macedonian Empire, which exceeded five million km^2. Note that, here, I am referring to the contiguous land mass of civilizations and excluding, in particular, the colonial conquests of maritime empires of the British, Spanish, and the Portuguese. Furthermore, although the Golden Horde and Mongol raids covered a vast geographic belt with an area of thirty-three million km^2 that stretched from the China Sea to central Europe, I treat this as an outlier, in that the era of the Golden Horde and Mongol raids did not typically culminate in stable government and state organizations following the Mongol invasions.

The smallest geographies, in contrast, were the Sultanate of Melaka of northern Sumatra, with about 1,650 km^2; the Sharqi Dynasty of Jaunpur in northern India, with about 4,000 km^2; Israel and the Kingdom of Judah, with 26,000 km^2 land mass; as well as the various North and Central American ancient civilizations, such as Mochica, Chavin, and Chimu, each controlling about 60,000 km^2 around the Andes region. Of those outliers in peak land mass, the societies that attained the largest geographic domains were all monotheists, with the exception of the various Chinese dynasties.

In terms of the general descriptives, of the 168 nonmonotheist civilizations in the sample, 26 were in the Middle East, 68 in Asia, 36 in Europe, 16 in Africa, and 22 in the Americas. Some of the notable nonmonotheist civilizations in the data include the Egyptian kingdoms (old, middle, and new), the early Anatolian civilizations (Hittites, Luvians, and Lydians), the Mesopotamian empires (such as Akkadians, Old Babylonian, and Assyrian), Iranian empires (Seleucid, Parthian, and Persian), various northern and southern Chinese dynasties (such as Xiongnu, Xian-bi, Xia, Shang, Song, and Ming), Indian dynasties (Shakas, Guptas, Viyajanagar, etc.), early American civilizations (Aztecs, Incas, and Mayans), as well as Alexander the Great's fleeting Macedonian Empire.

Of the 109 monotheist civilizations, 35 were in the Middle East, 38 in Europe, 17 in Africa, and 19 in Asia. Of those, 46 were Christian, 61 were Muslim, and only two were Jewish (Israel/Judah Kingdom, r. 1200 BCE–584 BCE, and Khazaria, r. 650 CE–965 CE). Besides Israel and the Judah Kingdom, among the notable monotheist civilizations were the Axum Empire, the Byzantine Empire, the Holy Roman Empire, the Carolingian Empire, the Portuguese and British Empires, which were all Christian; the Abbasids, the Umayyads, the Tulunids, the Fatimids, the Ayyubids, which were all part of the Arab caliphate dynasties; and the Mamluks, the Selçuk Empire, the Ottoman Empire, the Sultanate of Delhi, and the Safavids, which were all Muslim.

In order to better understand what monotheist societies entailed in terms of the interactions of religion and polities, consider the Carolingian Empire of Charlemagne, the Ottoman Empire, the Bahmani Sultanate, and the Mughals.

The defining characteristic of the Carolingian Empire was that its king, Charlemagne, was coronated by the Catholic Pope Leo III in 800 CE as the political leader of western Europe, crowned by God. During his reign, Charlemagne was driven by his desire to spread Christianity by conquering lands to his north and east, a feat that he executed quite successfully.

By contrast, the Ottoman Empire was observably more pluralistic in its sociopolitical and imperial policies, at least judged by the norms of its era. Conquered peoples were free to practice their religion as long as they paid the levied taxes. The Greek, Armenian, Jewish, and Frankish minorities practiced trade and commerce and lived in their more or less isolated communities throughout the empire in relative peace. But a career in the bureaucratic or military ranks required a Muslim identity, and the *devşirme* system, which was introduced by Sultan Murad I in the early fifteenth century, was the act of gathering and converting to Islam the young boys of the non-Muslim Ottoman populations who were raised in palaces or military barracks, with the intent of employing them in their adulthood in military or government posts.

The Bahmani Sultanate, which ruled in southeast India between the early fourteenth and early sixteenth centuries, also resembled the Ottoman Empire in that the Muslim groups dominated politically but the Hindu areas were granted some degree of autonomy and coexistence, facilitated by mutual noninterference (for related resources that relate ethno-religious heterogeneity with religious tolerance, see Chaney, 2008; Clingingsmith et al., 2009; and Jha, 2013).

The Muslim Mughal Empire was founded by the Chagatai Turkic ruler Babur and reigned in Northern India between the mid-sixteenth to mideighteenth centuries. While it became a politically and religiously intolerant regime later during the leadership of Aurangzeb, to which its seeds of decline are often attributed, the Mughals, too, were a religiously and politically tolerant society, especially during the reign of Akbar.

While this is an admittedly crude generalization, the societies classified as monotheist in this study resemble either the Carolingian Empire or the Ottomans and the Bahmani Sultanate in terms of the role of religion in their political, administrative, and social spheres.

Israel/Judah also has a peculiar role in that it represents the only historic civilization that adhered—unlike Khazaria, without a doubt—to Judaism. Nonetheless, it is also one society for which the exact date when it began to subscribe to the unambiguously monotheist version of Judaism is in question (Armstrong, 1993; Stark, 2001).

The Sassanian Empire, which ruled in parts of modern-day Iran and Mesopotamia between 208 CE and 651 CE, provides another interesting case. Its ruling class, nobility, and, for the most part, population, subscribed to Zoroastrianism. As noted previously, whether Zoroastrianism can be deemed monotheist is subject to debate. However, it is less contentious to acknowledge that Zoroastrianism represents an early precursor of modern monotheisms.

There were also eleven civilizations where the extent to which I could classify them by their theism changed sometime during their existence. They include the Roman Empire, the Ilkhanate Dynasty (of the Mongols), Khazaria, Takrur, the Qarakhanids, the Axum Empire, Cumans, Bulgars, Nubian kingdoms, Merovingians, and the Kievan Rus. We will classify these countries according to when they or their ruling classes converted to monotheism and declared it their state religion.

The Roman Empire formally converted to Christianity in 313 CE during the reign of Constantine. The Ilkhanate Dynasty adopted Islam when Khan Ghazan and his subjects converted to Islam in the late thirteenth century, immediately following the foundation of the Khanate in 1260.

Khazaria was a Turkic civilization that occupied a swath of land in the Caucasus to the northeast of the Black Sea between 650 CE and 965 CE. During the early reign of their state, Khazars practiced Turkic shamanism, but, either around 740 CE or 861 CE, the Khazar ruling class converted to Judaism. The extent to which the rest of the population adopted Judaism is subject to debate, but some archeological evidence seems to suggest that there were widespread shifts in the burial practices of the wider population, consistent with high rates of conversion to Judaism (for further details, see Brook, 2006, and Golden, 1980).

Takrur, an ancient west African civilization that lasted about half a millennium, converted to Islam around 1030. This is just about halfway through its reign. Cumans reigned in Transylvania from 1060 CE to 1237, but they converted to Catholicism during Prince Barc's tenure in 1227. Bulgars reigned in the Balkans between 679 CE and 1018 CE, and they converted to Orthodox Christianity much later during the reign of Boris I in 869. And while a precise date is harder to pin down for the conversion of the Qarakhanids, the available sources suggest it was rather early on. Nubian kingdoms of Nobatia, Pachoras, and Alwah converted to Christianity between 543 CE and 575 CE, due primarily to the work of two missionaries, Julian and his successor Longinus. They were all founded in the fourth century CE and existed for more than a millennium in east central Africa until the early sixteenth century. On this basis, in my analyses that follow, I will label them Christian.

The Merovingian King Clovis I converted to Christianity in 496 CE or 506 CE, which is immediately subsequent to the foundation of his kingdom in 476 CE. Kievan Rus reigned between 860 CE and 1150 CE and converted to Orthodox Christianity in 988 CE.

Among the civilizations that turned monotheist sometime during their reign, the Axum Empire stands out due to its isolated geography as well as its endurance too. It lasted for about seven centuries, from 270 CE to 960 CE, in what is today Ethiopia and parts of Yemen. Some folklore has it that the ark of the covenant in the Old Testament was actually stored in a monastery in Axum, although there are some alternative theories as to where it ended up. The first rulers of Axum were pagans and polytheists, and the empire grew to be an important trading center in Africa. It converted to Christianity in the fourth century CE after a "Christian philosopher by the name of Meropius, bound for India, was shipwrecked on the coast. Although he died, his two companions survived and when they began to spread to word of the gospels, they found a receptive audience" (Farrington, 2006, p. 64). Interestingly, Axum remained the only monotheist African society for another three centuries when, in the seventh century CE, the Arab Umayyad Dynasty began to conquer Northern Africa and convert the local populations to Islam.

There were also various monotheist and nonmonotheist empires that conquered massive swaths of territory, although they survived only for short periods of time: The Macedonian Empire lasted only forty years, but under the rule of Alexander the Great, it became a vast and mighty empire that extended from the Balkans to include Persia and parts of Egypt and the Middle East. The Mongol Empire lasted longer for about three centuries, but during the reign of Genghis Khan, it raided territories in the west and east so effectively and brutally that, between 1205 CE and 1260 CE, it managed to stretch from the China Sea to central Europe. Such was the case of the Empire of Tamerlane (the Timurids), which lasted barely more

than a century but became a powerful regional force at the turn of the fifteenth century in the Near East by triumphing over the Golden Hordes,
sacking Belgrade and temporarily ending the Ottoman Empire's rule in
Anatolia and the Balkans. The Islamic Seljuk Empire lasted only 157 years
but, moving west from its geographic origins in central Asia, was able to
enter Asia Minor in 1071 CE, which marked the beginning of the Turkish
presence in Anatolia that continues to this day. And the Arab Umayyads
were able to spread so rapidly between 661 CE and 750 CE that, by the
time the dynasty fell to the Abbasids in the middle of the eighth century,
the Arab Empires controlled the Arabian Peninsula; the Middle East; most
of southeastern Anatolia, Persia, North Africa, and the Iberian Peninsula.

2.4 Some Generalizations

On the basis of these observations and data, I now turn to various comparisons and generalizations. Table 2.1, for instance, shows that monotheist civilizations lasted significantly less than nonmonotheist societies,
with a typical nonmonotheist civilization enduring about 360 years
and a monotheist society lasting about 260 years. The monotheist societies attained a peak land mass of about 1.2 million km^2, which was
roughly 400,000 km^2 smaller than nonmonotheist societies. For comparison purposes, when the nonmonotheist civilizations of the Americas
are excluded, monotheist civilizations lasted about six decades short of
nonmonotheist civilizations, whereas their peak land mass was about
600,000 km^2 smaller than nonmonotheist societies. Hence the early
American civilizations lasted much longer than average, with about 640
years, but they occupied more concentrated areas during their reign.
Also, monotheist societies were distributed fairly evenly between Africa
and Asia but could be located anywhere in Europe and the Middle East.
By contrast, nonmonotheist establishments were predominantly centered in Asia and America.

The generalization of a "Christian Europe" and a "Muslim Middle East"
might be too much of a caricature. Nonetheless, as the middle section
of table 2.1 shows, 92 percent of the thirty-eight civilizations in Europe
were Christian and 96 percent of the thirty-five societies in the Middle
East were Muslim. Moreover, Asian civilizations were predominantly
nonmonotheist, with Hinduism, Buddhism, and Taoism dominating the
Asian religious landscape, and the Americas being home to no monotheist society.

Table 2.1   Dynasties, kingdoms, and empires (2500 BCE to 1750 CE)

Monotheist dynasties, kingdoms, and empires (109 observations)

Duration	Land	Europe	Africa	Middle East	Asia	Jewish	Christian	Muslim
25.6	1,217,531	38	17	35	19	2	46	61
Share of regional total (%):		51	51	58	22	. . .	. . .	. . .
Jewish (%)		0	0	3	5	. . .	. . .	. . .
Christian (%)		92	35	3	21	. . .	. . .	. . .
Muslim (%)		8	65	96	74	. . .	. . .	. . .

Nonmonotheist dynasties, kingdoms, and empires (168 observations)

Duration	Peak land	Europe	Africa	Middle East	Asia	America
35.8	1,621,008	36	16	26	68	22
As share of total in region (%):		49	49	42	78	100

Excluding the Americas (146 observations)

Duration	Peak land
31.6	1,820,441

Source: Iyigun (2010).

In table 2.2, I break down civilizations according to their theistic attribute by century. As shown in the first line of the table, only one of the sixteen societies on record was monotheist during the fourth century: the Christian Axum Empire in sub-Saharan Africa. By the eighth century, however, about one-fifth of all sovereign countries were monotheist, with one being Jewish (Khazaria) and three being Christian (Axum Empire, Byzantine Empire, and the Nubian kingdoms). By the twelfth century, more than 50 percent of all countries in the sample were monotheist. Within another three centuries, about 40 percent of the civilizations in existence were Christian, with about another 35 percent being Muslim. And, as shown on the last line, nearly 90 percent of seventeenth-century civilizations for which there exists data were affiliated with an Abrahamic monotheism.

The central observation thus is that there was a lot of variety and diversity in the historic record of human civilizations as well as some common

Table 2.2   A breakdown of civilizations by religion over time

	Total	Monotheist		Jewish		Christian		Muslim	
Century	No.	No.	%	No.	%	No.	%	No.	%
300–399 CE	16	1	7	0	0	1	6	0	0
500–599 CE	16	5	33	0	0	5	33	0	0
700–799 CE	20	4	15	1	4	3	11	0	0
900–999 CE	28	14	50	0	0	11	39	3	11
1100–1199 CE	39	21	53	0	0	19	48	2	5
1400–1499 CE	26	19	73	0	0	11	42	8	31
1600–1699 CE	18	16	89	0	0	12	71	4	18

Note this is a restricted sample (243 observations). Source: Iyigun (2010).

traits among them. All the same, as I will explore in more detail in the next few sections, adherence to monotheism did affect these civilizations in salient ways.

2.5   Hypothesis

The rudimentary facts outlined above provide good reason, I believe, why the evolution of societies that predominantly adhered to Abrahamic monotheisms warrants some attention.

Moreover, a host of questions could be motivated on the basis of my observations thus far: Why were monotheisms adopted fairly rapidly by numerous polities in Europe, the Middle East, and North Africa? Were there essential differences between monotheist societies and others? If so, what were these differences and how did they affect the evolutions of societies and polities? What were the channels through which religion and monotheisms influenced societies and polities? And, last but not least, what kind of impact did they have on the interactions and interplay between political and ecclesiastical authorities?

To briefly synthesize, if religious adherence was good for sociopolitical stability and monotheisms were easier to sustain as state religions due to the fact that they could imbue their affiliated ecclesiastical as well as political institutions with monopoly powers, then monotheist societies should have historically had various political and social advantages vis-à-vis the others.

To formalize, if (1) in Durkheimian fashion, moral and ethical considerations associated with *religion* serve as a *foundation for social stability*; (2) as argued by Diamond, *centralized government* and *organized religion* are *complements* in sociopolitical organization; and (3) in the spirit of Ekelund et al. as well as Barro-McCleary, *monotheisms* were naturally more effective in maintaining their *ecclesiastical dominance* within polities, then monotheist civilizations ought to have *endured longer* historically, and, to the extent that such stability conferred military, political, and economic benefits to societies as well, monotheist societies even ought to have *ruled over larger geographic domains*.

But what do the data say?

2.6 Identifying Monotheisms' Impact

We have already seen that monotheist civilizations lasted about nine decades less than pagan and polytheist cultures (280 years versus 360 years) in addition to ruling over geographic domains that were about half a million km^2 smaller (1.4 million km^2 as opposed to 1.8 million km^2). Of course, these are only driven by correlations, and there are other determinants of how long civilizations lasted and the geographic areas they were able to control.

I have already alluded to the fact that civilizations in the Americas lasted a lot longer than those in other regions, and those in Asia controlled larger geographic areas regardless of their religious orientation. Also, monotheisms became available to societies much later in time. Thus it is necessary to isolate the impact of these other determinants of duration and size of geographic domain to check if the theistic identity of societies played an independent role in those latter attributes. In addition, and as can be easily verified in figure 2.1, human civilizations tended to endure less over time.

Based on such observations, one can control for a whole bunch of observable factors that were potentially important for the size and the endurance of human civilizations. Then one can isolate the impact of adherence to monotheism on geographic domain and duration. Given the data set available, one would then like to see if the duration of each civilization was influenced by whether it was, according to our criteria, monotheist.

The estimation methodology and the complete technical details can be perused in the online technical appendix of this chapter. However, the bottom line is that, on the basis of the data I have just described covering 277 societies over the period between 2500 BCE and 1750 CE,

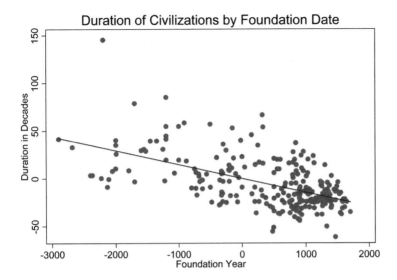

Figure 2.1 Civilizations endured less over time

whether a civilization adhered to monotheism was an important factor that affected the survival likelihood and duration of a civilization. For instance, a monotheist civilization that existed in the eleventh century was expected to last nearly two decades longer than an otherwise identical but nonmonotheist society.

This finding is neither driven nor influenced by geographic location; nor is it an artifact of whether Judaism, Christianity, and Islam were yet born, although the impact of monotheism on survival was declining over time for all societies (as shown in figure 2.1).

To give an idea, figure 2.2 provides duration estimates for monotheist versus nonmonotheist civilizations based on their dates of foundation (and after controlling for a host of important correlates of duration that I elaborated on previously). As shown, monotheist civilizations lasted noticeably longer than nonmonotheist societies all the way through the early nineteenth century.

While *adherence* to monotheism exerted a systematic positive effect on the duration of a civilization, there is also some evidence that the *birth* of Abrahamic monotheisms (i.e., Judaism) had a positive impact on survival, too. This might be indicative of two things: One, competition intensified between the three religious traditions as they started to coexist over time. Two, monotheism had a broader impact on human societies than what an indicator of adherence to a monotheism can capture and convey.

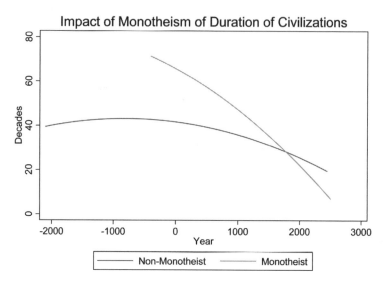

Figure 2.2 But monotheist civilizations typically lasted longer

So why is it that, in general, monotheist societies lasted about nine decades less than other societies but adherence to monotheism had a positive effect on endurance and survival over time? It turns out that there are both geographic and chronological reasons for this. As I have already shown, a society's geographic location influenced how long it lasted. This might have been due to the fact that continents differ a whole lot in the extent to which they can sustain population density levels. On this score, being located in Africa or the Middle East was "bad" and being in America was "good." On the other hand, there was a clear tendency of civilizations to endure less over time, and monotheist societies came to the historical scene much later.

What about the effect of adherence to monotheism on geographic size? While I have not found that the theistic attribute of the society had a positive impact on peak land mass, I have seen that the birth of monotheism in the early seventh century BCE provides a common break in the peak land mass attained by civilizations historically. Taking the lower estimates available, for instance, it can be seen that societies founded after 606 BCE had about 380,000 km² or roughly 25 percent larger land mass. All in all, it is clear that the birth of Christianity might have had an adverse statistically significant effect on peak land mass but not enough to offset the positive and significant impact of the birth of monotheism (i.e., Judaism).

On this score, it was not whether the civilization itself was monotheist that mattered. Rather, it was whether a civilization existed before or after monotheism became practiced among the Jews in 606 BCE. In particular, after monotheism was born in 606 BCE, a given kingdom, dynasty or empire had about 65 percent larger mass than a comparable civilization that existed before 606 BCE. And this was true for all civilizations, not just monotheist ones.

In line with earlier discussions, the location of a civilization was important too in predicting the peak landmass of historic civilizations. All else equal, being in America, where historically small sovereign establishments, such as the Mochica, Chavin, and Chimu civilizations existed, or in Africa, with its relatively smaller Soninke Dynasty, the Kingdom of Kongo, Meroe, and Napata-Kush civilizations, produced geographically smaller civilizations. The African adverse effect on size was quite substantial: whereas societies in the data set attained 2.1 million km² on average, all else equal, Africa generated a size of about 1.5 million km², which is about a 30 percent impact.

I have thus far made no particular distinction among Judaism, Christianity, and Islam and only focused on whether a society adhered to one of the three monotheisms. But it could be that the results—that is, adherence to a monotheist faith extending the duration of civilizations and enlarging their geographic control—are driven by Judaism, Christianity, or Islam alone. Nonetheless, controlling for the specific faith of each society shows that the duration of Jewish, Christian, and Muslim civilizations were all positively and statistically significantly influenced by their monotheist nature.

Interestingly, by separating the three monotheisms into Judaism, Christianity, and Islam, one can in fact see that the impact of monotheism seems to have had a religion-specific component when it comes to geographic control. Unlike the results on duration, adherence to a specific religion—Islam—did exert an additional positive impact on the geographic domain of civilizations historically. There is some evidence that Islamic societies spread over three times as large geographic domains as non-Islamic societies during their tenure. Thus Islamic empires seem to have been more successful than others in extending the reach of empire. This also reflects the fact that the influence of Islam grew within a relatively short time period subsequent to the birth of Islam in 622 CE.

In empirical studies like these, the direction of causality and omitted variables are always a concern. In particular, is it possible that the duration of societies and the size of their geographic domains were influencing their theistic characteristics and not the other way around? Or could there have been some other variables not accounted for that would explain both how long civilizations lasted over time and whether their administrative ranks—and most of their populations, in some cases—subscribed to and promoted monotheism? To be sure, there are various other issues that could be important here, such as the classification methodology employed and a consistent treatment of the dates of foundation and termination.

There are two factors that attenuate these concerns to some degree: First, one would have to bear in mind that, by ninth century CE, a vast majority of North Africa, the European continent, and the Middle East had become monotheist, with the local populations having subscribed to one of the three main monotheisms. Thus there is a structural time break in the adoption of monotheism in these geographic areas, roughly covering the period between 313 CE, when the Roman emperor Constantine I issued the Edict of Milan, which legalized Christian worship turning the Roman Empire monotheist, and the 751 CE Talas War between the Asian Turks and the Abbasid Muslims, which exposed Turks to Islam and led to their adoption of monotheism as well as its spread in Asia subsequently.

Second, recall that, in eleven civilizations in the data set, the rulers—and in some cases, most of the populations—converted to monotheism *after* the civilization was founded. In the case of all these societies except Khazaria, Takrur, Cumans, Bulgars, and Kievan Rus, the conversions occurred sufficiently late or early so as to enable one to classify Romans as nonmonotheist and the others as monotheist. In the case of Khazaria, Takrur, and Kievan Rus, there is a great deal more uncertainty about the date and extent of conversions that took place neither early nor late enough to aid with classification. In eight of the eleven cases, however, the classification employed was in the direction of attenuation. In any case, the statistical tests indicate that neither of the findings reported here rides on this classification issue.

What about the impact of other organized religions and faith in general, as opposed to monotheistic faiths? First, religion and beliefs in otherworldly divine beings were an integral part of all human cultures. Thus the effects picked up here should be interpreted broadly as the impact of monotheism vis-à-vis other belief systems. In addition, one can examine if monotheistic faiths imparted some effects on the stability of civilizations above and beyond those of other organized and widespread religions, such as Buddhism, Hinduism, Taoism, and Zoroastrianism. But doing so by accounting for monotheistic societies, on the one hand, and Buddhist, Hindu, Taoist, and Zoroastrian societies, on the other, it is not possible to identify that the latter had the positive and statistically relevant effects that monotheisms had on their adherents.

For further details and issues regarding the statistical analyses, see Iyigun (2010).

2.7 Monotheisms Reign Supreme

One way to interpret these findings is as follows: Abrahamic monotheisms are built upon true revelations. Consequently, they were destined to slowly wipe out the falsities of paganism, polytheism, and the like.

Be that as it may, this argument won't explain why monotheisms spread at the expense of other faiths, at least partly due to the fact that societies that adhered to monotheism lasted longer and spread wider. That is, monotheisms could have become the ecclesiastical norm among the historical societies of the Middle East, North Africa, Europe, and Asia without having an effect on the duration and dominance of civilizations. With such a transformation unfolding over time within societies, the latter would have slowly evolved into societies in which adherence to a monotheism would have gradually risen. Yet there would have been no effect on the size and longevity of human civilizations. Nevertheless, the role of monotheisms on human societies' durability and dominance seems to have been an important reason why at least Christianity and Islam spread rapidly in Europe, North Africa, and the Middle East between the fourth and ninth centuries. It is also why, for instance, after its meteoric rise in the Middle East and North Africa, Islam was able to penetrate deep into Far East Asia, India, and Indonesia, in particular.

Second, if monotheism did have a significant positive impact on the stability, endurance, and strength of civilizations in spreading over and controlling larger geographic domains, then this would imply that monotheistic religions should have begun to grow at the expense of other spiritual traditions. Indeed, the sociopolitical advantages reviewed in the opening chapter as well as the various religious conversions discussed in section 2.3 of this chapter amply illustrate that it would have been in the interest of rulers to pursue top-down policies of religious conversion. Of course, as some other conversion anecdotes suggest, there have been societies and times in which religious conversions cascaded, with individual conversions feeding on each other. Combined with the fact that an important characteristic of monotheistic faiths is particularism (i.e., that there is only One True God and One True Religion), the acceptance and spread of the main monotheisms yielded the specter of religious conflicts, too (Stark, 2001, pp 116–24).

However, there are strong and distinct disagreements and divisions within each of the three monotheistic religions. These are driven by doctrinal differences as well as individuals' tastes and preferences for religious intensity in their lives (Stark and Bainbridge, 1987; Stark and Finke, 2000): Judaism has its Orthodox, Conservative, and Reform denominations; Christianity has its Roman Catholicism, Protestantism, Anglicanism, and Orthodox Christianity; and Islam has the Sunni, Shi'a, and Sufism splits.

On this basis, it is incumbent upon us to acknowledge that, even within each monotheistic faith, there has existed the potential for and nearly countless realizations of internal conflicts regarding how to follow the Holy Scripture and the path of the One True God. Such observations have led many to conclude that ecclesiastical disagreements—whether they were driven by differences of opinion that are internal or external in nature—have historically have been sources of violent conflict.

Nevertheless, there are historical anecdotes suggesting that, at least when it comes to religious differences, there might have been a hierarchy of ecclesiastical affinity according to which societies and individuals formed alliances—that is, all else equal, external divisions generally trumped internal ones. That said, recorded history is never so clearly delineated, and there are various records of political alliances among Muslim and Christian secular rulers whenever their joint interests were aligned.

What I have established above is that societies that adhered to one of the three Abrahamic monotheistic religions had higher survival odds and reigned over larger geographic domains at their peak. Beyond the general impact of adherence to monotheism, I did not find much evidence that Judaism, Christianity, or Islam were associated with particular effects on the length of reign of civilizations historically. Unlike the results regarding duration, however, there is some evidence that adherence to a specific religion—Islam—was associated with an additional positive impact on geographic domain. Nevertheless, I have not yet identified any mechanism through which the three Abrahamic religions exerted these effects.

In an attempt to do so, the next chapter will offer a brief historiography of the early eras of Judaism, Christianity, and Islam. To that end, I will first explore the evolutions of the three monotheisms during the medieval era. I will then establish how Judaism, Christianity, and Islam spread between the fourth and eleventh centuries in Europe, North Africa, and the Middle East on the back of trade, violent conflicts, and missionary activities. And I will show that, once monotheisms became prevalent due to their inherent advantages vis-à-vis other theisms and as an artifact of their underlying fundamentals, faith-based conflicts and confrontations began to leave their mark in Europe and the Middle East.

THREE

Globalizing Abrahamic Monotheisms

Hume and Durkheim were right after all! Religion does promote social and political stability, but it is the monotheist kind that matters most. The belief and faith in One True God anchors the major monotheisms in human history, and as chapter 2 shows, there are common functionalist social benefits of Judaism, Christianity, and Islam. Indeed, the common functionalist traits of Abrahamic religions—in particular, Christianity and Islam—seem to have been the reason monotheist societies generally endured longer and expanded more swiftly.

It should come as no surprise then that, if monotheist societies were more durable and prone to expand, so were the particular faiths to which those societies adhered. All the same, while the mechanisms through which monotheisms expanded globally varied over time and among the three Abrahamic religions, they often involved proselytism, emulation, ties of commerce and trade, as well as forced conversions by conquest. And, as shown in this chapter, the extent to which Abrahamic faiths grew and spread on the back of either the functionalist benefits of monotheism or the more conventional channels of peaceful and violent contacts varied significantly.

3.1 Judaism

The birth of Judaism is typically dated at around 1200 BCE but there is a contentious debate as to when it became exclusively monotheist. According to one school of thought, it was not until the early seventh century, in 606 BCE (Armstrong, 1993, p. 61; Stark, 2001, pp. 24–25). A less disputed chronology involves the covenant Yahweh made with Moses on Mount Sinai around 1200 BCE. The covenant itself is proof that Yahweh was among multiple gods, although the children of Israel promised to only worship him upon their return to the Promised Land. According to the Bible, the Israelites were not true to their covenant and the establishment of Yahweh as the One True God of Judaism probably did not occur long after the Exodus (Armstrong, 1993, p. 22).

In any case, Toynbee (1946, p. 94) clearly articulates the impact of Judaism on its adherents:

In the power of their spiritual understanding the Israelites surpassed the military prowess of the Philistines and the maritime prowess of the Phoenicians. They had not sought after those things which the Gentiles seek, but had sought first the Kingdom of God; and all those things were added to them. As for the life of their enemies, the Philistines were delivered into Israel's hands. As for riches, Jewry into the inheritance of Tyre and Carthage, to conduct transactions on a scale beyond Phoenician dreams in continents beyond Phoenician knowledge. As for long life, the Jews lived on . . . today, long ages after the Phoenicians and Philistines have lost their identity. Their ancient Syriac neighbours have gone into the melting-pot and been reminted, with new images and superscriptions, while Israel has proved impervious to this alchemy— performed by History in the crucibles of universal states and universal churches and wanderings of the nations—to which we Gentiles all in turn succumb.

Judaism is also unique among the three Abrahamic monotheisms not only because it is likely the oldest surviving One God faith but also due to the fact that its growth and spread in the Middle East, North Africa, and Europe via Jewish proselytism is highly disputed. Rodney Stark (2001, pp. 52–59) makes a compelling case for why there probably was significant Jewish missionary activity in the medieval era. Relying on a variety of sources from theology, Stark identifies four factors that support the existence of extensive missionary activity by Jews in the medieval times: "First, Jewish doctrines set the goal of saving the entire world. Second, both Jewish and Roman writers testify to extensive, often very successful, Jewish proselytism, especially in the Greco-Roman diaspora. Third, estimated growth rates of Jewish populations, especially in the diaspora, strongly support the assumption of high rates of conversion. Finally, early Christian writers frequently reported large numbers of converts to Judaism."

Regardless of the extent to which Judaism grew and expanded in the medieval era on the back of missionary activities, it possessed two salient characteristics vis-à-vis the other two monotheisms. First, according to the Rabbinic view, which all branches of Orthodox and Conservative Judaism maintain, the Halakah (i.e., the Jewish law) establishes two strict rules for Jewish identity. Accordingly, a Jewish identity is assumed at birth through matrilineal descent—that is, only if the person is born to a Jewish mother. Or it can be acquired through the process of formal conversion, which can be a rigorous and lengthy process: Once a person decides to convert, the proselyte must learn the Jewish religion, law, and customs and begin to observe them. Only then is the candidate brought before a beth din (rabbinical court) that decides whether he or she is ready to become a Jew. If the proselyte passes this oral examination, the rituals of conversion are performed. If the convert is male, he is circumcised. Both male and female converts are immersed in the mikvah, a ritual bath used for spiritual purification. The conversion is finalized with the convert being given a Jewish name.

Moreover—and this is the second point—driven by the long history of captivity, abuse, and persecution, Jewish rabbinic leaders began to preach sometime during the first century CE the importance of literacy on the basis of the study and memorization of the Torah and the Talmud. Maristella Botticini and Zvi Eckstein (2005, 2007, and 2012) highlight the impact of destruction of the temple on Jewish literacy and occupational choices during the medieval era. In their own words,

Why were Jewish farmers (and Jews in general) literate whereas the rest of the rural population was illiterate at the beginning of the seventh century? The Jewish religion made primary education mandatory for boys in the first century when the high priest Joshua ben Gamala (64 CE) issued an ordinance that "teachers had to be appointed in each district and every city and that boys of the age of six or seven should be sent." In the first century CE, the Jewish warrior and writer Josephus underlined that children's education was the principal care among the Jews. After the destruction of the Temple in 70 CE, Judaism changed from a religion that was mainly concerned with sacrifices and ceremonies performed by priests in the Temple to a religion whose core was centered around learning the Torah. The synagogue became the center of this activity. From the second to the sixth century, Jewish leaders promoted further the learning and reading of the Torah and the recently redacted Mishna and Talmud by degrading the status of those who remained illiterate ("am ha-aretz"). The compulsory education for boys and the reading of the Torah, Mishna, and Talmud became the essence of Judaism. The monumental work of Goitein (1967–1988) from the documents of the Cairo Geniza provides extensive evidence of the full implementation of mandatory primary schooling for boys in the Jewish communities in the Mediterranean at the turn of the millennium.

This emphasis on literacy and value of human capital accumulation was to influence Judaism for many centuries to come, not only because it acted as an efficient screening device to sort out the less-committed coreligionists in the spirit of the "club religion" motives reviewed earlier, but also because such forward-looking policies equipped the Ashkenazi and Sephardic Jewish populations with skills valuable in commerce, trade, and government as they migrated and were often forced to relocate within Europe, North Africa, and the Middle East.

On this note, it is worthwhile to recognize that, while both Islam and Protestantism also advocate individuals to study the Holy Scripture directly themselves, thereby promoting literacy, Judaism stands out among the three Abrahamic faiths with its higher selectivity and literacy among its adherents. A plausible yet not the only credible explanation is that such distinctions could be attributed to the unique features of Halakah discussed previously.

3.2 Christianity

According to the Bible, Jesus Christ asked his inner circle to spread the faith. The Acts of the Apostles, the fifth book of the Bible in the New Testament, states that the Holy Spirit would give the apostles the powers to mimic some of the works of Jesus so they could spread his word and revelations (Farrington, 2006, p. 30). The momentum for Christian missionary works picked up when a conference of the eminent Christians in Jerusalem held in 49 CE affirmed that the Jews and Gentiles could be admitted to the faith. The subsequent spread of Christianity with the aid of missionary activities was so effective that, by the middle of the first century CE, there were churches in most of the main population centers of the Roman Empire.

Alas, the year 64 CE marks the great fire of Rome, for which the Roman emperor Nero held the Christian minorities responsible. Thus began the centuries-long Christian persecutions that ebbed and flowed within the Roman Empire until the early fourth century. But the major turning point for the faith came with the Edict of Milan in 313 CE, through which Constantine I adopted Christianity as the official state religion. Hence emerged a new "institutional" foundation for this new religion, upon which the financial, political, and social pillars were set for the Roman Catholic Church. Stark (2001, p. 62) elaborates,

[With Constantine's conversion], Christianity became "the most-favored recipient of near-limitless resources of imperial favor." . . . A faith that had been in humble structures was suddenly housed in magnificent public buildings. . . . A clergy recruited from the people and modestly sustained by member contributions suddenly gained immense power, status and wealth as part of the imperial civil service. . . . Because Christian offices had become another form of imperial preferment, it was the sons of the aristocracy who usually won the race. . . . Had the church been weaker, and especially had it not gained such a potent role in secular politics, the result might have been a relatively stable pluralism. . . . Instead, with the exception of Judaism, all other religions, including all new or less powerful brands of Christianity, were soon suppressed.

The rise of Christianity was so remarkable in the two-and-a-half centuries between 49 CE and the Edict of Milan in 313 CE that, by the early fourth century, it was the dominant religion throughout Anatolia, the Balkans, the Iberian and Italian peninsulas, Egypt, the coastal Mediterranean, western and central Europe, as well as most of the British isles. Stark (2001, p. 60) estimates that, in that same interim, over half the Roman Empire turned Christian, which corresponds to about thirty-three million people. Contrary to some prominent sociologists and theologians of Christianity, though, he is skeptical of the view that this substantial growth was the result of the work of missionaries alone and that an important part of it was perhaps due to the network ties of family and friends.

After Constantine moved the capital of the Roman Empire to Constantinople in the east in 324 CE, issues of jurisdiction, liturgy, and ecclesiastical doctrine became important, especially subsequent to the collapse of the Roman Empire in the west, which left the Byzantine Empire as the only heir of Rome. The subsequent history of Christianity is one of which various disagreements and disputes produced a diversity of ecclesiastical interpretations, which primarily if not solely revolved around the Holy Trinity. The Assyrian Church split from the Roman Catholic Church in 431 CE. The Coptic Church followed twenty years later in 451 CE. Then came the Great Schism between the Roman Catholic and the Eastern Orthodox Churches in 1054 CE, following numerous disputes and excommunications. That was followed by the Cathar/Albigensian uprisings in 1177 CE, the Waldensian movement in 1177 CE, the Lollardy splinter in 1350 CE, and the Hussites in 1415–19 CE, to name a few (Moore, 1994; Rhodes, 2005).

Thus were the seeds of plurality among the Christian ecclesiastical institutions sown and, come the Protestant demands for recognition five centuries later, an important precedent was already set.

3.3 Islam

Prophet Mohammed had no successors and, after his death in 632 CE, there were disagreements among his followers regarding who should assume the title of caliph, the leader of the Islamic *ummah*, or global Islamic nation. Some of Mohammed's followers decided that his father-in-law Abu Bakr should ascend the caliphate, whose successor would then be chosen by the spiritual leaders of Islam. However, some of Mohammed's other followers believed Mohammed wanted his cousin Ali ibn Ali Talib to succeed the first caliph, Abu Bakr.

In spite of that, both the Sunni and the Shi'a, as the followers of Abu Bakr and Ali ibn Ali Talib are now respectively called, recognized the reigns of the first four caliphs as legitimate. As a result, the Shi'a-Sunni split remained subdued throughout the reigns of the first four caliphs. But after *rashidun*, when the first four caliphs considered legitimate by both the Sunni and the Shi'a reigned supreme, Ali and his inner circle began to offer an alternative rule to the Sunni caliphs. The Sunni, under Mohammed's widow Ayşa's leadership, dissented. Five years later, in 661 CE, Ali and some of his followers were massacred in the city of Kufa in what is now central Iraq. Still, the Shi'a continued to recognize the legitimacy of caliphs from Ali's bloodline. And when Ali's bloodline died out after the twelfth caliph, the Shi'a declared that he would eventually return as their Messiah.

The Sunni-Shi'a split did nothing to stop or even slow the remarkable spread of Islam, although the ascendancy of Islam began before the sectarian split and during the reign of the second caliph, Umar, who was the founder of the Umayyad Dynasty. The Umayyads were the first Muslim Arab Empire that followed the Rashidun era, and their reign lasted slightly over a century, from 661 CE to 750 CE. But during the course of that brief interval of time, the Umayyad Empire's borders expanded from a narrow strip of the western range of the Arabian peninsula and a pocket of land on the Gulf of Oman to eventually encompass the Arabian peninsula, Egypt, and North Africa, Persia and the Middle East, as well as the Iberian peninsula. The Umayyads' reign was followed by that of the Abbasids, which itself lasted for about a century from 750 CE to 861 CE, and the grand Arab empires continued over roughly the same geographic domains with the successive reigns of the Tulunids, Fatimids, and Ayyubids until 1258 CE.

As discussed in chapter 2, the role of monotheism in societies' durability and dominance seems to have been an important reason Islam spread rapidly in Europe, North Africa, and the Middle East between the fourth and ninth centuries. It is also why, for instance, after its meteoric rise in the Middle East and North Africa, Islam was able to penetrate deep into to the Far East.

A notable comparison of Islam vis-à-vis Christianity reveals that the latter is more fragmented denominationally and ideologically. This seems somewhat of a paradox, given that both these Abrahamic faiths involved high entry barriers and enjoyed strong monopolistic advantages in their respective local religion markets. However, there are at least three observations one could make that are germane to this issue. First, as I will examine and investigate in later chapters, the interreligious rivalry and animosity between Christianity and Islam—and, in particular, the Ottomans' eastern European conquests just when Martin Luther was beginning to rise to prominence—might, at least in part, account for the sectarian and denominational proliferation of Christianity during the sixteenth and seventeenth centuries. Second, scholars such as E. L. Jones (1981) have long argued that the highly fragmented European political landscape could be the main culprit for why Europe was able to foster and accommodate a diversity of opinions and viewpoints, chief among them being the ecclesiastical variety. Finally, Islam being a "law-based" religion could help to explain this difference.

3.4 The Early Contacts

3.4.1 Mohammed and Charlemagne

The earliest contacts between the Islamic cultures of the Middle East and the Christian European societies began to take place during the first Arab dynasty of the Umayyads. In fact, one of the most momentous changes in medieval Europe is ascribed to these early contacts.

As is well known, Edward Gibbon (1776) attributed the fall of the Roman Empire in the fifth century to the Germanic barbarian raids from the north. But in his seminal work, *Mohammed and Charlemange* ([1937] 2001), the Belgian historian Henri Pirenne advanced the view that the rise of Islam was the real culprit for the downfall of Rome. Pirenne, at least implicitly, subscribed to the view that the monotheistic conflict between the east and the west trumped any cultural differences between the Germanic raiders and the Romans. In fact, in his view, the barbarians preserved the Roman culture and assimilated once they took control of the territories of the Roman Empire (Pirenne, [1937] 2001, pp. 147–48):

Nothing could be more suggestive, nothing could better enable us to comprehend the expansion of Islam in the 7th century, than to compare its effect upon the Roman Empire with that of the Germanic invasions. These latter invasions were the climax of a situation which was as old as the Empire, and indeed even older, and which had weighed upon it more or less heavily throughout its history. When the Empire, its frontiers penetrated, abandoned the struggle, the invaders promptly allowed themselves to become absorbed in it, and as far as possible they maintained its civilization, and entered into the community upon which this civilization was based.

By contrast, Pirenne leaves no doubt that the "armies of Mohammed" were driven by the rigors of a new faith and that not assimilation but conquest was on their minds. At the same time, he marvels at the swiftness with which Islam spread, especially when contrasted with the early diffusion of Christianity (Pirenne, [1937] 2001, pp. 149–50):

Preoccupied by the secular conflict, neither the Roman Empire nor the Persian Empire seems to have had any suspicion of the propaganda by which Mohammed, amidst the confused conflicts of the tribes, was on the point of giving his own people a religion which it would presently cast upon the world, while imposing its own dominion. . . . The Arab conquest, which brought confusion upon both Europe and Asia, was without precedent. The swiftness of its victory is comparable only with that by which the Mongol Empires of Atilla, Jenghiz Khan and Tamerlane were established. But these Empires were ephemeral as the conquest of Islam was lasting. This religion still has its faithful today in almost every country where it was imposed by the first Caliphs. The lighting-like rapidity of its diffusion was a veritable miracle as compared with the slow progress of Christianity. . . . Here the great problem is to determine why Arabs, who were certainly not more numerous than the Germans, were not, like the latter, absorbed by the populations of the regions which they had conquered, whose civilization was superior to their own. There is only one reply to this question, and it is of the moral order. While the Germans had nothing with which to oppose the Christianity of the Empire, the Arabs were exalted by a new faith. It was this, and this alone, that prevented their assimilation.

3.4.2 Holy Crusades

In the early eighth century, the Christian domains had retreated in the face of cohesive, effective, and determined Islamic armies of the Abbasids, thus surrendering the Iberian peninsula to Islam in 711 CE. It would not be for another eight centuries until those lands would be reclaimed by Christianity, and by the time Islam arrived in Anatolia via the Seljuk Turks, *al-Andalus* was firmly in Muslim control. But it was the decimation of the armies of the Byzantine Empire by the Seljuk warriors in the Battle of Manzikert in 1071 CE that had wide-reaching repercussions for Christian-Muslim relations.

With its eastern European flanks under an Islamic threat too, following the penetration of Anatolia by Muslim powers, Christianity began to feel the squeeze of the Islamic conquerors on its own turf. Moreover, the city of Jerusalem coming under Turkish control in 1077 CE meant that the European pilgrimages to the Holy City, which dated as far back as the fourth century CE, became dangerous if not impossible (Brundage, 2006).

Thus in such dire straits began the first of nine Holy Crusades, organized following Pope Urban's impassioned speech at the Council of Claremont in 1095. There are five different accounts of his historic speech, none of which is contemporary (Armstrong, 1988; Brundage, 2006). In the spirit of the material in chapter 2, they make clear the role of religion in uniting and galvanizing people and the importance of One God helping them take action (Brundage, 2006). In the words of Armstrong (1988, pp. 66–67),

[Pope Urban] called upon the knights of Europe to stop fighting one another and to band together against the Turks in a twofold war of liberation. First they should liberate the Christians of Asia Minor from the Turks; then they should march on to Jerusalem to liberate the Holy Land. There would be the Peace of God in the West and the War of God against Islam in the East—a perfect solution to the problems of Europe! . . . He used the words of Jesus which had hitherto summoned monks into the cloister: "Everyone who has left houses, brother, sisters, father, mother or land for the sake of my name will be repaid a hundred times over" (Mathew 19:29). He also seems to have reminded them that Christ had urged the Christians to be ready to die for his sake, as a Crusader would have to do.

The inaugural crusade that followed was the most successful of all, without a doubt. Five main expeditions of the First Crusade reached Constantinople in the winter of 1096, and the military campaign against the Turks began in earnest the following spring. After scoring victories in Anatolia, the crusaders sacked the city of Antioch in the summer on 1098; one year later, they took Jerusalem. In the two centuries between 1095 and 1291, there were about nine Holy Crusades, although, with various smaller scale missions taking place during that time interval, this number is subject to debate.

The power of religious identity and, in particular, that of monotheism is further revealed by the history of the Holy Crusades, as the Muslim response to the shock of the First Crusade was unification and power consolidation. To many scholars, this is why none of the subsequent crusades were nearly as effective as the first. For example, according to Brundage (2006, p. 287), "No subsequent crusading venture ever equaled, or indeed even approached, the success of the expedition of 1095–1099. Modern historians generally agree that the First Crusade succeeded as it did mainly because the Muslim powers of the Middle East at the end of the eleventh century were divided among themselves."

The Islamic response to the First Crusade began to take shape in mid-twelfth century. There is some debate about whether the elevation of the concept of jihad to a more prominent status in Arabic and Islamic writings coincides with this time period (Brundage, 2006, p. 288). By the late twelfth century, the countercrusade had reached full force with the Ayyubid leader Saladin recapturing Jerusalem in 1187 CE from the crusaders.

Another lasting legacy of the First Crusade was the establishment of three prominent Christian military orders in the Middle East, all of which were supported by the resources and commitment of western European secular and ecclesiastical powers. The Knights Templar, the Knights of Saint John, and the Teutonic Knights all were, in essence, Christian warrior monasteries. They were intended to protect the Holy Land from Muslim reconquest and safeguard Christian pilgrims. As I will show later, these orders, especially the Knights of Saint John, who relocated to Cyprus following the fall of the Kingdom of Jerusalem, were to play important roles in Muslim-Christian relationships throughout the sixteenth century.

In any case, the crusading enterprise shows the role and limits of faith-based cooperation and conflict. For one, the 1054 Orthodox-Roman Schism was still fresh in 1071 when Byzantine Anatolia fell to the Turks. And while the Turkish threat did not induce the two churches to reunite, it was enough for the Roman Catholic Pope Urban to rally Europe in support of Byzantine, despite the underlying currents of mistrust between the Orthodox and Roman churches.

Moreover, the Christian Crusades that began with the intent to liberate Jerusalem from the Muslims also mark the beginning of the Christian pogroms against the Jews as well as the specialized Crusades, like the Albigensian Crusade of 1209, which targeted the budding Christian reform movements. In this, one sees some tragic consequences of the One God/One Faith duality Stark and Niebuhr have emphasized. In Armstrong's own words (1988, p. 74),

The Crusaders had turned Urban's sophisticated Cluniac wars of liberation into a vendetta: they hounded the Jews as they would have hounded any other people who had killed their feudal lord. They believed that they were avenging the death of Christ, their lord, and that they were marching east to recover the Holy Land, which was his fief, his patrimony. Their aggressive religion was rooted firmly in their old chivalric traditions. Despite the Church's disapproval, hatred of the Jews continued to be an essential element in crusading. Every time a crusade was preached there was a fresh outbreak of pogroms. Sometimes people who could not go to the East felt that they were taking part in the expedition by killing Jews at home.

3.4.3 Moorish Spain (al-Andalus)

Al-Andalus, the Iberian peninsula under Islamic reign, defines a sanguine contrast in that cultures of all three monotheisms coexisted there for eight centuries. In some sense, the al-Andalus period in Iberia represents the prototype of the Ottoman administrations of the fifteenth through nineteenth centuries, under which some degree of religious and cultural freedoms was tolerated.

There are three aspects of cultural life and religious coexistence one should note about this period. First, the Umayyad Dynasty asserted its control on much of the peninsula in 711 CE, after which point, Christians, Muslim, and Jews lived together under Arabic rule in much of southern al-Andalus, as they also did under Christian rule in the Castile and Aragon Kingdoms in the north. Starting in the ninth century, the Spanish *Reconquista* began to take shape, with the Christian kingdoms up north pushing the frontiers southward into Muslim-held lands. By the mid-thirteenth century, Christian kingdoms had regained back most of the peninsula. The three monotheisms coexisted without major problems during this era, with the only exception being the Cordoban martyrs, a group of al-Andalus Christians "who provoked and achieved martyrdom at Muslim hands in the ninth-century Cordoba" (Constable, 2006, p. 307).

Second, it is important to recognize that the definition of peaceful coexistence back in the medieval era differed significantly from contemporary ideas of equality and social harmony. Both in Christian-held territories and in Muslim domains, the rights and obligations of religious minorities were subordinated to those of the majority, and they were spelled out in detail (Constable, 2006, pp. 327–34).

Third, starting with the Jewish pogroms of 1391, religious tensions reached a new height in the Iberian peninsula. Although many Iberian Jews converted to Christianity during this era in order to avoid religious massacre, many *conversos* remained under suspicion that they were still Jews in effect who continued to promote Judaism at the expense of Christianity. Thus began the infamous Spanish Inquisition, which was the design of Ferdinand of Aragon and Isabella of Castile to purge Iberia of all non-Christian elements.

This movement culminated in the expulsion of Jews from Castile and Aragon in 1492 and in other areas of the peninsula swiftly thereafter. A large number of these Sephardic Jews resettled in the Ottoman Empire during the reign of Sultan Beyazıt II (r. 1481–1512), who dispatched the Ottoman navy for their resettlement. The number of Sephardic Jews who were resettled in various parts of the still-fledgling empire—in particular, in Salonica, Avlona, Palestine, and Istanbul—is estimated to have totaled one hundred thousand (Kumrular, 2008, p. 24). Thereafter, the Jewish Ottoman community proved an invaluable asset for the empire, as they helped strengthen commerce and professional activities throughout much of the empire. This was in part due to the fact that Ottoman Turks were largely unequipped for business enterprises and their selection into military careers left commercial occupations to the minorities. But the Turks also distrusted the empire's Christian subjects whose countries had only recently been conquered by the Ottomans; hence, it was natural for them to prefer Jewish subjects to which this consideration did not apply (Inalcik, 1994).

For more details on the al-Andalus era in Iberia, see Chejne (1974), Jayyusi (1992), Kennedy (1996), Constable (2006), and Neusner (2006).

3.4.4 Medieval Islamic Science

As is quite well known, many scholars credit the Arab dynasties and particularly al-Andalus for preserving and advancing the discoveries of Greco-Roman traditions of philosophy, science, and literature at a time when they were at best being ignored in the Western world (Homerin, 2006). In fact, by the time the European continent was undergoing its intellectual reawakening with the Italian Renaissance, the influence of the Moors was quite apparent (Durant, 1950; Saliba, 2007).

Especially during the Abbasids reign in the eighth and ninth centuries, the Muslim empires' advances in literature, architecture, and the sciences were unrivaled, and it rubber-stamped the fact that the Arab civilizations went from chaos and anarchy prior to the advent of Islam to being the dominant and pioneering culture of the Medieval world subsequently.

To review only a handful of the Arab advances and contributions to the sciences and literature during that era, one could note al-Khwarizmi, who is credited with the first comprehensive study of algebra; al-Razi and Ibn Sina, two physicians whose works in medicine were translated into Latin and were very influential in the West for more than five centuries;

Ibn Battuta, who was the famed Islamic geographer of the medieval era; Jalal al-Din Rumi and Omar Khayyam, for their poetic works; Ibn al-Nafîs, who discovered pulmonary blood circulation; Taqi al-Dîn, who persuaded the Ottoman Sultan Murad III to build the leading observatory of its time in Galata, Istanbul; and Ibn Khaldun, for his seminal contributions to the principles of historical thought (Anglin and Hamblin, 1993; Lewis, 2002; Ghazanfar, 2006). Such intellectual vigor and dynamism was, to an important extent, the legacy of the Abbasid caliph Ma'mun, who established an academy in Baghdad in the early ninth century, where all the important scientific and literary Hellenistic works were translated to Arabic.

Jones (1981, pp. 175–76) makes it clear not only that the Muslim world was ahead of Europe and the West during the medieval era but also that its faith had something to do with it:

The strong point of the Islamic world of the Near East and North Africa lay in obtaining economies of scale by uniting one faith, one culture and the one Arabic language, a diversity of peoples from Spain across Asia. For a time this culture, occupying an area greater than the Roman empire, was most innovative. The "Arab Agricultural Revolution" which brought crops from India as far west of Spain was based on extensive culture contact and travel. . . . Ideas were also diffused in books to an extent beyond the dreams of Medieval Christendom. Large, well-lighted cities with universities and great libraries in Muslim Spain stood in contrast to the virtual hutments and spartan monasticism north of the Pyrenees. The generations are said to have passed into the thirteenth century without plague or famine. . . . Scientific and technological knowledge was absorbed from India and China and in some respects developed further. Even at later periods Europe had much to learn from Islam. . . . "Oriental" bloodstock reached eastern and central Europe only with the Turkish advances of the sixteenth century and only in the second half of the seventeenth century became an ingredient in the larger improved breed of horse essential to the growth of inland transportation. . . . When Thomas Jefferson was considering the grant of a patent for Oliver Evans's automated flour mill, [he found out that there] was already similar machinery in operation [in Egypt].

Mokyr (1990, pp. 39–44), too, acknowledges the superiority of the Islamic Arab cultures over their medieval European contemporaries and enumerates the various contributions of the medieval Muslims to technological progress in sailing, paper products, textiles, chemicals, and mechanical engineering.

In this regard, it is illuminating to consider what is more or less the conventional view about the state and sophistication of medieval Islamic science and literature—as it is implicit in the judgments of Jones and

Mokyr—and those of George Saliba (2007). The conventional view of Islamic knowledge during the medieval era is that, yes, it was very sophisticated by the European standards of the day, but this was because it had come into contact with Greco-Hellenistic ancient civilizations from which it bequeathed its crucial intellectual foundation. According to what Saliba defines as the *classical narrative*, such an intellectual foundation neither existed nor originated in the Islamic desert civilizations. Saliba's recent book, *Islamic Science and the Making of the European Renaissance*, is a detailed account and refutal of this viewpoint: the state of Abbasid literature and scientific knowledge in the late eighth and early ninth centuries was far too advanced for it to be explained by knowledge that had been imported from the Greco-Hellenistic civilizations alone, as the sophistication and novelty of the Abbasid works in science, astronomy, medicine, and algebra during that era demonstrate.

3.5 From Triumph to Confrontation

The rapid rise of Islam following its birth with the *Hicret* (exodus) from Mecca to Medina in 622 CE and the paths of conquest by the Arab dynasties of the medieval era subsequently made Iberia the center of interfaith contacts and relations between the early eighth century and early eleventh century. The historical record suggests that, for the most part, tranquility reigned in Iberia during this era, although the efforts of Christian kingdoms up north in the peninsula to reconquer lands held by the al-Andalus Arabs never dimmed. The fall of Byzantine Anatolia to the Muslim Turks in 1071, however, was a milestone in interfaith relationships because of its dire implications for Christian Europe. The Holy Crusades, which lasted close to two centuries, were mainly aimed at liberating the Holy Lands in the east, but their artifacts were the pogroms against the Jews in Europe, the violent suppression of Christian reform movements in southern France, and the eventual expulsion of Jews and Arabs from Iberia.

Hence, by the eighth century, the medieval world was predominantly a monotheistic domain and, by the turn of the fifteenth century, conflict and confrontation were part of its historic legacy.

Monotheism, Conflict, and Cooperation

FOUR

A Conceptual Framework

In the third part of the book, I will now turn attention away from the survival and spread of monotheisms and begin to focus on how religion influenced conflict and cooperation. I will also examine how some pivotal interfaith conflicts and intrareligious cooperations produced lasting effects in the sociopolitical and economic realms.

In doing so, the rest of the book is organized such that the impact of Islam on the Christian world will get a lot more early emphasis, especially in chapters 5 through 7. An examination of the influence of Christianity on the Muslim world—with particular emphasis on the role of the latter in the Near East and the Middle East—is the focus of chapter 11 and, to a less extent, the material in chapters 8 and 9.

Note that the interactions of Christianity and Islam with Judaism, which got some coverage heretofore, will for the most part recede to the background. This is, in part, due to the historical focus of the remainder of this book, which mainly covers an era when Muslim and Christian interactions dominated the relevant geographic landscape. It is also an artifact of Christianity and Islam accounting for more than half the world population and a majority of countries among their adherents.

To get this started, I would like to identify the conditions under which internal divisions within a monotheist religion would be subordinated to those between monotheisms and the conditions under which they would not. In particular, it will be useful to develop an analytical model that would help contextualize the incentives for conflict, the means through which conflict historically paid off, and how religious adherence came to bear on peace and conflict among societies.

The success of monotheisms in spreading and generating stability and durability for sociopolitical systems meant that, sooner or later, civilizations associated with Judaism, Christianity, and Islam would be in direct confrontation. While all monotheistic traditions agree on the oneness of God, they are in inherent disagreement over who the messenger of God is and, accordingly, which ecclesiastical clerical institutions ought to have domain over religious matters. Recall that sociologists brand this aspect of religion *particularism*—the idea that Judaism, Christianity, and Islam are all built on fundamental beliefs in One God and One Religion. Prominent scholars such as Rodney Stark (2001) and Karen Armstrong (1993, 2006) have suggested particularism as the cause of faith-based conflicts and confrontations in Europe, North Africa, Asia, and the Middle East, once Abrahamic religions exerted a religious monopoly in these geographies.

But conflict is of the same vintage as human history, and there was clearly no dearth of political and economic motives pitting rulers and societies against each other not only prior to monotheisms becoming the majority ecclesiastical norm in the Middle East, North Africa, and Europe but also thereafter. Furthermore, after the advent of monotheism, differences of ecclesiastical opinion among various sects of each religion were enough to produce seemingly irreparable rifts within societies that adhered to the same monotheist tradition.

In the words of Stark (2001, pp. 116–20),

It is precisely God as a conscious, responsive, good supreme being of infinite scope—the One True God as conceived by the great monotheisms—who prompts awareness in idolatry, false Gods, and heretical religions. *Particularism*, the belief that any given religion is the *only true religion*, is *inherent in monotheism* . . . . If salvation comes only through faith in Christ, then Jews are outcasts, bound for hell for practicing a false religion. By the same logic, if Yahweh is the One True God, then the ancient Greeks and Romans were idolaters—and even polytheists will take offense when others dismiss their Gods as fantasies or falsehoods. Thus, the two sides of particularism: the contempt for other faiths and the reaction by those held in contempt. But if monotheists believe there is only One True God, they have been unable to sustain One True Religion. Rather from the start all of the major monotheisms have been prone to splinter into many True Religions that sometimes acknowledge one another's right to coexist and sometimes don't. Hence, *internal* and *external conflict* is *inherent* in particularistic religion.

Observations such as these raise an important question: could differences among monotheisms override all other internal ecclesiastical rifts in determining the patterns of conflict and cooperation among societ-ies? Or, to state it more poignantly, when and under what circumstances could religious affinity and differences between Judaism, Christianity, and Islam drive violent conflicts and cooperation? (Readers who would like to be spared the analytical details can skip ahead to subsection 4.3.)

Once again, the existing literatures in economics, political science, and sociology provide the foundations upon which one can scaffold a useful analytical framework. Here, one can even borrow from existing work on evolutionary biology and psychology.

The tools of neoclassical economics were traditionally applied to a vari-ety of questions, but the supply side almost unequivocally involved aspects of *legal* production. And, to an overwhelming extent, it still does. A strong assumption inherent in the traditional neoclassical view is that property rights are well defined and secure; as a consequence, any individual who wishes to engage in productive activities can do so by taking into account the standard costs and benefits. In making such decisions and choices, one need not contend with whether the economic benefits of his or her activities could be appropriated through illegal means—nor is there an economic cost to ensuring a safe and relatively predictable environment in which people can engage in production. Perhaps more fundamentally, the standard neoclassical view of production does not entertain the question of whether an individual's time is more gainfully employed in production or crime, where the latter can even extend into various violent incarnations.

Despite this long-cherished and mostly useful tradition, there is no reason to take as given an environment in which an economy's resources and individuals' time are allocated to productive and peaceful uses only. This is all the more relevant for developing countries or the history of in-dustrialized nations; in weak institutional environments where property rights are not secure, it is more reasonable to consider the allocation of resources and time to all uses, including those that are of an extralegal nature.

Starting as early as the 1950s, a relatively small strand in the econom-ics literature has done precisely that: The notion that crime and violent conflict over the ownership for resources should be modeled as an alter-native to legal economic production was originally articulated by the Nobel laureate Trygve Haavelmo in his *A Study in the Theory of Economic Evolution* (1954). It was further developed by follow-up material such as Hirshleifer (1991), Grossman (1994), Grossman and Kim (1995), Gross-man and Iyigun (1995, 1997), Skaperdas (1992), Alesina and Spolaore (2005), Hafer (2006), and Konrad and Skaperdas (2012). This body of work is part of a broader literature on the importance of secure property rights in economic activity, with contributions such as Tornell and Velasco (1992) and Dixit (2004) to take but two examples. The incorporation of the means to engage in crime and appropriation has proven to be a fairly fruitful approach to modeling conflict, because it has directed the tools of economics to the study of some esoteric but important subjects, such as the illegal economy, state formation, violence, anarchy, military conflicts, and so on.

Broadly speaking, the key idea I advocate below is related to a body of work that focuses on the role of evolutionary survival dynamics on social and political norms and institutions. For example, Axelrod (2006) mathematically computes an evolutionary extinction model to illustrate how cooperation dominates noncooperative behavior in terms of long-term survival prospects. Bowles (2006, 2009) and Choi and Bowles (2007) study the emergence and sustenance of altruism versus hostility and conflict due to intergroup competition, and Levine and Modica (2013) show how serious external threats help sustain internal compromise and produce more efficient political institutions domestically.

In spirit, the framework below is most similar to Wright (2000). His view is that societies—in particular socioeconomic and political institutions—have evolved over time to reflect more complexity and interdependence between heterogeneous cultures and social groups. The main reason for this is that conflict and survival has been a constant in the history of humankind and, when faced with formidable external threats, societies have adapted to learn to cooperate with or at least tolerate the existence of other groups to thwart and deflect such threats—even if the involved parties have a long history of animosity and conflict.

In order to highlight the role of religion in cooperation and confrontation, in what lies ahead, I will modify a standard model of production and conflict in a couple of ways. First, I will discuss a world in which there are three countries or sovereignties. In standard models of conflict and crime between two actors, the efficacy of appropriation plays a key role in the allocation of resources between productive uses and conflict. When such models are modified to incorporate more than two actors, as I will do below, changes in the technology of appropriation can influence the patterns and timing of conflict, too. In particular, the emergence of a player with a superior technology can be sufficient for other agents to want to refrain from engaging each other in conflict and even trying to prop each other up in confrontations with their superior foes.

Second, I will incorporate into the model the economic and social influences of monotheism in line with what I have reviewed and documented thus far. In particular, I will assume the following:

1. Adherence to monotheism by a majority of society supports a stable environment in which production can be undertaken, with adherence to a common faith raising the return to production relative to the return to crime and conflict.

2. Monotheistic beliefs aid national defense, and religious differences propagate conflicts. Hence the intensity of conflict is higher when conflicting parties subscribe to different faiths.

These two modifications create a framework of analysis according to which religious beliefs influence productivity at home and religious differences affect the intensity of violent conflict abroad. One should then be able to infer when and under which conditions religious affinity or lack thereof would drive and sustain violent conflict and cooperation among different societies.

The online technical appendix of this book exposits all details of the analytical model that underlies the following discussion.

4.1 An Outline

To simplify things as much as possible, consider a world in which there are only three countries, each under the rule of an autonomous sovereign. These countries are assumed to be lined up geographically contiguously in such a way that only one of the countries (say, country **B**) shares common borders with the other two, whereas the remaining two countries only neighbor country **B**. In this sense, as I will show shortly, country **B** is cursed with bad geography.

Each country's sovereign has the authority to tax his resource base at a rate of his choosing. He can then use the proceeds to bankroll the military. Thus, in every period, sovereigns choose how much to tax their subjects and, conditional on how their tax revenue converts into military resources and capability, decide whether to engage in military conflict.

Each of the countries in our world is endowed with some initial resource that can be used as an input in production. Think of this resource as land or labor. While it is not necessary to make a distinction about what the countries' endowments might be, there are at least two plausible interpretations. First, one can literally think of the endowments as the wealth of landowners, in which case a lump-sum tax would represent a pecuniary and required payment made by landowners to the sovereign. Alternatively, the countries' endowments could be interpreted as some fixed units of available manpower. In that case, the tax imposed could be viewed as the soldiering time mandated by the sovereign.

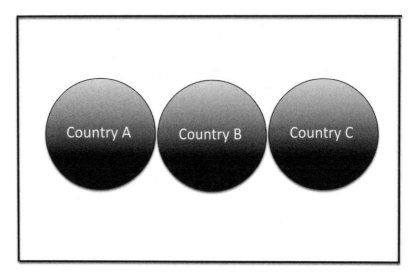

Figure 4.1 Country **B** neighbors both countries **A** and **C**. The latter only neighbor country **B**.

In order to keep things as simple as possible, I will assume that no military conflict can end in stalemate; one side unambiguously wins, and the victor takes full control of the resources of the defeated. The likelihood that any one country wins a military confrontation is determined by the relative resources allocated to war by both sides, as well as each country's potency in military conflict. The latter might be a function of various other determinants, not the least of which includes war technology.

The decisions to allocate resources to military conflict and engage in warfare are independently made, but in equilibrium, they will be conditional on each other. For instance, a sovereign can bankroll his military but choose not to attack his neighbor, in which case the sovereign will retain his resources until the next period, provided that the neighboring states refrain from an attack.

For heuristic purposes, assume that only two countries can be in conflict at any one time and only neighboring countries can engage in warfare. Consequently, the two peripheral countries **A** and **C** can engage each other only after country **B** is defeated and conquered. In other words, I rule out three-way wars but not cooperation and collusion. As long as one can establish the stability of one-on-one wars at any given time as equilibrium outcomes, this will prove to be an innocuous assumption.

In such a setup, there are four possibilities in regard to the pattern and timing of conflicts between the three countries. To begin with, it is possible that two countries form a military alliance against an odd one out. But such a partnership will always require a commitment on the part of the countries involved. The commitments would have to bind not only the resources allocated to the joint war effort but also how the spoils of war would be divvied up in case of victory. This is not a trivial problem although economists have established a fairly good grasp of the difficulties involved in implementing mechanisms of commitment that would make such an alliance feasible. Nonetheless, this issue is beyond the scope of what I would like to pursue here and, as a consequence, I assume that no country can overcome the commitment problems involved in forging military alliances.

This still leaves three scenarios of conflict and peace to analyze: In one scenario, depicted in figures 4.2 and 4.3, countries A and B engage in a military conflict, while country C does not interfere. Then, depending on the outcome of that conflict, country C engages either country A or country B subsequently (although figure 4.3 assumes that A won its war with B). At the end of two periods, there will be one country left standing with all the resources at its disposal.

A second scenario is similar to the one above, with the roles of countries A and C reversed: countries B and C engage in a military conflict at the outset, while country A sits on the sideline. And, in the following period, country A confronts the winner of the war between countries B and C.

In a third scenario, peace prevails indefinitely, although this does not imply that no country chooses to arm militarily. And even though I ruled out three-way wars by assumption, I will check the conditions under

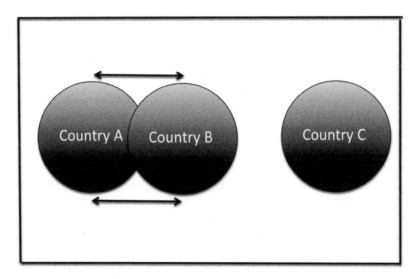

Figure 4.2 In the first period, countries **A** and **B** are at war. Country **C** does not interfere.

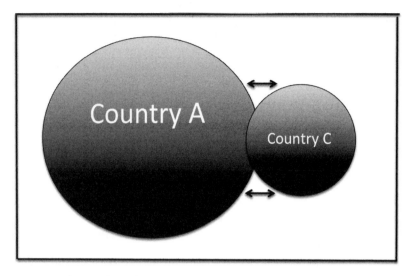

Figure 4.3 In the second period, country **A**, which defeated country **B**, confronts country **C**.

which the third country would find it in its interest to wait to confront the winner of a first-stage war between the two other countries. This will then ensure that the first and second scenarios described above are sustainable outcomes.

By examining the sustainability of each of these three scenarios under various alternatives, I will then be able to predict patterns of conflict and cooperation in different states of the world.

4.2 Resources, Conflict, and Territorial Conquests

I will now describe the key predictions of the model in nontechnical, user-friendly terms and qualitatively explain the main intuition behind those predictions.

Consider the economic costs and benefits of engaging a neighbor in military conflict. If a sovereign expects to be attacked by a neighbor, then arming to meet the challenge is the rational thing to do. When a sovereign taxes its populace and/or resource endowments at the optimal level, then the outcome of the war will be determined by the relative superiority of the two countries' military technologies alone. In this case, the likelihood of prevailing over the enemy might still be small, but without a military defense, the war will surely be lost and the sovereign will be no more.

Alternatively, take the costs and benefits of military action for a sovereign who does not expect to be imminently attacked. This sovereign would not need to tax its populace or resource base if it chooses peace over war, and it would be guaranteed to survive at least one period. Of course, come the next period, there is no guarantee that peace would still prevail. Nonetheless, the cost to a benevolent sovereign of choosing to arm and engage its neighbor in military conflict immediately would be the loss of output due to higher taxes. The benefit, by contrast, would be the capture and control of the neighboring sovereign's resources or endowments, although this benefit would be associated with the risk that the military conflict could be lost and the sovereign's reign abruptly terminated.

It should now be clear that, for a sovereign who possesses an important military advantage vis-à-vis its neighbor(s), the net benefit of initiating a military confrontation would be relatively large because, by doing so, the sovereign can capture additional resources without much risk to its own sovereignty. By the same token, it should also be fairly evident that relatively weak sovereigns would refrain from initiating violent confrontations with their neighbors because they would recognize that doing so would be tantamount to suicide.

But what happens in more intermediate cases, when differences in military might are not too large? First, consider the case of fairly high égalité when all three countries possess roughly similar levels of military capability and are endowed with identical resource bases. If that were the case, the odds of prevailing over the enemy in a conflict would be roughly equal at around 50 percent for all countries. This would describe a situation in which farsighted and forward-looking sovereigns will choose peace over war, as a consequence of which peace can indefinitely prevail between the countries. This is akin to the situation in which there is a significant military buildup that sustains a peaceful equilibrium initially defined in Grossman and Kim (1995) and perhaps best exemplified by the Cold War era that lasted over three decades. In particular, even though resources need to be allocated to potential military action, wars could be avoided so long as the rulers prefer to maintain their original endowments to a war with a 50 percent likelihood of triumph. With rulers who are less patient with less concern for the future, neighbors can engage each other in warfare, with the winner of that confrontation taking on the country that initially remained idle.

Moving along, there are two other cases that are perhaps more intriguing: First, suppose that a periphery sovereign is relatively weak, whereas the other two are stronger and equally potent militarily. The most likely pattern in this case is one where the buffer country engages the weaker periphery country first, with the showdown between the two militarily superior foes taking place next. The reason for this should be self-evident: when two equally matched countries engage each other in conflict, the odds of victory are fairly even, which makes the risk of such a conflict relatively high. In contrast, engaging a weaker foe is relatively risk-free for a periphery country because the latter is most likely to prevail. By the same logic, a periphery country not engaged in conflict initially would find it optimal to wait for the winner of an existing conflict, again due to the fact that, if it did engage the buffer country in conflict, the odds of victory would be roughly even.

Now entertain a final scenario: Suppose that a periphery country possesses superior military capability, while the other two are inferior and roughly similar. In this situation, the militarily superior country will engage the buffer country without delay. The relevant implication is that, if there had been a longer running or simmering feud between the other two countries, they would have had to put that on hold when faced with the threat of a militarily advanced peripheral rival.

All in all, when one periphery country is relatively weak in terms of its military technology and its resource base, which together determine the likelihood that the country will win a war, and the other two are matched fairly evenly, the weak periphery country is engaged in military conflict first. This is followed by a (potential) showdown between the evenly matched countries, but if a periphery country is dominant compared with the other two, then it engages the buffer first, followed by its (likely) confrontation with the weaker foe next. Then the latter country benefits because it is spared a first-stage conflict regardless of how weak it is militarily against the buffer.

In addition, it is in the interest of countries that are spared an early conflict to aid the weaker of the two opponents in the first-stage confrontation without yielding a permanent advantage to the weaker side. This is because first-stage conflicts always involve a militarily superior foe; the survival odds and the expected payoff of countries that are not engaged in conflict in a first-period conflict rises if the militarily superior country is eliminated. But, as I have already noted, a lack of a commitment mechanism can be a hindrance to following this strategy.

4.3 What's Faith Got to Do with It?

So far, I have remained silent about how religion factors into all this, but, on the basis of the material in chapters 2 and 3, I can now incorporate faith and belief in One God into my analysis.

If, as in the words of Rodney Stark, monotheisms are characterized by *particularism*—the belief that any given monotheism is the One True Religion—and provide the basis of the vigor with which adherents of different monotheist faiths engage each other in conflict historically, as empirically documented by political scientists such as Richardson, then one can capture this idea simply by parameter differences in the model that come to bear on conflict intensity. In particular, holding constant resources devote to warfare, one can consider that the intensity and efficacy of violent conflict rises when the latter involves adherents of different monotheistic creeds. Of course, one still needs to acknowledge that other factors, such as warfare technology, drove differences in military effectiveness across societies. All the same, I conjecture that the military effectiveness of a country was, all else equal, higher when it engaged a country with a different religious belief and that the same was true to a lesser extent when two countries that subscribed to different sects of a shared religion were in direct confrontation.

I will now interpret the main findings: For religious affinity to foster cooperation among parties that could otherwise be in conflict with one another, the resources at stake need to be meaningful and outside external threats need to be credible and grave enough. And given how religion comes into play here, the likelihood that an outside threat would be viewed as "grave" would be that much higher when the threat comes from those who subscribe to a different religion. The emergence of an outside military threat by a society that is of a different religious faith could breed coexistence among others, however fragile and contingent the latter might be on the sustenance of the threat. Instead, if either an outside threat is not credible enough or what is at stake is not sufficiently significant, then preexisting rifts among countries of similar or identical religious and cultural affinities could continue to grow. In those cases, the emergence of an outside threat with a different religious or cultural creed can even entice some degree of cooperation—however implicit—between sovereigns of different faiths.

The evidence presented on patterns of conflict and cooperation in section 1.4 of chapter 1, indeed, suggests that, all else equal, human societies of different religious persuasions were prone to settle their differences through violent conflict. As we saw there, religious conflicts not only persisted over time but also lasted longer and were typically more fatal. These observations are in line with Richardson (1960, pp. 233–39), who documented that differences of religion, especially those of Christianity and Islam, have been causes of wars and that, to a weaker extent, "Christianity incited war between its adherents." Along these same lines, recall that Richardson found no conflict in his data set that arose because two sides identified with the same religion, nor did he observe any conflict that was restrained because the involved parties adhered to different religions. Instead, conflicts arose and persisted due to religious differences, or they were subdued or eventually contained, primarily because the actors involved coreligionists.

I will conclude this chapter by making two observations, one of which is relevant for the material in part 1 and another that will be applicable when I review the impact of Ottomans on western Europe.

In chapter 2, I reviewed the various sociopolitical advantages of monotheism vis-à-vis polytheism or atheism. In chapter 3, I documented that indeed monotheistic faiths had a significant survival advantage. In the context of the analysis here, this would be tantamount to the emergence of a foe that dominates others with the sophistication of its military technology. In such a case, this exercise suggests that if there are existing feuds among other countries, those might still take precedence over engaging the militarily superior, monotheist foe; that the monotheist country would not necessarily engage others in military conflict immediately; and that the likelihood the monotheist player would eventually dominate and conquer others is relatively high.

Also, if one of the periphery countries is militarily superior to the other two, which share a common faith, and it subscribes to a different faith than others, then according to my framework, the likely pattern of conflict among these countries will be such that the periphery will engage the buffer immediately. This would be the case even if the other two countries would have been in conflict, save for the military threat by the periphery country.

Bear these in mind as we move along and explore next how religious rivalries influenced—in some crucial aspects permanently—the sociopolitics of Europe and the Middle East following the rise of the Ottomans in Anatolia during the fifteenth century.

FIVE

The "Dark Side" Rises

Mamma, li Turchi!
ANONYMOUS, ITALY

5.1   From Local Tribe to Global Empire

5.1.1   Foundations

By the late tenth century or the early eleventh century, there were dramatic demographic and political changes taking place on the eastern coasts of the Aegean Sea as well as in eastern Anatolia and Persia. These changes were to have serious historical repercussions in the next half a millennia and shift the stage of Christian-Muslim conflicts from the western Mediterranean and the Iberian Peninsula to Anatolia and the Middle East.

Historians date the start of the contacts between Muslim Turks and Byzantine Christians to the Battle of the Manzikert in 1071. There is some debate regarding how the Turks began to move westward from central Asia and start to change the demographic makeup of Asia Minor in the eleventh century. While some of these views reflect a *pull theory*, arguing that Anatolia suited the Turks nomadic lifestyle, others are based more on a *push conjecture*, according to which the Mongol and Golden Horde raids forced the Turks to flee westward.

One finds the arguments for these not necessarily mutually exclusive theories in the writings of Imber as well as Kafadar. Kafadar (1996, pp. 2–4), for instance, opines on some of the demographic implications of the Turks' Anatolian debut:

According to most historical traditions, the immediate ancestors of Osman [the founding father of the Ottoman Empire] arrived in Anatolia with the second great wave of Turkish migration from central Asia, which took place in the wake of the Chingisid onslaught in the early thirteenth century. . . . The earlier wave, the tail end of the *Volkermanderungen* in a way, had occurred in the eleventh century when large numbers of Turkish tribes, belonging primarily to the Oguz dialect group and to the Oguzid idiom of Inner Asian political discourse, crossed the Oxus and moved toward western Asia. . . . In any case, ongoing friction in eastern Anatolia in the eleventh century led to the fateful encounter of the Seljuk and Byzantine armies in Manzikert in 1071. . . . The Byzantine defeat at Manzikert was to be followed by deeper and more frequent raids or plain migration by Turkmen tribes into Asia Minor. . . . Before the end of the eleventh century, most of Anatolia was divided up among petty potentates led by Turkish warriors, Armenian princes, Byzantine commanders, and Frankish knights arriving with the First Crusade.

Imber (2002, pp. 4–6) articulates the reasons for the demographic and political changes in Anatolia and, in particular, the Turks' increasing presence:

From being primarily Greek and Christian in the eleventh century, by 1300 Anatolia had become primarily Turkish and Muslim. The origins of this change lie in the eleventh century. In the mid-century a confederation of Turkish tribes from Transoxania conquered Iran, and in 1055, occupied Baghdad, establishing it as the capital of the Great Seljuk dynasty. The consequence of these events was not simply to establish a new ruler in Baghdad, but also, with the influx of Turks from central Asia, to alter the ethnic balance of the Middle East. . . . A convenient date for marking the beginning of this phenomenon is 1071. In this year the Great Seljuk Sultan defeated the Byzantine Emperor at Manzikert in eastern Anatolia. . . . The collapse of Byzantine defences and the appearance of a Muslim dynasty undoubtedly encouraged the immigration of the Turks. So too did geography. It seems that the Turks who had migrated from Transoxania to the Middle East were, in the main, seminomadic pastoralists, and Anatolia was well suited to this way of life. . . . In 1243, a Mongol army—part of an invading force which, by 1258, had conquered Iran, Anatolia and Iraq—defeated a Seljuk army at Kosedag and reduced the Sultan to the status of vassal. . . . The Mongols were a pastoralist people, and needed the grasslands of the newly conquered Seljuk territory not only for their flocks, but especially for the horses that were essential for their military success. It seems very likely, therefore, that competition from the Mongols forced many Turkish pastoralists to seek new lands in the West.

Thus, as Imber notes, came the fall of the Seljuk Turks at the hands of the Mongol raiders in 1243. The Seljuks disappeared from the stage of history but not without setting in motion the demographic and political changes in Anatolia and the east Aegean, which led to the birth of the Ottoman Empire.

After the demise of the Seljuk Turkish Empire at the end of the thirteenth century, Anatolia became a breeding ground for many small feudal Turkish states. The Ottoman tribe (*beylik*) was one of these states, being founded by Osman I around the Anatolian city of Eskişehir in 1299. Under the sultanate of Osman, who moved the capital of his fledgling settlement soon after its foundation to Bursa, eighty-two miles northwest of Eskişehir, the Ottoman beylik consolidated its power, dominating the other Anatolian Turkish derebeyliks and capturing territories in the Aegean at the expense of the Byzantine Empire and in eastern Anatolia against the Persians.

During the fourteenth century, the beylik grew rapidly, capturing territories in the Balkans as well. Osman I's achievements were followed by the reigns of Orhan I, Mehmed I, and Yildirim Beyazıt (the Lightning Bolt) when Ottoman rule began to extend over the eastern Mediterranean and the Balkans. After defeat in Battle of Plocnik, the Turkish victory at the Battle of Kosovo effectively marked the end of Serbian power in the region and paved the way for Ottoman expansion in eastern Europe.

There is not much doubt that the Ottomans' Muslim religious identity influenced their objectives and policies of conquest, which were oriented toward the Christian world to their west. But the sultans—at least the early ones who came to rule in the fourteenth and fifteenth centuries—also understood and made effective use of alliances with Christian rulers, which mainly took the form of strategic intermarriages as well as policies of divide and conquer. In fact, it is with the help of such maneuvers that the Ottomans gained their first foothold in Europe. In the words of Imber (2002, pp. 9, 10),

It was Orhan, too, who first established an Ottoman bridgehead in Europe. He achieved this by exploiting a civil war in Byzantium between the rival Emperors Kantakouzenos and Palaoilogos. Kantakouzenos sought allies among the Turkish rulers of western Anatolia and, in 1346 formed a pact with Orhan by marrying him to his daughter Theodora. The strategy was successful and, in 1347, Kantakouzenos entered Constantinople and proclaimed himself Emperor, with John V as his co-regent. It was, however, Orhan who gained most from this arrangement. In 1352, as war raged between John V and Kantakouzenos' son Matthew, the father summoned help from Orhan, granting his troops under Süleyman Paşa a fortress on the Gallipoli peninsula. This was the first territory that the Ottomans occupied in Europe.

In their geopolitical calculations as such, the early Ottoman rulers were aided by some of their European counterparts who, like Francis I of France, were more than willing to form tactical alliances with the Ottomans in their attempts to divide and conquer Europe. The active cooperation of Francis with Süleyman should be seen in this light.

The early rulers also understood the value of power consolidation and securing their rear flanks. Partly as a consequence, the fledgling empire engaged in warfare with other local Muslim rulers in Anatolia periodically during the fourteenth century. During the reigns of Murad I, Beyazıt I, Mehmed I, Murad II, and Mehmed II, there were numerous confrontations with the Karamans in Anatolia and the Safavids as well as the Mamluks in the Middle East, all of which were rival Muslim civilizations that competed with the Ottomans for dominion in the region (for more details, see Shaw, 1976, pp. 22–79).

5.1.2 Government and Polity

In its early days and pretty much through the interregnum period in 1402–13, the Ottoman government and its institutions—if they can be labeled as such—reflected the seminomadic and pastoralist lifestyle of the central Asian Oguz Turks from whom the Ottomans descended. But as time wore on, the evolution and growth of the empire left its political and administrative institutions under the influence of three traditions: the central Asian or Turkic heritage upon which the early administrations were founded; institutions of Sunni Islam and the Sharia law, courtesy of the influence of the early Islamic Umayyad and Abbasid empires of the seventh and eighth centuries; and the impact of the Byzantine Roman culture that permeated, for the most part, through the influence of the sultans' Balkan wives and the devşirme class, which was instituted by Murad I in the early fifteenth century. In chapter 7, I will explore in full detail the political influences of the imperial wives and the Ottoman harem on the empire's foreign and conquest policies.

During the early era, the Ottoman rulers carried the title of bey and they had full political and military control. In the words of Shaw (1976, p. 22), "As tribal leader, frontier bey, and then independent bey, the Ottoman leader carried the government and military command more or less in his saddle." Only with the transformation of the Ottoman clan from an Anatolian tribe to a regional power in the Aegean and the Middle East, then to an Empire in the Balkans as well, did the Ottoman leaders adopt the title of sultan. Early on, culture and customs helped settle internal disputes, and the Ottoman bey interfered in disputes among public administration and military leaders rarely; when he did, it was typically as a mediator.

In its prime, maturity, and decline, the Ottoman hierarchy involved two main branches, with the military and bureaucratic order on the one side and the religious order on the other. The latter was composed of the Islamic clergy, the Ulema, who interpreted and enforced the Islamic laws. The military and the bureaucracy answered first and foremost to the sultan, then to his grand vizier, and then to the Ottoman *porte* (the sultan's court). The top echelons of the military and administrative hierarchy were composed predominantly of Turkoman members with few Christian converts. Their roles switched from administering tax levies and collection in peace time to waging military action and taking booty in times of war. The Ottoman system according to which higher-ranking military personnel oversaw nonoverlapping geographic domains to carry out these duties was called the *timar*. The division of labor in the empire was along the lines of religion and ethnicity: only Muslims could hold military and administrative positions within the government, while the minority Christians and Jews dealt with commerce, crafts, and trade.

As the empire grew, so did the duties of the sultans' deputies, the viziers. Some of them exercised considerable power. The sultan enjoyed absolute power and, in theory at least, was personally involved in every governmental decision. In the Ottoman experience of government, everything representing the state government was issued from the hands of the sultan himself. The sultan also assumed the title of caliph, or supreme temporal leader of Islam, after Yavuz Sultan Selim conquered Egypt and took de facto control of the Arabian peninsula in 1517. With the caliphate, the Ottoman sultans became the guarantors of security for the two Muslim Holy sites, Mecca and Medina. But as caliph, the sultan was responsible for Islamic orthodoxy, too.

In this regard, Shaw (1976, p. 85) makes a distinction between the Ottoman sultans' adoption and use of the title caliph versus "Servant and Protector of Holy Places." However, the religious significance of either title is still clear:

The Ottomans did use the title caliph for a time after the conquest of the Arab world, but this was only practiced among Muslim rulers after they achieved something of distinction. It was in fact by the much more important titles of sultan and "Servant and Protector of the Holy Places" that Selim and his successors sought to be remembered—the idea of caliph being used only to emphasize their preeminence in the Islamic world and right to promote and defend the Muslim religion and law. By extending the gazi tradition, the Ottoman sultans came to stress their role as leaders and defenders of the entire Islamic world, thus using a new interpretation of the caliphate to establish Ottoman mastery over Islamic peoples.

With imperial growth came also institutions and government structures commensurate with the state of affairs. The Ottoman public and military administration began to evolve with imperial growth in order to accommodate the changing needs of the state. Even dating back to the reigns of the second and third sultans, Orhan and Murad I, distinct changes were beginning to materialize: public administration was being separated from that of the military and a distinction was being drawn between the treasury of the sultan and that of the government (Shaw, 1976, p. 23). But it was Süleyman the Law Giver who transformed the Ottoman law and institutions to reflect its evolution from a regional power in the Middle East to one of a world empire (which will be discussed in more detail later).

5.2   Gaza, Islam, and the Ottoman State

The origins of the Ottoman Empire and, in particular, the sufficient causes of its success as a world power are matters of intense debate (Kafadar, 1996). On one side, there are those, like H. A. Gibbons and Rudi Paul Lindner, who saw in the Ottomans' success the artifacts of the demographic and sociopolitical turmoil of Anatolia in the thirteenth century and the realpolitik skills of the early Ottoman rulers combined with their heritages of Byzantine public administration and military organization. But others, such as Paul Wittek and Mehmed Fuat Köprülü, advocated the Gaza-ideology hypothesis as the defining key aspect of the Ottomans' rise to imperial heights.

The central tenet of the Gaza thesis is that the early Ottoman conquerors were driven and motivated by an ideology of holy war in the name of Islam and that Ottoman power was essentially built on that commitment.

As Cemal Kafadar articulates in full detail in *Between the Two Worlds: The Construction of the Ottoman State*, those who dismiss the gazi mentality of the early Ottoman rulers do so on grounds that the empire recruited non-Muslims into the military ranks; often fought against other Muslim civilizations, such as the Mamluks, the Karamans, and the Safavids; typically did not use force to convert conquered peoples to Islam; and so on. But according to Kafadar (1996, pp. 78–81), such arguments are based on a rigid and inflexible interpretation of the gazi mentality:

With respect to gaza, the first thing to be noted is that it is not synonymous with *jihad* even though [Lindner and Gibbons] use the two terms interchangeably or use one English term, "holy war" for both as if there were no appreciable difference. But there clearly was such a difference. . . . Jihad should not be understood as incessant warfare to expand the adobe of Islam or a mentality that recognizes a permanent state of war. . . . Accommodation was not necessarily outside the pale of "Islamic law." Furthermore, jihad is defined by most canonical sources as a war undertaken when the world of Islam or the peace of the umma is threatened. There is thus a defensive quality to it. . . . Nevertheless, a difference between jihad and gaza was maintained whereby the latter term implied irregular raiding activity whose ultimate goal was the expansion of the power of Islam.

Thus a credible view among Ottoman historians articulates that faith and the promotion of Islam in particular were motivating factors for at least the early rulers of the Ottoman state in their imperial conquests. Upon reviewing and analyzing some relevant data, I will have more to say on this topic at the end of chapter 7.

5.3 Western Conquests

By the end of the fourteenth century, the Ottoman Empire was in full control of Asia Minor, most of the Balkans, and the eastern Mediterranean, and it seemed virtually unstoppable in its mission of bringing to an end the Byzantine Empire's long reign in eastern Europe.

For many early Ottoman sultans, the capital of the Byzantine Empire, Constantinople (*Istanbul* in Turkish), was a highly prized target. This was not only for the city's geostrategic locale between the continents of Europe and Asia, sitting at the crossroads of the major land and maritime trade routes during the medieval era and providing the only access point between the Mediterranean Europe and the Black Sea ports of southern Russia; it was also for its symbolic value as the seat of the Eastern Orthodox Church as well as the center of a once-mighty Christian empire that lasted over a millennium and played an active role in instigating the Christian Crusades against the Muslims during the eleventh and twelfth centuries. Indeed, some of the most monumental Ottoman fortifications on either side of the Bosphorus Strait had been planned with the capture of Istanbul as the main goal: in 1393, Yildirim Beyazıt (the Lightning Bolt) had the Anadolu Hisarı built on the Anatolian shore of the Bosphorus and, in 1452, Mehmed II (the Conqueror) followed through with the construction of the Rumeli Hisarı on the other side of the strait.

The capture of Constantinople and the fall of the Byzantine Empire still had to wait until the reign of the seventh Ottoman sultan, Mehmed II, the Conqueror, because, despite Beyazıt I's expansionary orientation toward the West, the Asian Turco-Mongol warlord Tamerlane succeeded in decimating the Ottoman military decisively and swiftly in the Battle of Ankara in 1402, taking as prisoner Beyazıt and his wife. Thus began the Ottoman Interregnum, which lasted eleven years until 1413 when the empire regrouped under Mehmed I (*Çelebi*), who overcame the claims of his two half-brothers for the sole possession of the Ottoman Sultanate. Thereafter, the empire quickly regained its momentum of the late thirteenth century and began consolidating more territories in the Balkans and the Middle East.

5.3.1 The Golden Era

Constantinople eventually fell to the Turks on May 29, 1453, with the Byzantine Empire surrendering to the twenty-one-year-old Sultan Mehmed II, thereby extinguishing the Byzantine Empire and putting the seat of the Eastern Orthodox Church within Muslim control.

Under Mehmet II's tutelage, the empire even went as far as establishing a beachhead garrison on the Italian peninsula in 1480, with the intent of uniting the Roman Empire under *Dar al-Islam*. Mehmet's death a year later abruptly halted those plans. Nonetheless, the period between the end of the Interregnum in 1413 and the Lepanto Naval Battle in 1571, when the Ottoman naval fleet was soundly defeated by the galley fleet of the Holy League thus marking the first time the Ottoman military suffered a convincing defeat against the Europeans, epitomizes the pinnacle of the empire's military and political prowess. During this century and a half, the Ottomans barely lost a military campaign against its rivals in Europe, Middle East, North Africa, and the Arabian Peninsula.

The successive reigns of Mehmed II (the Conqueror), Beyazıt II, Selim I (the Grim), and Süleyman (the Magnificent) represent the golden age of the Ottoman Empire. Furthermore, each and every one of those sultans played historically important roles regarding the impact of the Ottoman Empire on European secular as well as ecclesiastical authorities. It is with this in mind that I briefly review their sultanate tenures.

Fatih Sultan Mehmed (the Conqueror), 1432–81

Mehmed II succeeded the Ottoman throne twice. In 1444, when he was only twelve years old, his father, Sultan Murad II, abdicated the throne to live a life of ascetic reflection in Balikesir. Given the age of his son at the time, one could only hope that he had trusted the state with the grand vizier, Çandarli Halil Paşa. A Janissary Corps revolt coupled with Mehmed II's inexperience in matters of state was enough for Murad II to return to the helm two years later in 1446, where he remained for another five years until his death.

Mehmed II ascended the Ottoman throne a second time, in 1451, at the age of nineteen. From the start, his main goals were to capture Constantinople and turn the Ottoman state into a world power. On May 29, 1453, he succeeded in his first objective at the age of twenty-one, after a month-long siege of the prized city marked the end of the Byzantine Empire.

The early part of Mehmed II's reign then was centered around rebuilding and repopulating Constantinople. But his whole tenure was defined by almost constant warfare and imperial conquest—in the east, the west, the Mediterranean, and the Middle East. The Ottoman gains came at the expense of the Karamans in Anatolia, the Genoeans in the eastern Mediterranean, the Bulgarian and Wallachian princes in the Balkans, and the Holy Roman Empire in Europe.

When Mehmed II, the Conqueror, died in 1481 in preparation for yet another eastern conquest and the year after he established a beachhead garrison on the Italian peninsula with the intent of bringing the Roman Empire under Dar al-Islam, the Ottoman Empire had ended the millennial reign of the east Roman Empire. It had conquered the seat of Eastern Orthodox Christianity—its church, the *Hagia Sophia*, being converted to a mosque. Neither in the west nor the east could this have gone unnoticed—and it didn't—but Mehmed II's lifelong ambition and pursuit of imperial conquest left the Ottoman treasury in dire straits and the population in hardships due to the heavy tax burdens necessitated by Mehmed II's conquests. This is one reason his successor Beyazıt II's reign was a hiatus of peace and relative tranquility.

Yavuz Sultan Selim (the Grim), 1465–1520

Selim I's accession to the throne did not come without challenge, but Selim subdued his brother Ahmet's claims to the throne by defeating his army in Yenisehir and executing him. His tenure saw a rapid growth in the Janissary Corps and the devşirme class, on both of whom Selim relied to defeat Ahmet. His eight-year reign was one of the shortest of all the Ottoman sultans, but by the time he died, he had doubled the empire's territories "by adding . . . the former Safavid territories in eastern and south-eastern Anatolia; all the territories of the Mamluk Empire in Egypt,

Syria, Lebanon, Palestine, and the Hejaz; and, in addition, Tunis and Algiers in North Africa" (Imber, 2002, p. 48).

Perhaps most importantly, Selim I acquired the title of Sunni caliph in 1517 with his Egyptian conquests against the Mamluk Empire and his control of the holy cities of Islam, Mecca, and Medina, the latter due to the newly acquired allegiance of the Bedouin tribes who lived on the Arabian Peninsula. Thanks to Selim, from 1517 until 1924 after the Ottoman Empire ceased to exist, all the Ottoman sultans were not only the rulers of a vast and influential empire but also the temporal leaders of the Islamic Sunni ummah, or the global Sunni nation.

Kanuni Sultan Süleyman (the Magnificent), 1494–1566

The apogee of Ottoman prowess and grandeur, the reign of Süleyman lasted forty-six years, the longest of all Ottoman sultans. His accession was peaceful because he had no brothers to challenge his claims. Despite the fact that the empire grew under the tutelage of his two successors, Selim II and Murad III, the reign of Süleyman is remarkable for not only its military achievements but also the institutional innovations introduced in the Islamic world in general and the Ottoman state in particular. This is the main reason Süleyman was referred to as *the Magnificent* in the west but as *the Lawgiver* at home and in the east.

In the words of Shaw (1976, p. 87),

Süleyman attempted to build a system of justice to end the possibility of violent and arbitrary actions such as those of Selim and Mehmed II, and he substituted a new emphasis on protection for the lives, property, and honor of individuals regardless of religion. A day after taking the throne, he decreed that soldiers should pay for all provisions taken along the paths of their campaigns in Ottoman or enemy territory. Taxes were levied only according to the ability to pay, with the extra taxes and confiscations of his predecessors prohibited. The system of courts previously established was enlarged . . . the administration was reorganized . . . [and] only merit was considered in the appointment, assignment and promotion of officials.

His military career was best exemplified by his prolonged conflict with the Holy Roman Empire and the House of Hapsburg—in particular, his campaigns against the King of Hungary, Ferdinand. Süleyman's support of the Hungarian Protestant estates' choice of John Szapolyai as Hungarian king and his victory against Austria-Hungary in the Mohacs battle of 1526, which in turn gave him the rights of arbitration between the Hapsburgs and the Hungarian estates, kept him involved with Austria-Hungarian

Figure 5.1 Sultan Süleyman, the Magnificent (painting by Titian Vecellio, around 1539, The Kings Academy)

affairs. His 1521 capture of Belgrade but, more important, his 1529 siege of Vienna, which was deflected only with the help of a Holy alliance, were watersheds in solidifying European views of the Muslim Turkish threat.

The Ottoman navy achieved formidable might only during Süleyman's reign, and, as a result of this, the Ottomans began to control the eastern Mediterranean Sea. Süleyman's eastern campaigns against the Safavids in the early 1530s added Baghdad and various eastern outposts in Anatolia to the Ottoman domain. And during his close to half-century tenure, Süleyman captured other crucial territories in the Gulf, the Red Sea, the Aegean, and Moldavia.

Figure 5.2 shows a map of Europe, North Africa, and the Near East in 1300 CE, and figure 5.3 shows the same geographic region at the turn of the eighteenth century.

There are two striking aspects of the comparison between the two periods. One is the overwhelming territorial gains made by the Ottoman Empire, most of which took place between the mid-fifteenth century and the end of the sixteenth century. The empire was barely a year old in 1300 CE, but, by the end of the sixteenth century, the Ottomans controlled the

Balkans; had conquered the city of Istanbul (in 1453), thereby ending the Byzantine Empire and giving the Ottomans full control of the Bosphorus and the Dardanelles Straits; had gained important military victories against Hungary in central Europe, such as the capture of Belgrade in 1521 and the Mohacs Battle victory in 1526; had established a garrison in Otranto of the Italian Peninsula in 1481; and had put the capital of the Austrian monarchy, Vienna, under what eventually turned out to be the first of two unsuccessful sieges in 1529. For further references on the history of the Ottoman Empire, see Faroqhi (2004), Kinross (1979), Inalcik (1973), Karpat (1974), Shaw (1976), and Goodwin (2000).

Although not shown in figures 5.2 and 5.3, one can also verify that a significant degree of political consolidation accompanied the Ottoman expansion in continental Europe. Although I do not expound on this issue until later in chapter 9, this consolidation is indicative of another channel through which the Ottomans potentially affected Europe: According to a relevant hypothesis, military threats necessitate the formation of larger states in order to sustain military establishments commensurate with such threats. See, for example, Tilly (1992) and McNeill (1984) as well as Kennedy (1987) for some conceptually relevant discussions, as well as Iyigun, Nunn, and Qian (in progress) for some relevant empirical analyses.

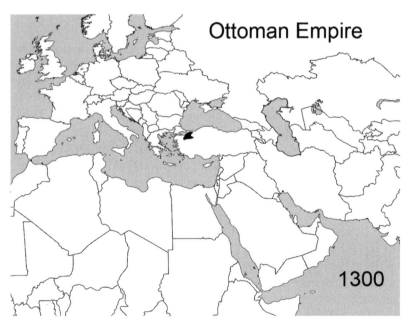

Figure 5.2 Ottoman Empire circa 1300 CE

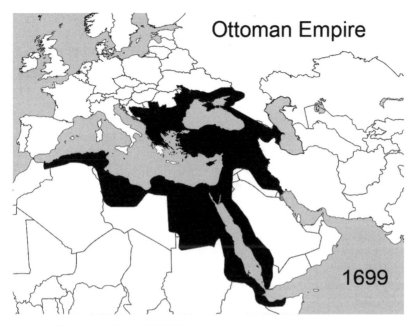

Figure 5.3   Ottoman Empire circa 1699 CE

The capture of Istanbul by the Ottoman Turks in 1453 was a serious blow to continental Europe because of its strategic importance for medieval trade and commerce. A number of sea and overland routes passed through the city, and its fall in 1453 necessitated an instant shift in the commercial center of the continent toward the Atlantic seaboard countries (see Anderson, 1967, p. 32).

Following Istanbul's fall, perhaps the most alarming development for continental European powers was the establishment of an Ottoman garrison at Otranto, Italy. Shaw (1976) asserts that Mehmed II had made it an explicit goal for his navy to spearhead an Ottoman occupation of Italy, "which seemed ripe for conquest due to the rivalries then endemic among Venice, Naples, and Milan as well as divisions caused by the political activities of the pope." When Otranto fell to the Ottomans in the summer of 1481, "Rome panicked, and the pope planned to flee northward along with most of the population of the city. At the same time, a new Crusade was called and support came from the Italian city-states, Hungary and France" (Shaw, 1976, pp. 69–70).

Leaving aside for a moment the notion that Gaza drove the Ottomans' westward imperial orientation. The political and military rivalries between the Ottoman Empire and the secular and ecclesiastical European powers still had something to do with Islam versus Christianity. This is indicated by the political science literature perused in the first part of the book—that differences of religion, especially those of Christianity and Islam, have been causes of wars and that, to a weaker extent, differences among the Christian denominations incited wars.

The bottom line is that the gains made by the Ottomans in eastern Europe in the late fifteenth and early sixteenth centuries were perceived as an existential threat to the survival of the continental European states. To be sure, the Ottoman advances were neither the first realized by Muslims on the continent nor among those that penetrated deepest the western and central parts of the continent. However, there can be little doubt that, by the late fifteenth and early sixteenth centuries, the Ottomans represented an organized and effective Islamic military power that was gradually and systematically encroaching upon Europe. This had major repercussions for Europeans not only because of the empire's religious motives of conquest but also as a consequence of the much longer history of religious rivalries inherent in the monotheisms of Christianity and Islam.

It is also worthwhile to recognize how the devşirme system might have influenced the Ottomans' imperial geographic orientation, and it is equally important to note how religious differences provided a backdrop against which the Ottomans' relationship with the outside world evolved via harem politics. The devşirme system fed the empire's top administrative ranks, its elite Janissary Corps, and often an important chunk of the harem power structure, due to the wives and mothers of sultans who were themselves converts. Various historians have asserted that, as the Ottomans' Balkan possessions grew in the sixteenth century and the harem as well as the palace administrative hierarchy began to evolve to reflect the changing demographics of the empire, the geographic orientation of the Ottomans' military expeditions evolved accordingly. Stanford Shaw (1976, p. 47), for instance, claims that the empire began to direct its territorial aspirations away from the Balkans and continental Europe toward the Middle East and North Africa as the influence of those with ethnic backgrounds from the Balkans grew within the harem and the palace hierarchy. (For an elaborate and interesting account of the Ottoman harem politics and power structure, see Peirce, 1993.)

If religious identities and allegiances were—and perhaps still are—as vital as this book has made them out to be, how were the social and political dynamics of Europe, in the continental east particularly, as well as those of the Ottoman Empire itself, altered?

In the next chapter, I will examine one of the major effects of the European-Ottoman interactions on Europe itself. Then, in chapter 7, I will explore how the Ottomans' own internal politics and policies evolved as a result. And in part 4, I will attempt to identify the subtler but longer-lasting sociopolitical and institutional ramifications of the European and Ottoman relationship.

SIX

Ottomans' Faith and Protestants' Fate

There were numerous challenges to the ecclesiastical monopoly of the Roman Catholic Church in Europe in the fourteenth and fifteenth centuries, but neither of those movements got off the ground.

Among the best known failed reform attempts were the movements instigated by John Wycliffe and Jan Hus. Wycliffe died in 1384 after he was fired from Oxford, and the movement he inspired, known as Lollardy, was suppressed and had to go underground. Jan Hus was burned alive in Constance in 1415. The Albigensian and Waldensian heresies in Southern France were suppressed by the Albigensian-Cathar Crusade, which was spearheaded by Pope Innocent III in 1209 and lasted twenty years (Armstrong, 1988, pp. 389–99; Hill, 1967; Hillerbrand, 1968; MacCulloch, 2003).

By contrast, the birth, survival, and growth of Protestantism in the sixteenth century and subsequently of its various offshoots, such as Zwinglianism, Calvinism, and Anabaptism, came to represent a watershed in European history. But how did Lutheranism and its offshoots proliferate while previous reform attempts failed?

According to the conventional historiography, the invention of the printing press by Johannes Gutenberg in 1450 was the critical communications innovation that helped Lutherans avoid the dismal fate of their predecessor reformists.

This chapter is based on Iyigun (2008).

According to another, not mutually exclusive claim, however, it was no coincidence that the Lutherans were able to survive and prosper just around the time when the Ottoman territorial gains and threats in Europe were at their peak.

Indeed, the Ottoman Empire peaked in strength, influence, and military might late in the fifteenth century and the early part of the sixteenth century, which coincided with a budding Lutheran movement. Hence it should come as no surprise that many historians associated the Ottoman Empire's prowess with the proliferation and perseverance of the Lutherans. A number of historians, such as Benz (1949), Fischer-Galati (1959), Setton (1962), Coles (1968), Inalcik (1973), Kortepeter (1972), Shaw (1976), Goffman (2002), and MacCulloch (2003) have articulated such.

Precisely how the Ottomans aided and abetted the Reformation is subject to debate. But the historical analyses of the period suggest that the Ottomans' were either a distraction for the House of Hapsburg and the Catholic Church, a bargaining opportunity for the Protestant German Diets, or both. Some historians emphasized that the empire's expansionary goals and achievements at the expense of Europeans made it an urgent priority for the Hapsburgs to deal with the Ottoman threat—even if that came at the expense of other pressing matters.

Yet others stressed how the Ottomans' European presence factored in the strategic bargaining between the Hapsburgs, the Catholic pope, and the leaders of the nascent German Protestant movement. The give and take between the two camps revolved extensively around Ferdinand's need for manpower to fight the Ottoman Turks in exchange for temporary peace and even the Church's official recognition of Protestantism.

6.1 Charles, Francis, and Ferdinand

As for the Ottomans' distractionary role, the central theme is that the Ottomans' territorial aspirations in Europe and their success in realizing those without much meaningful resistance early on made it fairly urgent for both the Pope Charles Ferdinand nexus and the Protestants to cooperate and deflect the Ottomans. On this point, Stanford Shaw (1976, pp. 60, 61) notes that the Hapsburgs had to take the Ottoman danger seriously, especially after the fall of Constantinople in 1453: "With the conquest of Constantinople [by the Ottoman Sultan Mehmed II] the Muslim world acknowledged Mehmed as leader of the Holy War against

Christianity. . . . Mehmed also began to see himself as heir not merely to eastern Rome but to a worldwide empire. Byzantine and Italian scholars surrounding him encouraged grandiose ideas of world dominion."

Shaw (1976, p. 94) highlights the sociopolitical ramifications of the Hapsburgs having to deal with the Ottomans when he states, "What [the Ottoman Sultan] Suleiman had done was to shock Austria and most of Europe by the depth of his penetration, causing Charles to make concessions to the Protestants in Germany to gain their support, a major factor in the subsequent survival and expansion of the Lutheran movement throughout western Europe."

Goffman (2002, p. 110) also hones in on the fact that, save for the Ottomans at the gates of Vienna, Luther and his followers would have gone the way of their reformist predecessors in Southern France:

[The siege of Vienna in 1529] was a moment in which one might have expected fear and loathing to grip Europe. Luther certainly expresses such emotions; but also perceptible in these passages and elsewhere in his text is a grudging esteem for a government that not only accorded non-Catholic Christians the right to reside and worship but also was the arch-enemy of his own arch-enemies, the Pope and the Holy Roman Emperor. Other religious reformers reiterated Martin Luther's uncertainties. The principal paradox for all of them, perhaps, was that even though the Ottomans posed a dire threat to Christendom, and especially to the Christian state, nevertheless, it was the Catholic world—and above all its Pope, represented by these same reformers as Anti-Christ—that was most immediately threatened. The Ottoman Empire pounded away at the "soft underbelly of Charles V's empire, and it was Charles and his Pope who had sworn to force Luther, John Calvin and other Protestants to renounce their convictions. Many Protestants understood that only the Ottoman diversion stood between them and obliteration. . . . It is certain that the Ottoman threat as much as the dynastic claims and political ambitions in Italy distracted Charles V from his declared intent of crushing the Protestant revolt to his north."

According to Coles (1968, pp. 109–10), European rulers and the Catholic Church took comfort in the fact that buffer territories existed in eastern Europe, mainly in the Balkans, between their possessions and the Turks. But that mind-set was punctured with the fall of the Byzantine Empire and Ottomans' territorial expansion in the Balkans.

In his book *Ottoman Imperialism and German Protestantism: 1521–55* (1959, p. 9), the historian Stephen Fischer-Galati establishes how the Hapsburg brothers were looking to exploit the Ottomans' Middle Eastern entanglements in order to shore up their defenses:

Since [the Ottoman Sultans] Bayezit and Selim spent most of their reign either in Istanbul or fighting in the Middle East, the Emperor thought of exploiting this situation to strengthen Eastern Europe against [the Turks]. These plans . . . could not be executed without the help of dependable allies, as the Turks were much more formidable than the mercenaries of the Venetians or the French. . . . To obtain support from the West, Maximilian [Charles V's predecessor] turned once more to the Diets. . . . He was not altogether unjustified in asking their assistance, as some Germans at least seemed interested in undertaking a crusade against the "enemy of the faith."

Perhaps it is the Reformation historian MacCulloch (2003, pp. 54–55) who best articulates the Ottomans' role in distracting the House of Hapsburg from swiftly putting down the nascent Protestant reform movement to its north. To MacCulloch, by the time Charles V could muster the strength and resources to deal with the Protestants, as he attempted to do in the 1546–47 Schmalkaldic Wars, it turned out to be too little, too late:

The trail of catastrophe [left in the wake of the Ottomans in eastern Europe] signaled [to the Christians in western and central Europe] the failure of the crusading enterprise on Europe's southern and eastern flanks, where crusades had achieved so many military advances and annexation of territory against Islam. . . . In the aftermath of Hungary's fall, the emperor Charles V tried hard to get the rulers of western Europe to finance more traditional crusades. Even as late as 1543, Henry VIII, far away in England, was prepared to sponsor a nationwide campaign to raise money for his brother monarch's effort (despite their being on opposite sides of the Church's schism), but the general political will had gone amid the bitterness of the Reformation. Martin Luther went so far as to consider Charles's effort futile, because he considered that the Turks were agents of God's anger against sinful Christendom—and no one could resist God. Indeed, the Turkish invasions were, paradoxically, good news for Luther. If Charles V had not been so distracted in his efforts to save Europe's southeastern frontier, he would perhaps have had the will and the resources to crush the Protestant revolt in its infancy in the 1520s and 1530s. When Charles did strike, it was too late.

Thus for the Hapsburgs and the Catholic papacy, the Ottoman threat took precedence over the Protestant issue. From the perspective of Charles and Ferdinand, it would have been prudent to deal with the Protestants when the Ottomans were concentrated on their own domestic discords or engaged in confrontations elsewhere.

In the words of Shaw (1976, p. 189), "During and after the struggles against the Celalis and Persians, the sultans' ministers managed to keep peace in Europe and settled whatever problems that arose without any resumption of hostilities. This effort was successful largely because the Hapsburgs were enmeshed in the Thirty Years' War [against the Protestants] and wanted to avoid conflict with the Ottomans at all cost."

There are various other relevant sources to peruse on this topic, such as Charriere (1848), Ursu (1908), and Zinkesien (1854), which Fischer-Galati (1959) provides as his original sources in French and German.

6.2   The German Diets, Austria-Hungary, and the Papacy

Did the German Diets and the nascent Reformation forces actively exploit the Islamic threat from the east? According to various prominent historians, the answer is "yes" because the German Diets seem to have repeatedly capitalized on the Hungarian King Ferdinand I's persistent need and demand for soldiers in order to extract strategic concessions from the Catholic Church and the Holy Roman emperor.

On this point, Inalcik (1973, p. 38) comments that "at first Luther and his adherents followed a passive course, maintaining that the Ottoman threat was a punishment from God, but when the Turkish peril began to endanger Germany the Lutherans did not hesitate to support Ferdinand with military and financial aid; in return they always obtained concessions for the Diets. Ottoman intervention was thus an important factor not only in the rise of national monarchies, such as in France, but also in the rise of Protestantism in Europe."

Along the same lines, Fischer-Galati (1959) details how the bargaining between the House of Hapsburg and the German Diets, representing the early Protestant movement between the 1520s and 1550s, evolved in response to the Turkish advances in eastern Europe. His detailed accounts make it clear that Ferdinand could not muster enough help from his elder brother Charles V, who was concentrating his resources and attention in the West to confront the French Emperor Francis and the Italian city-states. But Ferdinand needed resources and manpower in order to contain the Turkish threat. This left the German Diets and the budding Protestant Reform movement as his only realistic allies.

In elaborating on the meeting of the Diet at Worms in 1521, Fischer-Galati (1959, p. 16) makes the following relevant observation: "From as early as 1521, Ferdinand showed grave concern over the Turkish position in eastern Europe. He realized that the renewed Ottoman aggression, if left unchecked, could bring disaster to Hungary and even perhaps Germany and the Hapsburgs' Austrian possessions. . . . At least until 1526, Ferdinand believed that Hungary could be saved if aid could be secured;

hence, from 1521 until the battle of the Mohacs [in 1526] he was a fervent advocate of assistance to Hungary."

Thus it is that Ferdinand repeatedly turned to the German Diets to ask for their assistance. But the Diets always seemed reluctant to contribute funds or manpower to the Hapsburgs. Fischer-Galati (1959, pp. 19–24) documents this in detail when he notes how, by 1522, the situation had worsened because the Turks had captured Belgrade:

The increased danger had been appreciated by Charles as early as August 1521 when he asked the German estates for favorable consideration of Louis' anticipated demands for help. . . . The clamors for assistance brought no immediate results except for the appointment of a commission to meet in Vienna with representatives of nations threatened by the Turks to determine the extent of the danger and the amount of aid needed. . . . Before 1524 the religious and the Turkish questions were basically separate issues; however, it was clear to the German Diets that the religious question, though not directly associated with the Turkish one, took precedence over it.

It is hard if not impossible to discern whether the Germans' "wait-and-see" attitude initially was due to their view that the Turks were primarily Hungary's problem or they were holding out hope that Ferdinand's situation would become more precarious with further Turkish advances, on the back of which they could wrangle a better deal from the Hapsburgs. One thing is clear: The German Diets' stance began to change as the Turkish gains in Europe accumulated and Ferdinand became more desperate.

Following the Diet of Speyer in the summer of 1526, the Germans not only became more vocal about their demands to link the Protestants' official recognition with aid to Hungary but also increased the extent to which they came to the aid of Ferdinand when the Turkish advances threatened to be detrimental even to the Germans.

Fischer-Galati (1959, pp. 19–24) identifies that Ferdinand began to cave in to at least some of the German Diets' demands as early as 1526:

By the summer of 1526, when a new Diet met at Speyer the Hungarian situation had become critical. The Turks were about to launch a decisive campaign against [Hungary] and Ferdinand was gravely concerned. . . . The Diet, however, was not swayed by his arguments. . . . The estates declined to consider the question of assistance to Hungary before solving the German religious problem. . . . [Ferdinand's] alternatives were limited: he could either accede to the wishes of the estates or dissolve the Diet. Turkish pressure on Hungary was too great for him to choose the latter alternative; therefore he reluctantly agreed to the former.

Figure 6.1 Martin Luther (painting by Lucas Cranach the Elder, 1528, Veste Coburg Castle)

The subsequent negotiations between the Protestants and Ferdinand-Charles reflected persistent attempts by the Protestants to link the provision of funds and men to Hungary with the resolution of their religious conflict with the Catholic Church. At the same time, Ferdinand's main concern was to get the Diet to commit troops and funds in defense of Hungary without yielding too many concessions to the Protestants in exchange. Their wrangling lasted until 1529 when the Ottomans put Vienna under siege.

The Ottomans' move against the Hapsburgs' Austrian possessions was too much of a threat to keep the two sides entrenched in their own positions any longer. As a result, "Germans, irrespective of religious affiliation, prepared to defend the Empire against the Infidel. All these factors convinced the Protestants that they could not withhold their support and they participated in the campaign that ended with the Turkish withdrawal from Vienna. Disregarding factional interests, the Protestants rallied to the defence of the Empire in 1529. But this was the last time that they joined in anti-Turkish hostilities without first securing concessions in religious matters. After the siege of Vienna, Lutherans' fate and assistance against the Turks became more and more closely interrelated" (Fischer-Galati, 1959, p. 35).

Ferdinand, who became Holy Roman emperor following Charles V's abdication of the throne in 1556, negotiated the Treaty of Passau with the Lutheran elector Maurice of Saxony who was at war with the emperor. In 1555, he signed the Peace of Augsburg, which culminated in roughly one-half century of peace to Germany's warring religious factions. The Peace of Augsburg is widely recognized as the date when the Holy Roman Empire officially recognized the Lutheran Protestant movement.

Even after the peace treaty, Kortepeter (1972, p. 196) makes it clear that the attempts to link the Protestants' recognition with the Ottoman threat lasted well into the seventeenth century. While the Peace of Augsburg was a recognition of the Protestant legitimacy by the Holy Roman Empire, it did not directly involve the Catholic Church and turned out to be a temporary reprieve.

Indeed, much of the Counter-Reformation period got under way in earnest after the success of the Holy League at Lepanto in 1571, when the Holy Empire fleet decimated the entire Ottoman navy and scored the first major victory for Europeans against the Ottomans. This sea battle marked not only a significant setback for the Ottoman naval prowess in the eastern Mediterranean Sea, which the Ottomans never dominated again, but also the first major victory of the European powers against the Ottoman Turks. Hence the period of truly violent sectarian conflict in Europe during the Thirty Years' War (1618–48) coincided with a period of tranquility with the military weakness of the Ottomans. As Anderson (1967, p. 60) concludes,

It became apparent after the Battle of Nördllingen (1634) that the Catholics could not hold northern Germany, nor the Protestants, southern. This ought to have ended the war, but it rumbled on for thirteen terrible years, until, after lengthy negotiations, a spirit of compromise prevailed and finally, in October of 1648, the Peace of Westphalia was signed. . . . Although it had ostensibly been a war of religion, the bloodletting did not appreciably alter the ecclesiastical picture of the continent. The Peace of Westphalia reaffirmed the Peace of Augsburg and added the Reformed Churches to its recognized list. . . . With the exception of the lands of the Austrian Hapsburgs where the Counter-Reformation gains were to be allowed to stand, the areas that were Protestant or Catholic in 1624 were to remain so.

Anderson's account makes it clear that, by the time the House of Hapsburg and the Catholic establishment were pitted against the Protestant Reformers to their north in 1618, the German Protestant Reformers were no longer the budding reform movement they used to represent in the early sixteenth century but a much more formidable opponent. And it was not until the Peace of Westphalia at the end of the Thirty Years' War that religious pluralism became the accepted norm by the House of Hapsburg as well as the Catholic Church.

6.3 Deals with the Infidel

The extent to which European rulers and minorities from different Christian denominations coalesced with the Ottomans varied. Even as early as the late fifteenth century, the Catholic Popes Innocent VIII and his successor Alexander VI cooperated with the Ottoman Sultan Beyazıt (Frazee, 1983, pp. 19–22). In exchange for financial and security concessions from the Ottoman Empire, the former agreed to permanently jail Beyazıt's younger brother Cem, who had sought the aid of the Knights of Saint John to succeed the Ottoman throne.

In the sixteenth century, Francis I, the king of France, was eager to cooperate with the Ottomans and lean on this alliance for his geopolitical rivalry with the Hapsburgs and the Italian city-states (i.e., the brief, French-Ottoman joint military campaign against the Duke of Savoy in the mid-1500s). To this end, Francis signed a treaty with Süleyman the Magnificent in 1535. According to Kinross (1979, p. 204),

[The treaty] permitted the French to carry on trade throughout the Ottoman Empire, by payment of the same dues to the Sultan as were paid by the Turks themselves. . . . [The treaty] granted complete religious liberty to the French in the Ottoman Empire, with the right to keep guard over the holy places, and amounted in effect to a French protectorate over all Catholics in the Levant. The treaty put an end to the commercial predominance of Venice in the Mediterranean, and obliged all Christian ships—with the exception of those of the Venetians—to fly the French flag as a guarantee of protection.

Political alliances between Poland-Lithuania, Sweden, and the Ottomans became more prevalent in the seventeenth century, and England began to trade cannon, gunpowder, lead, and woolens with the empire (Kortepeter, 1972, p. ix).

Various scholars have documented that the Ottomans' deliberate policies of low taxes and religious toleration generally helped to "divide and conquer" Eastern Orthodox Christian communities of the Ottoman territories from the Catholic West, at least until the eighteenth century.

Faroqhi (2004, pp. 37, 64) discusses the Ottomans' direct involvement in aiding the Protestants by accepting the relocation of Huguenots from France to Moldavia, then an Ottoman territory, as well as the Ottomans' indirect support of the Serbian Orthodox immigrants against the Hapsburgs in some Balkan protectorates. As Kuran (2004a) argues, however, the evolution of the political and social institutions in western Europe and the simultaneous stagnation of the Ottoman state jointly helped patch the divisions between the Christian Ottoman diaspora and the Europeans over time. For references, see also Kafadar (1996), Shaw (1976), and Karpat (1974).

In the grand scheme of things, however, Ottoman-European cooperation remained an exception to the rule, and it carried significant social stigma. It is primarily because European courts, noblemen, and publicists rallied against the alliance of Francis with the Ottomans—for instance, when Charles and Francis ended their conflict and acceded to the wishes of the pope who explicitly wanted to unite Europe against Islam (Shaw, 1976, p. 98; Faroqhi, 2004, p. 33).

6.4 Hypothesis

The anecdotal evidence and the relevant historiography thus suggest that the Ottomans' military prowess and the Protestants' eventual success in bringing to an end a millennium and a half of sectarian monopoly within Christianity were intertwined.

Nevertheless, this is ultimately an empirical issue that revolves around two fundamental questions: First, was the Ottoman threat to the Catholic Church and the existing European ecclesiastical authorities perceived to be more serious than that of the Protestant reformists, to an extent that the Ottoman conquests produced de facto intra-European peace? Second, were religious differences the reason the timing of the Hapsburg confrontations with the Lutherans depended inversely on the timing of the Ottomans' European conquests?

Luckily, there is some relevant data to test these and other related questions. To that end, I will make use of data on violent conflicts for a two-century interval between 1451 and 1700, which was compiled by Peter Brecke of the Georgia Institute of Technology. The data suit our purposes because they contain a comprehensive and annual documentation of all violent confrontations in Europe, the Middle East, and North Africa for the era immediately prior to the Industrial Revolution and the period surrounding the Protestant Reformation.

6.5 Data Sources and Definitions

The primary data source for the analyses below is a conflict catalog being constructed by Brecke (1999, in progress). It is a comprehensive data set on violent conflicts in all regions of the world between 1400 CE and the present. It contains a listing of all recorded violent conflicts with a Richardson's magnitude of 1.5 or higher that occurred during the relevant time span in five continents. Richardson's index value of 1.5 derives from the fact that the logarithmic value of thirty-two or more deaths corresponds to a magnitude of 1.5 or greater. While the catalog is still under construction, it is virtually complete for Europe and the Near East. This portion of the catalog will be utilized in a variety of statistical analyses discussed in the remainder of this book.

For each conflict recorded in the catalog, the primary information covers the number and identities of the parties involved in the conflict; the common name for the confrontation (if it exists); and where and when the conflict took place. On the basis of these data, there also exists derivative information on the duration of the conflict and the number of fatalities, which is unfortunately available for less than a third of the total number of observations. Supplementary data come from a variety of sources: to cite two, for population measures and urbanization measures, I use the estimates by Chandler (1987) and McEvedy and Jones (1978) and, for distance measures, I use the "City Distance Tool" by Geobytes (which can be found at http://www.geobytes.com/CityDistanceTool.htm).

Using the European subset of the conflict catalog data, I generated annual observations for the period between 1450 CE and 1700 CE. I focus on this time interval due to the fact that the Ottoman Empire's era of dominance is formally defined as the period between 1453 CE and 1699 CE (see, for example, Shaw 1976, pp. 55, 224). However, using alternative estimates where the interval of time is defined more narrowly or wider, one can derive similar results.

6.6   A Descriptive Look

I will start by noting some salient aspects of European and Ottoman conflicts and demographics at the time. Between 1451 and 1650, there was on average one new Ottoman military action initiated in continental Europe roughly every three years and about one new Ottoman engagement domestically or in other regions every five years. This compares with roughly three violent conflicts every two years among or within continental European countries themselves. The highest number of intra-European conflicts recorded in any given year was six in 1519; the number of conflicts between the Ottoman Empire and Europe was three in 1551; and the highest number of domestic conflicts in the Ottoman Empire or military excursions in other regions was three in 1526.

Now consider the number of aggregate or cumulative conflicts, defined as conflicts that were initiated in any given year as well as the ones started earlier that were still ongoing then. Looking at such conflicts, the range of intra-European feuds was between as few as one (in 1454 and 1547) and as high as eleven (in 1478, 1620, 1625, and 1626); the range of Ottoman and European engagements was between zero (in numerous years) and five (in 1463); and the range of Ottoman internal conflicts and conflicts elsewhere (aggregate) was identical to the range of newly initiated conflicts—between zero and three.

Both European and Ottoman population levels are negatively correlated with violent conflicts in Europe (either between Ottomans and Europeans or among the European countries themselves), but they are positively associated with the number of Catholic-Protestant engagements. This reflects the fact that population levels manifest a positive time trend and the Protestant-Catholic confrontations were concentrated in the later part of the sample period.

A salient observation is that the raw correlation between the number of Ottoman conquests in Europe and that of violent conflicts among the Europeans themselves is negative but fairly low.

6.7   Main Findings

The online technical appendix of this chapter, which is based on Iyigun (2008), provides the details of my empirical approach and statistical results. In what follows, I will run through a bird's eye view of the main statistical relationships.

For starters, I will try to establish whether the Ottomans' military excursions in Europe impacted the patterns of wars within continental Europe after accounting for the roles of various other relevant factors in influencing conflict patterns in Europe.

To that end, one would want to account for the date of conflict due to the fact that there is a time trend that political scientists have established long ago. According to research by Woods and Baltzly (1915), Richardson (1960), and Wilkinson (1980), reviewed in chapter 1, and more recently Brecke (1999), there has been a secular decline in warfare in Europe since the fifteenth century, despite the observation that the eighteenth century was the most tranquil of all centuries on record. Moreover, as some historians have argued, the influence of the Ottoman Empire on Europe was at its pinnacle from the capture of Istanbul in 1453 to the Lepanto sea battle in 1571, in which the Holy Empire fleet decimated the entire Ottoman navy and scored the first major victory for Europeans against the Ottomans. To many historians, this sea battle marked not only a significant setback for the Ottoman naval prowess in the eastern Mediterranean Sea, which the Ottomans never dominated again, but also a psychological momentum shift. Taking into account these two issues, it is prudent to control for the year of conflicts within continental Europe.

Next, I will account for the population levels of continental Europe because it is quite plausible for there to be links between population levels and violent conflict. Indeed, this would be in line with the positive check on population growth discussed by Malthus. On this basis and in various alternative estimates, I will also control for the population level in the Ottoman territories.

I would also like to control for the average length of intra-European conflicts as well as Ottoman military engagements at any given time on the basis of a potential relationship between the length of conflicts and their frequencies. The idea is that, the more protracted conflicts a sovereign was engaged in, the fewer conflicts (or more, for that matter) he could initiate.

Since the main idea involves the Ottomans' imperialistic threat to continental Europe subsiding their own squabbles, implicit in this hypothesis is the notion that the impact of the Ottomans on European sovereignties' military proclivities should have decreased with distance from the Ottoman frontier. For this reason, one should also account for the average distance of continental European conflicts from the Ottoman capital, Istanbul. A corollary of this reasoning dictates that the farther the Ottomans' military engagements from those in Europe, the smaller their impact on European affairs. Thus I will include the average distance of the Ottomans' other military engagements from Istanbul.

6.7.1 Ottoman Wars and Intra-European Violence

I will begin by exploring the timing and frequency of violent confrontations initiated in Europe between 1451 CE and 1700 CE. Based on a variety of empirical estimates and calculations and controlling for a host of related observable factors discussed above, the data show that the timing of intra-European feuds were *inversely* related to the timing of Ottomans' European conquests, although this effect was subsiding over time. Nevertheless, the statistical analyses also reveal some other pertinent patterns and links surrounding Ottoman conquests and intra-European conflicts.

For instance, recall that the Ottomans' presence in Europe might have influenced intra-European conflicts by pushing those conflicts away from the Ottoman frontier, altering neither their frequency nor their intensity. But controlling for the distance of conflicts from the Ottoman capital Istanbul reveals that the deeper the Ottomans penetrated into Europe, the greater their impact on subduing intra-European feuds. This result is consistent with the idea that, regardless of how close or distant potential conflicts were to the Ottoman frontier, the Ottomans' military activities had a negative and statistically significant impact on all intra-European feuds. Then, taking this idea seriously, one can see if the ratio of the number of intra-European conflicts in any given year to the average distance of these conflicts to the Ottoman capital was influenced by the intensity of Ottomans' European military activities. In essence, this adjustment enables one to see if the Ottomans affected intra-European conflicts regardless of how close the latter were to the Ottoman-European frontier. The results reveal that, even with an adjustment for distance from the Ottoman frontier, the number of Ottoman military actions in Europe had a statistically significant and negative impact on the number of intra-European conflicts.

As another alternative test of the idea that Ottoman military involvements in Europe had a stronger discouraging effect on intra-European violent feuds that were closer geographically, one can also test if the average distance of within-Europe violent conflicts from the Ottoman capital, Istanbul, was affected by the Ottomans' military activities. The Ottomans had a positive and statistically significant effect on European conflicts in all relevant specifications. Thus when Europeans were engaged in violent feuds among themselves, it was more likely that their confrontations took place in parts of Europe that were farther away from the Ottoman frontier when the Ottomans were militarily active in continental Europe. In particular, an additional Ottoman military engagement in Europe in any given year raised the average distance of intra-European violent conflicts from Istanbul by about 140 to 320 miles. This suggests another channel through which the Ottomans' military ventures in eastern Europe and the Balkans helped suppress intra-European conflicts on the whole continent. And it is further indication that their impact was not solely concentrated on the buffer territories within geographical proximity of the Ottoman frontier.

In addition to the direct effects of the Ottomans' European military conquests and confrontations on intra-European violent feuds, my empirical investigations have also revealed some intriguing peripheral findings. For example, there seems to have been a rather significant decline over time in the Ottomans' impact on intra-European feuds, which is in line with what one would expect: The Ottomans were quite formidable between 1451 and the end of the sixteenth century, and the chink in their armor came only with the 1571 Lepanto Sea Battle. Although the empire recovered swiftly from that debacle at sea and restored its fleet within a couple of years, by the seventeenth century, it was well into its stagnation period and was no longer the feared and loathed Islamic power it used to be. I found that the count of Ottomans' military engagements elsewhere (including its own civil discords and domestic uprisings) had a positive and significant effect on intra-European violent confrontations. Indeed, if the Ottoman threat was able to subdue intra-European conflicts, it is possible that its wane due to the Ottomans' being bogged down in conflicts away from its European frontier might have stimulated and helped resume intra-European rivalries.

6.7.2 Ottomans and the Protestant Reformation

The third and final relevant aspect I will examine, in particular, is a pure count of the historically well-documented Protestant-Catholic confrontations.

What we see here is consistent with the hypothesis that the Protestant Reformation was aided and abated by the Ottomans' European aspirations: the number of the Ottomans' military engagements in Europe, for the most part, did exert a negative dampening impact on the number of Catholic-Protestant feuds. This impact tended to decline over time, although in any given year, an Ottomans military conquest in the Balkans or eastern Europe reduced that number anywhere between roughly 25 percent and 40 percent.

In all three different tests discussed above, one should note that the Ottomans' military engagements outside Europe typically had positive and statistically significant effects on intra-European wars and conflicts—that is, the tendency for the intra-European feuds to escalate, as measured by all three of my European violent confrontations measures, rose as the Ottomans got bogged down in domestic uprisings in their own territories in Anatolia, the Middle East, or North Africa or as they undertook campaigns in the east, the north, or the south against other rivals, such as the Persian or Russian Empires.

Results like these verify that there was indeed a negative link between the Ottomans' military activities in Europe and those between the European actors. In particular, the intensity of military engagements between the Protestant Reformers and the Counter-Reformation forces, such as the Schmalkaldic Wars (1546–47), the Thirty Years' War (1618–48), and the French Wars of Religion (1562–98) did depend negatively and statistically significantly on the Ottomans' military activities in Europe.

Moreover—and this has serious repercussions for my hypothesis—the impact of Ottoman military conquests in Europe did not weaken, and it persisted with distance from the Ottoman frontier. Together with the fact that the simple correlation of the number of Ottoman wars in Europe and that of intra-European violent conflicts is negative but fairly low, this finding contradicts an alternative hypothesis that the Ottomans forced their neighbors to engage them for survival but did not impact other Europeans.

6.8 At the Dawn of an Oasis of Prosperity

I will conclude this chapter by quickly reviewing what these findings suggest from a longer-term and broader perspective.

For starters, we have seen that domestic conflicts, rivalries, and even cooperation can be influenced by outside threats. As I briefly reviewed in the chapter introduction, there were various calls for and attempts at religious reformation in Europe prior to the Lutheran era, although the Catholic papacy prevailed over them, usually by force. But when, in 1517, Martin Luther appeared at the steps of the castle church in Wittenberg and nailed his Ninety-Five Theses on the door, things were a bit different. Luther was very convinced that the Turks pounding away on Europe's eastern frontiers was God's punishment of Europe for straying from the true faith and the divine path. And he did view the Ottomans as less of a problem than the pope, who to him represented the antichrist. My analyses provide support to those who claim that Turks were, to some important extent, the Protestants' blessing. Politics make strange bedfellows, but apparently realpolitik had some precedents in medieval Europe, too.

There are ramifications of these results for the literature on the history of European economic development. Various authors have argued that the non-European, peripheral regions contributed to European development between the fifteenth and twentieth centuries. For example, Pommeranz (2000) emphasized that production by British, Portuguese, and French colonial plantations helped raise the threshold for Malthusian mechanisms in Europe. Berg (2005) and de Vries (1994) focused on the role of desirable imports altering the Europeans' labor-leisure trade-off. And Abu-Lughod (1989) argued that technological transfers from the East—in particular, China—were important to the West. By contrast, the findings here suggest that European military and political competition with its periphery might have affected its sociopolitical and economic history in a serendipitous and hitherto neglected fashion as well.

Last but not least, these findings impinge upon the historical relevance of differences of faith between the Europeans and the Turks, Christians versus Muslims, and One True Religion versus two or more accepted faiths. Put differently, the emergence of a formidable threat to the Hapsburgs and the Catholic Church in the early sixteenth century, regardless of its religious affiliation and sympathies, could have aided the Protestants. That the Ottomans were Muslim and their sultan intended to bring Europe into Dar al-Islam might have had no relevance. This is certainly a credible viewpoint. Nonetheless, the findings above represent a serious challenge to it.

First, if the Ottomans were merely a faith-neutral distraction for the Hapsburgs because they were a credible military threat to the Hapsburgs' eastern European possessions, then this would have sufficed for the Protestants to make maximum use of the relative calm up north. But I have documented that the Ottomans' military presence in Europe had quite a large impact not only on the Protestant-Catholic confrontations on the continent but also on all intra-European feuds in general. Moreover, I was able to verify that this dampening effect persisted with distance from the Ottoman frontiers in Europe.

Second, recall from the material in chapter 5 that the common scholarly view regarding the foundations of the Ottoman state is based on the *Gaza ideology*, which asserts that early Ottoman sultans were driven to Western conquests by motives of holy war in the name of Islam.

The data used in this chapter show that, during the two-century interval between 1451 and 1700, the Ottomans were involved in seventy-nine military excursions in Europe, whereas over the same time interval, they dealt with only forty-eight conflicts elsewhere. By perusing the various credible sources on Ottoman history (such as Shaw, 1976, and Goffman,

2002), one can classify each of those conflicts by whether they were initiated by the Ottomans. Doing so does not turn out to be very difficult but is quite illuminating; except for some cases in which border skirmishes preceded the onset of military hostilities between the Ottomans and their rivals, the historical accounts make it clear how each confrontation began. This tally identifies the Ottomans' ambitions of European conquest: of the seventy-nine Ottoman wars in Europe, fifty-five were initiated by the Ottomans (which corresponds to about 70 percent of all European-Ottoman engagements), but of the forty-eight Ottoman confrontations elsewhere—of which six were Anatolian uprisings—only eighteen were initiated by the Ottomans (accounting for 38 percent of all Ottoman military activities elsewhere). Moreover, the proportions of war initiated by the Ottomans in Europe showed a rapid decline, but there is no discernible pattern in those elsewhere. For example, in the period between 1450 and 1550, Ottomans engaged Europeans in thirty-seven conflicts; of those, thirty-two began with some Ottoman initiative (which is more than 85 percent).

This reveals that the Ottomans had a clear intention to expand westward and conquer *Dar al-Harb*. With this, as well as Kafadar's account of the origins of the Ottoman rise, it is rather difficult to argue that, at a time when the Ottomans were swallowing European landscape in big chunks, European powers were oblivious to this intent. This is all the more relevant when one bears in mind that some of these European institutions were the ones that played an active role in organizing Holy Crusades against the Muslims between the eleventh and thirteenth centuries.

If existential outside threats help calm the waters and induce *internal* disputes to be set aside—even temporarily—could the evolution of domestic sociopolitical institutions subsequently reflect this history, especially if the *external-threat-cum-cohabitation* leads to the survival of fringe and theretofore marginalized groups?

On this point, one needs to recognize that the fluidity with which civilizations, empires, and societies have appeared on and disappeared from the historical stage as a result of foreign animosities is a testament to the fact that domestic power struggles were often rendered irrelevant in their long-term impact on domestic institutions. Nevertheless, riding on the back of the Ottomans' implicit aid, the survival and official recognition of Protestantism and its various offshoots, such as Calvinism, Zwinglianism, and Anabaptism, had a profound impact on the European religion market. That religious pluralism generated competition between different Christian denominations is a direct corollary of the spatial competition model of Hotelling (1929) applied to the religion market and espoused more recently by Barro and McCleary (2005).

In what lies ahead, I will further explore the extent to which religious and ethnic identities factored in the interactions between the Christians of Europe and the Muslims of the Ottoman Empire and the Middle East. Then I will analyze the long-term political ramifications and manifestations of this history on European and Middle Eastern societies.

SEVEN

Those Harem Nights

In earlier chapters, I explored the sociopolitical advantages of the Abrahamic monotheisms, on the back of which Christianity and Islam, in particular, were able to spread and become dominant fairly swiftly by historical standards. I then identified that, once Christianity and Islam became dominant in Europe and the Middle East, respectively, religious identities and differences did play a role in influencing patterns of intra-European conflict. And precisely because the Islamic Ottoman threat to the Catholic monopoly in Europe dominated the challenges posed by the Lutherans, I showed that religious identities and rivalries came to bear on the evolution of Christian denominations. In this chapter, I will show that ethnic and religious identities might have had subtler influences on Ottoman and European interactions as well.

The conventional studies of conflict and war overwhelmingly, if not solely, emphasize differences between social groups (Richardson, 1960; Wilkinson, 1980). This is primarily driven by the view that religion and ethnicity are two fundamental components of *culture capital*, the differences in which that can produce wholesale *clash of civilizations*. According to the *club theory*, religious and ethnic norms persist and are accentuated because they help maintain adherence and loyalty to different faiths and ideologies (see, for instance, Huntington, 1996; Landes; 1998; Inglehart and Baker, 2000; Iannaccone, 1992; and Berman, 2000). Taking

This chapter is based on Iyigun (2008).

this perspective, then, religiously motivated wars are primarily about societies and not their rulers.

Political leaders' motives for war and peace have been studied quite extensively in more contemporary political economy contexts (Hess and Orphanides, 1995, 2001; Glaeser, 2005). However, the degree to which rulers themselves are driven by religious motives or the extent to which their own identities and cultural ties influence the patterns of international war has never been examined. A serious impediment for such an investigation has been the difficulty involved with observing variations in the rulers' ethnic or religious identities, independent of those of their own societies at large.

In a related vein, there exists a strand within economics that promotes the notion that *culture matters*. It is primarily on this basis that the channels through which cultural beliefs, views, and traits are passed from one generation to the next have also been of interest to economists. Among the recent but influential papers in the economics literature on the intergenerational transmission of cultural traits, a salient example is provided by Fernandez, Fogli, and Olivetti (2004), who argue that cultural traits or attitudes are transferred from mothers to sons.

Ottoman history is relevant for all this due to three reasons. First, as I have already shown in chapters 5 and 6, the empire had a profound and lasting impact in Europe, the Middle East, and North Africa, especially during the apogee of its power between the fifteenth and seventeenth centuries. Most of the Balkans and eastern Europe remained under Ottoman imperial rule for centuries, and many countries there today reflect the remnants of various institutional features inherited from the Ottomans. Indeed, some of the fundamental contemporary political problems of the Middle East and the Balkans are, at least in part, attributed to the empire's rapid disintegration during the late nineteenth and early twentieth centuries (MacMillan, 2002).

Second, I have already discussed how the Ottomans were motivated by the Gaza ideology, at least during the empire's early era running through the end of the sixteenth century. Hence, to the extent that *Gaza* accurately describes the Ottomans' imperial predisposition and their geopolitical objectives, it provides a useful yardstick with which one can gauge and quantify the influence of other relevant determinants of conflict and war.

Third, within a fairly swift period of time following its foundation, the empire became a multiethnic and multireligious civilization with many important posts within the military, administrative, and palace hierarchies routinely being held by converts to Islam from the Balkans, the Mediterranean, and the Black Sea.

With the data set mentioned in chapter 6 at my disposal, I can exploit the Ottomans' unique imperial history to examine whether cultural preferences, beliefs, and values persisted intergenerationally between the sultans and their mothers in perpetuating or diverting conflicts and war. Whereas Gaza is put forward as the reason the Ottomans initiated more conflicts in the West and the reason, on the eastern fronts, more conflicts were started by Ottomans' rivals, another—not necessarily mutually exclusive—hypothesis claims that the imperial harem wielded considerable political power in Ottoman affairs. And various historians have suggested that the members of the harem with different ethnic or religious backgrounds often lobbied the sultan to influence the geography of Ottoman conquests (Shaw, 1976; Peirce, 1993; Goffman, 2002; Imber, 2002).

In what follows, I will document that Gaza was important for understanding the Ottomans' imperial motives but was not sufficient. What also mattered almost as much was the sultans' ethno-religious identities. In particular, due to the fact that the Ottoman throne successions were deliberately noninstitutionalized and highly random events, there is a great deal of variation in the ethnic and religious backgrounds of the Ottoman queen mothers. On this basis, one can establish that, while Ottoman conquests were predominantly in the West until the mid-1500s, the ethnic background of *valide sultan* (the queen mother) was an important and independent determinant of whether the empire engaged in military conquests in Europe versus North Africa or the Middle East. To quantify, the reign of a sultan with a European maternal ethnic background was enough to offset more than 70 percent of the empire's Western orientation in imperial conquests. By contrast, the reign of a sultan with a European matrilineal descent mostly had no discernible influence on the empire's Eastern conflicts, while a Muslim matrilineal genealogy typically boosted the Ottomans' military ventures in Europe.

It is difficult, if not impossible, to discern how general these results are. But on some level, they are a testament to the deep roots of ethnic and religious identities. This is because conversions to Islam, even and particularly among the elite of the harem hierarchy who had influence on Ottoman policymaking, seem not to have been enough to maintain loyalty to the "holy cause." The ethno-religious identities of the sultans' inner circle played a significant and independent role in subverting the imperial ambitions of the empire toward the Middle East and North Africa. It is on this basis that one can account for the distinct geographical patterns of and shifts in the Ottomans' history of imperial conquest. This is also why the findings below relate to economic development as well. Ethnic and religious polarization is an important determinant of civil as well as interstate conflicts, with the latter having significant adverse effects on long-run economic growth. The findings below suggest that the intergenerational transmission of underlying ethnic and religious identities might be strong enough to have persisted and perpetuated over generations, even when individuals—voluntarily or involuntarily—converted to official or state religions.

The idea that cultural preferences, beliefs, and values may persist intergenerationally—and that they may do so based on motives beyond pecuniary cost and benefit calculus—has solid roots in economic theory, political science, and psychology. The literature on the economics of cultural transmission, in particular, provides the foundation for the analyses and interpretations below. For example, one highly relevant framework is exposited in Bisin and Verdier (2001). In their model, children's preferences are acquired from their parents through a process of adaptation and imitation, whereby parents' efforts to indoctrinate their offspring depend on the social and cultural environment. If family and society are closer substitutes in the transmission of cultural values, parents socialize with their children more intensely when the traits they wish to impart on their offspring are common only to the minority. According to Bisin and Verdier (2001), parents evaluate their children's actions from their own preference perspective. Hence as is implicit in the analyses that follow, a mother always attempts to socialize her children according to her own cultural preferences. For example, see Peirce (1993), Imber (2002), Goffman (2002), and Shaw (1976).

In this vein, the role of women in Muslim civilizations in general and the Ottoman Empire in particular has been—and continues to be—extensively debated. Peirce (1993) details the power of imperial women in the Ottoman harem, and other Ottoman historians, such as Shaw (1976) and Inalcik (1973), also review this topic at some length. The empirical analyses discussed below lend some credence to the view that women—in this case, the queen mothers in particular—had influence and extensive power in decision making in an inherently Islamic and powerful empire.

All the same, it is important to qualify the channel through which the Ottoman royal women might have had a bearing on Ottoman political and military actions. As I will demonstrate below, I find some evidence that the harem politics played less of a role in influencing the sultans in state matters, but that, more likely, the sultans acted cognizant of their family legacies. In this, my findings are more in line with a channel of cultural transmission between the valide sultans and their ruling sons.

7.1 Trends in Ottoman Conquests

When one examines the Ottomans' geographical patterns of conquest, it is not difficult to discern a westward orientation from the foundation of the empire running through the reign of Beyazıt II, later giving way to more frequent conquests in the Middle East and North Africa in much of the sixteenth century, during the reigns of Selim I (the Grim) and Süleyman I (the Magnificent).

Figures 7.1 and 7.2 show Europe, the Middle East, and North Africa 115 years apart, in 1451 CE and 1566 CE, respectively. As can be seen in figure 7.1, in 1451 CE, the Ottomans controlled only parts of Asia Minor in the east, although it had full sovereignty in all the Balkans and a significant chunk of southeastern Europe, too. By the mid-sixteenth century, however, they had not only expanded their territorial control in eastern Europe (a history already surveyed in chapter 5) but also made significant conquests in the east and the south. Hence one can clearly establish how the Ottomans primarily turned eastward for imperial expansion during the sixteenth century. Indeed, all the Arabian peninsula and most of North Africa—with the notable exception of the northwestern coastal regions remaining under the control of the Kingdom of Morocco—were under Ottoman rule by 1600 CE. For detailed references on the history of the Ottoman Empire, see Faroqhi (2004), Kinross (1979), Inalcik (1973), Karpat (1974), Shaw (1976), and Goodwin (2000).

7.2 The Harem Hierarchy and Genealogical Links

The imperial harem, *harem-i hümayûn*, was the sacred, private quarters of the Ottoman sultan, who was "God's shadow on earth" (Peirce, 1993, pp. 5–7, 17, 24). Throughout the middle of the sixteenth century, the imperial harem consisted only of an administrative quarter, which was inhabited only by males, including the sultan himself and the top echelons of the palace hierarchy. Toward the end of the century, however, when another private quarter to house the immediate family of the sultans was established, it too began to be called the imperial harem. This inner sanctum included the wives and concubines of the sultan as well as his imperial offspring.

The Ottomans typically relied on slave concubines for reproduction, although the sultans were legally married to as many as four wives. The thinking went that the slave concubines had no officially recognized lineages, which made them immune to vested familial interests. By contrast,

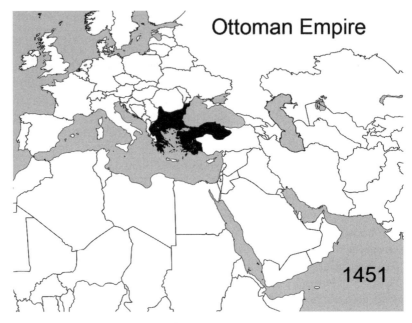

Figure 7.1   Ottoman Empire circa 1451 CE

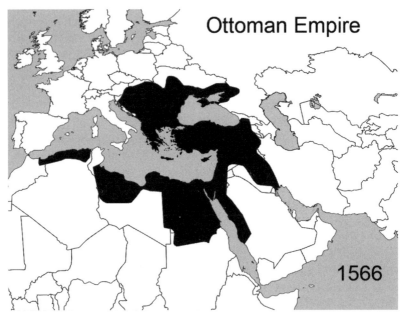

Figure 7.2   Ottoman Empire circa 1566 CE

wives were feared to have vested interests in their maiden family's affairs. This led to the preference of slave concubines for royal reproduction, although the findings below suggest that the system of "reproduction through concubinage" was not foolproof to identity politics either.

That Ottoman imperial wives and mothers played an influential role in shaping, directly or indirectly, Ottoman administration and practices is well established. For instance, Stanford Shaw (1976, p. 24) discusses the influence of the wives and queen mothers on Ottoman policy making:

Beginning in the Seljuk times and continuing into the fourteenth century, Byzantine and other Christian women were taken in to the harems of Seljuk, Turkoman and early Ottoman rulers. The mother of the Seljuk ruler Izuddin II was the daughter of a Greek prince. Izuddin II is said to have been secretly baptized and to have followed strong Greek influence at his court. Orhan's wife Theodora, daughter Cantacuzene, is said to have remained a Christian and to have provided help to the Christians of Bithynia while she was in the Ottoman court. Murat I and Bayezit I had Christian Greek mothers. Murat married the Bulgarian princess Tamara and the Byzantine princess Helena. Bayezit married Despina, the daughter of the Serbian prince Lazar. All these women brought Christian advisers into the Ottoman court, influencing Ottoman court practice and ceremonial as it evolved in this crucial [fourteenth] century.

Peirce (1993, pp. 6, 7) describes in more detail how the harem hierarchy was typically controlled by the mother queen, valide sultan: "The imperial harem was much like the household harem, only much more extensive and with a more highly articulated structure. . . . The larger the household, the more articulated the power structure of the harem." Invariably, but more so after the sixteenth century, the harem hierarchy functioned under the control of the mother queen, valide sultan. More to the point, her influence transcended the harem boundaries because the empire itself was accepted as the personal domain of the royal family. According to Peirce (1993, p. 7),

Women of superior status in this female [harem] society, the matriarchal elders, had considerable authority not only over other women but also over younger males in the family, for the harem was also the setting for the private life of men. . . . The authority enjoyed by the female elders transcended, in both its sources and its effects, the bounds of the individual family. In a polity such as the Ottomans, where the empire was considered the personal domain of the dynastic family, it was natural that important women within the dynastic household—in particular, the mother of the reigning sultan—would assume legitimate roles of authority outside the royal household.

While the institutional powers of the valide sultan solidified with the establishment of the inner sanctum of the imperial harem in mid-sixteenth century, she exerted influence over the eventual sultan long before that. Again, referencing Peirce (1993, p. 24),

From the middle of the fifteenth century, and possibly earlier, when a prince left the capital for his provincial governorate, he was accompanied by his mother, whose role was to preside over the prince's domestic household and perform her duty of "training and supervision" alongside the prince's tutor. But when the queen mother emerged as an institutionally powerful individual toward the end of the sixteenth century, there were two generations of "political mothers" related to the single politically active male of the dynasty, the sultan. . . . With the lapse of the princely governorate, the entire royal family was united in the capital under one roof, rather than, as previously, dispersed throughout the royal domain. There was now only one royal household, over which the senior woman, the sultan's mother, naturally took charge.

Goffman (2002, pp. 124–25) takes exception to the canonical account of the imperial women: according to such historiography, the era of "the sultanate of women," which roughly spanned the period between the mid-sixteenth century to mid-seventeenth century, was a manifestation of the decline of the empire. To Goffman, the prominence of valide sultans in Ottoman state affairs was more of a statement about the maturity and preparation of the sultans:

Many voices . . . echoed this condemnation of female meddling in politics; many commentators both contemporary and modern considered this trend ruinous. There is another way to consider the situation, however. The imperial prince's mother's principal task long had been the training and protection of her son. In the fifteenth and sixteenth centuries her job was finished when her well-prepared and grown-up offspring defeated his brothers and gained the sultanate. In the seventeenth century, however, when her ill-prepared son became sultan despite youth or the incompetence spawned by a lifetime of seclusion, it can be argued that it was appropriate that the *valide sultan* remained as his guide.

It is important to point out that Ottoman throne successions were deliberately noninstitutionalized and highly random events. The only established rule was *unigeniture* and, starting in the 1450s, *infracticide* (Inalcik, 1973). For more details on the Ottoman succession struggles between 1300 and 1650, also see Imber (2002, pp. 96–115). Goffman (2002) states, "[When one sultan died], one of his sons, rather than his many brothers and sons, succeeded him . . . the road toward unigeniture remained rocky, its institutionalization a matter of luck as well as strategy. Beyazid, for example, probably was able to eliminate his elder brother Yakub because it was Beyazid who in 1389 was on the battlefield at Kosovo when his father fell. . . . Yakub, meanwhile, had the misfortune to be far away in Anatolia." Peirce (1993) also makes this point succinctly when she declares, "the history of Turkish states, the Ottomans included, demonstrates a number of options for succession, none of them regarded as illegitimate or unconstitutional. . . . However, the prevailing tendency in most Turkish states was to avoid restrictions on eligibility and to regard all males as having a claim to eligibility for succession. In theory, the will of God, who had bestowed sovereignty on the dynastic family, would determine in each generation which of its scions should emerge victorious."

Imber (2002, p. 98) goes a step further to ascribe the resilience of the Ottoman Empire to its two principles of succession:

The first, which seems to date from the earliest days of Ottoman rule, was that Ottoman territory was indivisible. The sons of Beyazid fought each other to the death rather than split up the lands that remained to them after Timur's victory. The second principle was that none of the sultan's heirs enjoyed primacy in the succession. The sultanate passed to whichever one of them could eliminate the competition. . . . Ottoman subjects were, it seems, prepared to accept as ruler almost any legitimate heir to an Ottoman sultan, without regard to any order of precedence.

Finally, an essential observation is that the royal offspring were predominantly born to concubines who were themselves slaves captured in various non-Muslim domains and converted to Islam. Imber (2002, p. 89) notes, for instance, that "throughout its history, the Ottoman Dynasty continued to reproduce through slaves, but between the fourteenth and early sixteenth centuries it was also the custom to restrict each consort's reproductive life to a single son." While the maternal genealogical links of sultans' are somewhat debated, most credible accounts confirm that, with the exceptions of at most five of the nineteen sultans who ruled over the empire during the three centuries between the fifteenth and seventeenth centuries, all sultans had non-Turkish maternal origins.

Table 7.1 lists a genealogical map of all Ottoman sultans between 1400 CE and 1909 CE. These genealogies, more or less, mirror the Ottomans' military conquests and territorial gains. In the five centuries discussed below, the empire had thirty-one sultans. In terms of matrilineal backgrounds, five were Turkish; four were Venetian; four others were French; and the rest were Serbian (three), Greek (three), Polish (two), Albanian

Figure 7.3 Sultan Süleyman's powerful wife and Selim II's mother, Hürrem Sultan (anonymous painter, the Topkapı Palace Museum)

(two), Bosnian (two), Russian (two), Romanian, Bulgarian, Genoan, and Circassian.

Some of these genealogical links are debated and contested, as there are various claims about the maternal ethnic ancestors of some of these sultans. For instance, an alternative claim about the maternal genealogy of Mehmed II is that he had a Serbian mother instead of Turkish mother, and the maternal genealogy of Beyazıt II is indicated as Serbian or French in some sources, instead of Albanian. A second hypothesis for the ancestry of Süleyman I involves a mother of European descent rather than a Turkish/Crimean one. In what follows, I will adhere to the primary genealogical classification, although, later on, I will discuss how alternative classifications impact the main findings. As a potentially valuable reference, the last column of table 7.1 lists the years when the queen mother was alive during her son's reign.

Table 7.1 shows that six of the Ottoman sultans—roughly 19 percent of the total thirty-one—had Muslim matrilineal descent, with five sultans

Table 7.1   Ottoman sultans and their genealogical links (1400 CE to 1909 CE)

Name	Period of reign	Mother's name	Genealogy	Overlap
Beyazıt I	1389–1401	Gülçiçek Hatun	Greek	—**
Mehmed I	1413–21	Devlet Hatun	Turkish	—
Murad II	1421–44, 1446–51	Emine Hatun	Turkish	1421–49
Mehmed II	1444–46, 1451–81	Hüma Hatun	Turkish	—
Beyazıt II	1481–1512	I. Gülbahar Hatun	Albanian	—
Selim I	1512–20	II. Gülbahar Hatun	Turkish	—
Süleyman I	1520–66	Ayşe Hafsa Sultan	Turkish	1520–34
Selim II	1566–74	Hürrem Sultan	Polish*	—
Murad III	1574–95	Nurbanu Sultan	Venetian*	1574–83
Mehmed III	1595–1603	Safiye Sultan	Venetian	1595–1603
Ahmed I	1603–17	Handan Sultan	Greek	1603–5
Mustafa I	1617–18, 1622–23	?	Albanian	—
Osman II	1618–22	Mahfiruz H. S.	Serbian	1618–20
Murad IV	1623–40	Kösem Sultan	Bosnian	1623–40
İbrahim I	1640–48	Kösem Sultan	Bosnian	1640–48
Mehmed IV	1648–87	Turhan Sultan	Russian	1648–82
Süleyman II	1687–91	Saliha D. Hatun	Serbian	1687–89
Ahmed II	1691–95	Hatice Muazzez S.	Polish*	—
Mustafa II	1695–1703	Emetullah R. G. S.	Venetian	1695–1703
Ahmet III	1703–30	Emetullah R. G. S.	Venetian	1703–15
Mahmut I	1730–54	Saliha Sultan	Greek	1730–39
Osman III	1754–57	Şehsuvar Sultan	Serbian	1754–56
Mustafa III	1757–74	Mihrişah Sultan	French	—
Abdülhamit I	1774–89	Rabia Sermi S.	French	—
Selim III	1789–1807	Mihrişah Valide S.	Genoese	1789–1805
Mustafa IV	1807–8	Ayşe Seniyep. S.	Bulgarian	1807–8
Mahmut II	1808–39	Nakşidil Sultan	French	1808–17
Abdülmecit	1839–61	Bezmialem Sultan	Russian	1839–53
Abdülaziz	1861–76	Pertevniyal Sultan	Romanian	1861–76
Murat V	1876	Şevkefsa Sultan	French	1876–76
Abdülhamit II	1876–1909	Tirimüjgan Sultan	Circassian	—

Sources: Shaw (1976) and Peirce (1993).
(?) denotes some degree of uncertainty about genealogy; (*) represents Jewish decent; and (**) denotes an unknown interval of mother-son overlap, in which case no period of overlap is assumed in the empirical estimates. The column *Overlap* lists the period of each sultan's reign when both the sultan himself and his mother, the valide sultan, were alive.

who reigned in the fifteenth and sixteenth centuries possessing Turkish heritages and one other who reigned in the late nineteenth century of Circassian origin. By contrast, there were twenty-three sultans—about 75 percent of the total—who had European backgrounds, with twelve of those, or 39 percent of the total, drawing from a Balkan matrilineal heritage. And while sultans with Turkish genealogies were clustered early on during the empire's rise in the fifteenth century, those with European maternal origins were spread more uniformly, covering the fifteenth, sixteenth, seventeenth, and nineteenth centuries by varying extent and spanning the eighteenth century entirely.

7.3 Hypothesis

If the imperial harem exerted a significant amount of political and familial influence in Ottoman affairs and the valide sultan, whose genealogical background varied, was the top of the hierarchy, a natural question to ask is whether and to what extent the political and familial influence of the imperial harem played a role in the Ottomans' conquests. In fact, even without the Ottoman harem influencing political and military affairs, the sultans themselves could have been impartial to their ethnic and genealogical backgrounds in deciding Ottoman military plans. All this was playing out, of course, against the backdrop of the Gaza ideology defining the imperial objective of the empire from its foundation. In the next section, I examine the validity of this idea.

Note that my central contention here is still grounded in the analytical framework exposited in chapter 4. On that basis, even though one of the main Ottoman conquests and territorial expansion motives was provided by a religious ideology that aimed to make gains against the Christian West, when an Ottoman sultan with stronger Christian maternal ties ascended the throne, the Ottomans' conflicts against the West ought to have turned relatively less likely.

I now combine the genealogical information listed in table 7.1 with the data on the Ottomans' wars and battles by geographic region in the fifteenth through the twentieth centuries, the latter of which was put to good use in chapter 6. Then I investigate whether the ethnic and religious matrilineal identities of the Ottoman sultans came to bear on the Ottomans' conquest and war patterns in the East versus the West.

To be more precise, I tally up Ottoman wars by the reigns of the thirty-one sultans who ruled the empire between 1400 and 1909 and identify them by geographic region—that is, fought in the East against non-Europeans versus fought in the West mainly against the Christians. Then I statistically explore if the number of newly initiated conflicts between the Ottoman Empire and European powers during a sultan's reign was influenced at all by his matrilineal genealogical links. Specifically, I see if the maternal background of sultans has any predictive power in explaining the frequency and timing of the Ottomans' conflicts in the East or the West.

7.4 Main Results

In the empirical analyses that underlie this discussion, there were other variables included, such as—but not limited to—the length of reign of the sultan, the year of his ascension to the throne, estimates of the average Ottoman and European population levels during the sultan's reign, and an indicator for each of the three centuries during which the sultan ruled.

Consistent with my approach in the previous chapter, I include the year and century when the sultan began to rule in the estimates because there has been a secular decline in warfare in Europe since the fifteenth century. I include the dummy for the year of the Lepanto War to examine if the Ottomans' patterns of military activity were altered following their first decisive defeat against European allied forces in 1571. I also control for the age at which the sultan ascended the throne as well as his length of reign, to identify if those had systematic discernible effects on Ottoman military activities.

For a fuller treatment of this topic and all the relevant statistical issues, see the online technical appendix as well as Iyigun (2013). However, in general, the statistical analyses show that a European matrilineal link comes to bear negatively on the likelihood of an Ottoman conflict in the West, against the Europeans. What is more telling is that the European matrilineal link alone can explain more than 40 percent of the variation in Ottomans' European engagements.

Of the other explanatory variables considered, one sees—without much surprise—that sultans who ruled longer were more likely to have had a European engagement. And when the estimates incorporate three more variables related to the reign of sultans and their maternal links—namely, the year in which the sultan took the throne, an indicator of whether the sultan's rule overlapped at all with his mother's life, and the number of years the sultan's rule and valide sultan's life overlapped—there are once again find statistically significant and negative European matrilineal effects, with none of the controls besides the length of reign exerting an influence on the Ottomans' European campaigns.

In addition, the impact of a European matrilineal descent on the Ottomans' military activities is very large even when a long list of controls are introduced, with European matrilineal descent lowering the Ottomans' European conflict propensity by about two-thirds.

7.5 Discussion

I will now make some salient observations that relate to this analysis. First, the estimated effects of maternal lineage implies that, while Ottomans engaged its European foes once every three years on average, they did so once every decade when a sultan with a European matrilineal descent was at the helm. To put this in further context, recall that, of the ninety-three Ottoman-European military conflicts, sixty-three were historically documented to be initiated by the Ottomans (roughly about 68 percent) but only seventeen out of fifty-two Ottoman confrontations with other sovereigns and groups elsewhere (including Anatolia) were instigated by the empire itself (about 33 percent). Even more remarkable is the fact that most of the Ottomans' European ventures were front-loaded: in the period between 1401 and 1550, Ottomans engaged Europeans in fifty-one conflicts; of those, forty began with some Ottoman initiative (which is close to 80 percent). Thus when one factors in the fact that some Ottoman-European wars were initiated by the Europeans, the impact of having a European matrilineal descent becomes even larger.

Next, there is the issue of reverse causality and the possibility that the patterns and locations of Ottomans' military activities having come to bear on the matrilineal genealogy of sultans and not the other way around. However, the historiography of Ottoman throne successions allows one to address this issue fairly confidently. As I have already noted, Ottoman throne successions were deliberately noninstitutionalized and highly random events. Ottoman procreation norms, throne successions, and the institutional features of the harem were all designed to ensure competition among the sultans' brothers and male offspring for succession. In this, there is a de jure basis for why the valide sultans' identities were not driven by Ottomans' European affairs. Of course, this does not rule out the possibility that the valide sultans' identities were de facto influenced by Ottoman-European affairs.

From this latter perspective, there are two issues that complicate the empirical analyses: One, due to Ottomans' patterns of conquest, which were front-loaded with eastern European and Balkan territorial gains, it is possible that the harem composition began to tilt heavily in favor of a European presence because of the Ottomans' European conquests. That, in turn, could have made it more likely for Ottoman sultans to have a European matrilineal descent. Note, however, that the basic mechanism through which Ottomans' conquests were affected by the sultans' ethnicities or matrilineal religion would remain the same, although there would be long lags involved in that case.

Two, it is also possible that internal or external political developments might have been the channel through which the Ottomans' conquests came to bear on the identity of Ottoman sultans, but the history literature on this topic does not specifically suggest that this may have been the case. Goffman (2002, p. 186) does note that Europeans (in particular, the Italians) had envoys in Constantinople in attempts to "collect information about and predict the actions of a foreign and dangerous nemesis" at a time when the conventional international diplomatic ties did not yet exist, but there is no indication that such foreign interactions had success in penetrating or influencing the politics of the harem.

The chronology of the matrilineal genealogies of Ottoman sultans reveals very little persistence in ethnic identities, but there is stronger persistence more broadly when one examines religious identity or classifies valide sultans according to whether they had Turkish roots. Specifically, of the thirty-one succession transitions, there are only five instances in which the ethnicity of two successive valide sultans coincided and one where three successive mother queens shared the same Turkish background. In contrast, there were twenty-four transitions where the queen mothers had different ethnic identities. Of course, there is clustering of Muslim queen mothers over the period between 1413 and 1566, with only one of the six queen mothers over that time interval having a European lineage. However, it is difficult to discern whether this persistence in religious identities across the queen mothers was due to internal or external political dynamics.

7.6 Mom Knows Best?

Turning to how a European matrilineal background might have come to bear on the Ottomans' European conflicts, there are at least two possible channels through which maternal genealogy might have mattered for Ottomans' imperials quests. One is that the Ottoman imperial harem was an institution that played a typically varying but influential role in determining the empire's political actions, and the most powerful member of its hierarchy was the valide sultan. Alternatively, it is also possible that the harem played no role in influencing the sultan in state matters, but the sultans acted cognizant of their family legacies, presumably and in part because their mothers' cultural heritage was transmitted intergenerationally as part of their upbringing. Obviously, the analyses I have discussed above cannot fully distinguish between these two channels. Nonetheless, it does verify that ethnic lineage—and perhaps religious identities, too—was a strong enough influence on Ottoman matters so as to almost completely nullify one of the founding motives of an inherently Islamic empire.

All the same, one can try to exploit the fact that the private quarters of the imperial harem were built only in the mid-sixteenth century, around 1566. Recall that the private quarters of the Ottoman harem were added later, and, as a consequence of this, the role of the harem in Ottoman politics is believed to have risen. This is why, for example, Peirce (1993, chapter 4) labels the era between 1566 and 1656 the "age of the Queen Mother."

If it was primarily the political influence of the harem that drove Ottoman conquests and not the sultans' ethnic and cultural matrilineal upbringing, then it is plausible that the queen mothers' influence should have risen after the private harem quarters were built. Nevertheless, controlling for the addition of the new harem quarters neither yielded meaningful effects nor altered the impact of European matrilineal descent on the Ottoman conflicts reported earlier. In fact, all the estimates for European matrilineal descent were in line with the magnitude of those presented above.

On a related note, there is another possibility that needs to be entertained: since the Janissary Corps as well as the top echelons of the Ottoman military and administration relied on converts to Islam whose origins lay in conquered lands, it is possible that they—not valide sultans nor the sultans' ethnicities themselves—account for the changes in the pattern of Ottoman conquests. There are two issues to bear in mind in this regard. First, the ethnicity details for the military and palace hierarchies are not available, but these details are available for the queen mothers. Second, political power was still concentrated but, nonetheless, more diluted among the viziers and the top echelons of the Janissary Corps. As such, one would expect less of an impact from the ethnic and religious backgrounds of a member of these institutions.

In this vein, one should also be able to detect that the periods when the queen mothers were alive (listed in the final column of table 7.1) and in charge of the harem were different. Consider this: if harem politics were the main culprits of the patterns of Ottoman warfare but not the intergenerational links of cultural transmission (which presumably were in place even when the sultans were much younger and not in charge), then the impact of the sultans' matrilineal ties should be conditional on the extent to which the mothers were alive and in charge of the royal harems. It is with this idea that one can account for the number of years when the reign of a sultan overlapped with his mother's life as well as the interaction of the latter with either European or Muslim matrilineal descent as additional explanatory variables. Doing so, one detects additional support for the intergenerational transmission channel.

7.7 Cultural Identity, Ethnicity, and Religion

What about ethnicity versus religion? In particular, is it possible to ascertain whether it was ethnic or religious matrilineal ties that mattered more in the patterns of Ottoman conquest? At some level, this is obviously difficult to discern because most of the sultans' mothers were Turkish and Muslim or Christian and non-Turkish (which meant European, with the exception of the Russian Orthodox mothers of Mehmed IV and Abdülmecit). So it is quite difficult, if not impossible, to dissect whether it was religious or ethnic ties that affected the sultans' conquest motives. However, the fact that Ottoman sultans had diverse ethno-religious matrilineal backgrounds could also be useful to assess whether ethnic ties mattered more than religious identity. The idea is that, if it was religion that mattered more, then the incentive to divert Ottomans away from Europe ought to have still remained high after the mothers' ethnic home regions fell to the Ottomans.

To test this idea, one can in fact account for each queen mother's ethnicity and take that in tandem with the date at which that ethnic region came under Ottoman control (if it did at all). If ethnicity mattered more than religion, then sultans with ethnic ties to certain geographies would have been less likely to initiate hostilities against those areas. The downside of this exercise is that, of the maternal ethno-regional backgrounds, only the Balkans (those of Serbian, Greek, Albanian, Bulgarian, and Bosnian descent) came under the control of the Ottomans, typically around the mid- to late fifteenth century during the reign of Mehmed II (the Conqueror). And only one sultan, Beyazıt I, had a mother of Balkan descent prior to the Balkans being transferred to Ottoman control. All the same, one can actually account for the period during which the Balkans were under Ottoman control in tandem with whether the queen mother was of Balkan descent. Doing so, one sees that sultans with Balkan matrilineal descent engaged in less European wars there *before* the region fell under Ottoman control. Equally interesting is the fact that, for the Ottomans' confrontations with non-Europeans, the conflict-propagating role of a matrilineal Balkan tie was more pronounced *before* the region became an Ottoman territory. In general, one can interpret this as suggestive of the idea that ethnicity and nationalities, not so much religion, drove some of these results. Alas, given that these findings hinge on the rule of only one sultan, Beyazıt I, they should be interpreted with a great deal of caution.

On this point, recall that membership in the Ottoman harem, bureaucracy, or public administration required a Muslim identity. Thus all wives and queen mothers were either Muslims at birth or converts to Islam of Christian or Jewish backgrounds. (A possible exception was Orhan's wife, Theodora, who might have retained her religion even after becoming an imperial wife. However, Orhan is the second Ottoman sultan with his reign corresponding to a much earlier period before 1400.) In this, there is some implication that ethnic and religious identities had some latent persistence.

Finally, one should note in passing that the results regarding the political role of the valide sultans could, in theory, be indicative of political alliances substituting for conflict, as opposed to the effects of religious and ethnic sympathies. But this would have been more pertinent if the Ottoman mothers had mostly been women from powerful European families, in which case one could have attributed reductions in conflict to the Ottomans' ability to reach negotiated settlements with European states when a member of the nobility was in the sultan's court. As I have illustrated thus far, however, Ottoman mothers were either ethnic Turks, as they typically were during the early Ottoman era, or concubine slaves, as they were during most of the rest of the Ottoman history.

In closing, I have just examined an argument that is as unknown in the Middle East as the Ottoman impact on Europe is in Europe (discussed in chapter 6). The role of women in Muslim civilizations in general and the Ottoman Empire in particular has been extensively debated. Indeed, Peirce (1993) details the power of imperial women in the Ottoman harem, and other Ottoman historians, such as Shaw (1976) and Inalcik (1973), also review this topic at some length.

The empirical analyses discussed above lend some credence to the view that women—in this case, the queen mothers in particular—had influence and extensive power in decision making. They suggest that the religious, ethnic, or cultural identities of the sultans' inner circle played a significant and independent role in subverting the imperial ambitions of the empire toward the Middle East and North Africa. Hence there is evidence in Ottoman history that the rulers' *individual* identities as much as those of their societies more broadly were important in the long run for maintaining conflicts, conquests, and wars on ethnic or religious grounds.

PART FOUR

Pluralism, Coexistence, and Prosperity

EIGHT

Culture, Clashes, and Peace

8.1 Ethnicity, Religion, and Conflict

The first part of this book established that the three Abrahamic monotheist religions survived and spread among the polities in the Old World over a relatively short period of time. Part 2 explored how this might have been a manifestation of comparative advantages inherent to monotheistic faiths. Part 3 showed that, once monotheisms were pitted against one another, *differences among* them were strong enough to typically trump and relegate *disagreements within* them.

The fourth and final part of this book illustrates that such dynamics did have some serious and lasting repercussions for the organization of societies as well as their polities, insofar as Europe and the Middle East are concerned.

To start with, religious and ethnic fractionalization plays a prominent role in the growth and development literatures and has been repeatedly shown to have a wide array of adverse social and institutional effects. In various studies, ethnolinguistic differences have been identified as having detrimental effects on sociopolitical cohesion, thereby eroding the quality of institutions, the commensurate government policies, and long-run economic growth. See, for instance, Easterly and Levine (1997), Alesina et al. (1999, 2003), La Porta et al. (1999), Mauro (1995), and Caselli and Coleman (2013). Religious fractionalization, by contrast, often exerts a positive if not always statistically significant

The next two chapters are based on Fletcher and Iyigun (2009).

effect on economic growth, presumably because such fractionalization is an indicator of sociopolitical tolerance and religious freedoms. For further details, see Alesina et al. (2003).

While the associated literature suggests that fractionalization has an indirect influence on economic growth, various scholars have shown that the standard measures of ethnic or religious fractionalization have a quantitatively and statistically negligible impact on the propensity of violent conflicts within countries (Fearon and Laitin, 2003; Collier and Hoeffler, 2005, 2007; Miguel et al., 2004; and Ray and Esteban, 2007). It is on this basis that economists and political scientists have often refuted the "Huntington hypothesis," whereby differences of ethnic, religious, and cultural identities are the ultimate determinants of conflict (Huntington, 1996).

The observed levels of fractionalization are a manifestation of population movements, conflicts, and evolving political borders in the very long run. Thus the standard approach for estimating the impact of fractionalization on institutional quality and economic growth has involved maintaining time horizons that are long enough to isolate the impact of fractionalization on economic outcomes but are also short enough that measures of fractionalization remain more or less constant. In practice, this strategy has yielded studies that cover two or three decades. Still, the extent to which ethnic, linguistic, or religious fractionalization evolves and changes over time is subject to some debate, although there is more of a consensus that religious fractionalization is the most malleable and responsive to changes in the external environment. See, for instance, Alesina et al. (2003). A dissenting view is provided by Campos and Kuzeyev (2007), who argue that ethnic fractionalization evolved more rapidly than linguistic and religious fractionalization in twenty-six former communist countries over the period between 1989 and 2002.

In the following two chapters, I will investigate the extent to which the religious or ethnic identities of conflicting parties came to bear on various forms of fractionalization and political borders in the long term. In this chapter, I will particularly examine the long-run determinants of contemporary fractionalization across countries along the ethnic, linguistic, and religious dimensions. I will particularly focus on the impact of violent confrontations over the course of medieval and post–Industrial Revolution history on religious fractionalization. Covering 953 violent confrontations that took place in 52 countries in the Middle East, the Near East, Europe, and North Africa over half a millennium between 1400 CE and 1900 CE, I will then document how the frequencies and types of conflict influenced contemporary levels of religious and, to some extent, ethnic and linguistic fractionalization, too.

8.2 What the Data Say

For these analyses, I once again turn to Brecke (1999, in progress). Recall that, for each conflict recorded in Brecke's catalog, the primary information covers (1) the number and identities of the parties involved in the conflict, (2) the common name for the confrontation (if it exists), and (3) the date of the conflict. On this basis, there also exists derivative information on the duration of the conflict and the number of fatalities, but the latter are only available for less than a third of the sample.

Fletcher and I worked with two cuts of these data: one that covered the five centuries between 1400 CE and 1900 CE and another that spanned the two hundred years between 1400 CE and 1600 CE. The broader, half-millennium cut yielded a total of 953 conflicts, while the narrower data set resulted in 502 observations. We then identified the geographic locations of each conflict and assigned each to one of the fifty-nine countries that exist today in Europe, the Middle East, the Near East, or North Africa. To be specific, we first identified the theater(s) of conflict for each of the observations in the Brecke data set using multiple sources, including but not limited to the Oxford *Atlas of World History* (2002), the Rand McNally *Historical Atlas of the World* (2005), the *Encyclopedia Britannica*, Levy (1983), and Shaw (1976). Then we identified the longitude and latitude of each of the battle or conflict locations. We first digitized this information and then used it to tally the different kinds of conflicts and violent confrontations that occurred between 1400 CE and 1900 CE within the borders of the fifty-nine countries in our sample. Then we augmented this information with the fractionalization data constructed by Alesina et al. (2003). For some other peripheral data, such as population measures, polity and democracy scores, and city distance calculations, we relied on McEvedy and Jones (1978), the "Polity IV Project," and the "City Distance Tool" by Geobytes (http://www.geobytes.com/CityDistanceTool.htm). The location of the conflicts in the data set by century is depicted in figure 8.1.

In terms of the patterns of warfare and conflict, one sees that Austria, France, Germany, Italy, Poland, Russia, Spain, and Turkey were most

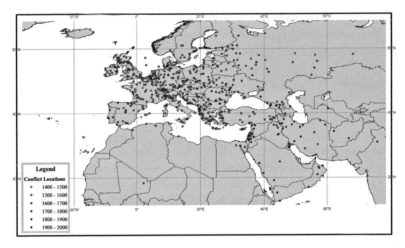

Figure 8.1   Conflicts by geographic location over six centuries (Iyigun, Nunn, and Qian, in progress)

often the theaters of conflict. Adjusting for country size, some of those countries remain high on the list, although the incidence of violent conflicts in Germany, Russia, and Turkey adjusted for their geographic size is relatively low. Of the fifty-nine countries in the sample, predominantly eastern European and Balkan countries, such as Albania, Greece, Austria, Bulgaria, Turkey, and Ukraine, saw the most Muslim on Christian conflicts. But in Spain and Russia, too, there were a significant number of conflicts pitting Muslim against Christian players. And in six of the countries in the sample, including France, Germany, and Switzerland, there were violent confrontations between Protestants and Catholics. Although not shown, the data also cover four countries—Belarus, France, Portugal, and Spain—where one or more pogroms took place between 1400 CE and 1900 CE.

The final step involved classifying conflicts by the actors involved. If a violent conflict pitted a predominantly Muslim society against Christians, such as the Ottomans versus the Hapsburgs at various occasions during the sixteenth and seventeenth centuries or the Russo-Circassian Wars between 1832 and 1864, Fletcher and I labeled that conflict as one involving Muslims against Christians. If the conflict included coreligionist groups, such as the Napoleonic Wars in Europe or Russia in the nineteenth century or the Ottomans against the Safavids or Mamluks in the sixteenth century, then we classified it as Christian versus Christian or Muslim versus Muslim. And for those conflicts that explicitly had a religious dimension, such as the various Protestant or Huguenot revolts against the Catholic establishment in Europe during the fourteenth, fifteenth, or sixteenth centuries and various Jewish pogroms that occurred in Europe dating back to the eleventh century, w\e classified them as Catholic-Protestant confrontations or pogroms.

As for the broader geographic distribution of conflicts historically, most intra-Christian conflicts were witnessed in Europe and Russia; Muslim versus Muslim confrontations typically occurred in Anatolia, the Middle East, and the Arabian Peninsula; and conflicts pitting Christians against Muslims were generally in the Balkans, the Iberian Peninsula, Russia, and Anatolia.

A descriptive look at the data reveals that the countries that are most religiously fractionalized today include the eastern European and Balkan countries, such as Bosnia and Herzegovina, Slovakia, Czech Republic, Hungary, and Moldova. This is more or less the set of countries that lay in the buffer zone between Christianity and Islam, as defined by Huntington (1996, p. 159). This buffer zone for Christianity and Islam is roughly defined by a north-south split of the European continent from Asia, running "along what are now the borders between Finland and Russia and the Baltic states (Estonia, Latvia, Lithuania) and Russia, through western Belarus, through Ukraine separating the Uniate west from the Orthodox east, through Romania between Transylvania with its Catholic Hungarian population and the rest of the country, and through former Yugoslavia along the border separating Slovenia and Croatia from the other republics. In the Balkans, of course, this line coincides with the historical division between the Austria-Hungarian and Ottoman empires."

There are other highly fractionalized countries located in western and central Europe as well, such as the Netherlands, Switzerland, Germany, and the United Kingdom, as well as others in the Middle East, such as Jordan and Lebanon. By contrast, those countries that are religiously most homogenous typically have Muslim majorities, such as Algeria, Tunisia, Turkey, and Yemen.

While there are a priori reasons to think that the interactions of people with different ethnic or religious backgrounds might have been more frequent in the buffer zones, they do not necessarily suggest the higher frequency of ethnic and religious interactions produced a positive or negative net impact on fractionalization. On the one hand, it could have been that minorities were either oppressed or forced to convert with more frequency by societies that subscribed to majority religions in the buffer zones, thereby leading to forced conversions to the monotheistic religion or to a syncretized form of religion (sects) that was marginally tolerated by the dominant faith. Such dynamics would have produced more religious homogeneity in the buffer zones. On the other hand, buffer zones could have been areas with more religious porousness, especially if the more intense nature of ecclesiastical competition in them enabled more proselytizing and voluntary conversions. In that case, religious diversity would have been higher. For these reasons, it is incumbent to acknowledge—and, in the statistical analyses, explicitly control for—the special nature of the buffer zones in the dynamics of ethnic and religious fractionalization.

Moving along, note that countries are more religiously fractionalized than they are ethnically or linguistically. At the same time, there is also a higher level of cross-country variance in religious fractionalization. There were close to 18.3 conflicts within each country in the sample over the five-hundred-year interval between 1400 CE and 1900 CE. Among these conflicts, there were on average 3.3 violent confrontations per country that involved Muslim and Christian sides; there were 0.73 that pitted Catholics against Protestants and 0.096 of Jewish pogroms per country. Catholic versus Protestant conflicts lasted much longer on average than those between Muslims and Christians, which in turn lasted much longer than Jewish pogroms and other types of violent confrontations. Conditional on the fact that there was at least one such type of confrontation within country borders over the interval between 1400 CE and 1900 CE, a typical Protestant versus Catholic conflict lasted more than 3.5 years, whereas Muslim on Christian conflicts lasted roughly 3 years and Jewish pogroms on average did not last even half a year.

Using the longer timespan covering the period between 1400 CE and 1900 CE, the average year of conflicts was 1644, with Muslim on Christian wars occurring on average around the year 1626 and Jewish pogroms being dated around the year 1500 CE. By contrast, when I restrict the time coverage to the two-century interval between 1400 CE and 1600 CE, those dates are respectively revised as 1512 CE, 1547 CE, and 1451 CE.

There is a positive but relatively low level of correlation between religious fractionalization and the two other fractionalization measures, although that between religious and linguistic fractionalization is the higher of the two measures. By contrast, the correlation between ethnic and linguistic fractionalization is still positive but much higher. Religious fractionalization exhibits a negative and relatively low correlation with Christian on Muslim conflicts, but it shows a positive and modest correlation with Protestant and Catholic wars and a low positive correlation with Jewish pogroms. The correlation of religious fractionalization with the duration of different kinds of conflict varies, too, with the correlation of religious fractionalization and the duration of Muslim versus Christian conflicts being the only one that is slightly negative. The geographic correlations of religious fractionalization confirm that the Balkans and eastern Europe are highly fractionalized, whereas the Middle East is not. Finally, I document that religious fractionalization rises with distance from the equator and ethnic fractionalization falls with it, while linguistic fractionalization is barely related to equatorial distance.

8.3 Key Findings

I would now like to shift our primary focus—that is, the link from long-term patterns of conflict—to various measures of social fractionalization. As usual, readers who are interested in the methodological and statistical details should peruse the online appendix. For further details, they could also refer to Fletcher and Iyigun (2009).

Based on a variety of alternative statistical estimates and different sets of controls, Fletcher and I found that religious fractionalization across countries depends negatively and significantly on the *frequency* of Muslim versus Christian confrontations as well as those among the Muslim groups themselves. By contrast, the extent to which countries are religiously diverse depends typically positively—though not significantly—on violence between Protestants and Catholics.

Figure 8.2 depicts the causal estimate of the impact of the frequency of violent conflicts between different Muslim groups within each of the fifty-nine countries in this sample between 1400 CE and 1900 CE. One can visually confirm that the two are negatively related. Figure 8.3 also displays a similar association, this time between the frequency of conflicts between Christians and Muslims within countries over the half millennium covering 1400 CE and 1900 CE, albeit somewhat less strongly than figure 8.2. As shown in figure 8.4, no such link can be found, however, when one examines the impact of conflicts between Catholic versus Protestant adversaries on religious fractionalization.

These results buoy the thesis that the long-run incidence and patterns of religious conflicts—in this case, those between Muslims and Christians and among the Muslims themselves—did impact the contemporaneous extent of religious fractionalization within countries. The role of historical conflicts in influencing modern-era fractionalization is quite large, especially when one considers the impact of intra-Muslim conflicts and Christian-Muslim confrontations on

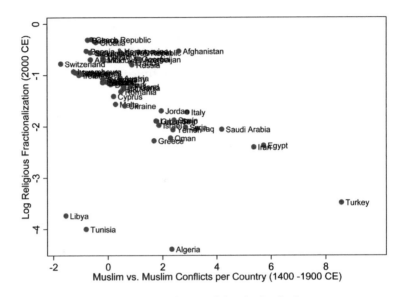

Figure 8.2 The effect of intra-Muslim conflicts on religious fractionalization

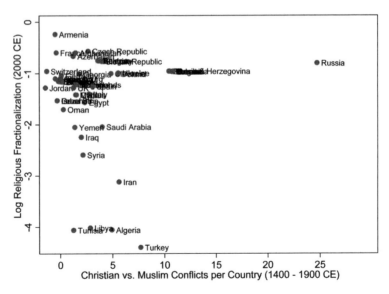

Figure 8.3 The effect of Christian versus Muslim conflicts on religious fractionalization

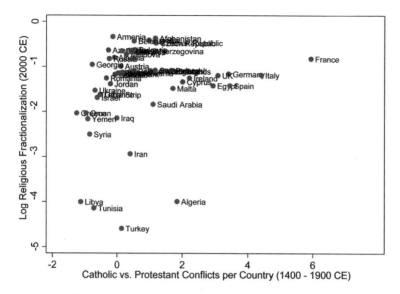

Figure 8.4 The effect of Catholic versus Protestant conflicts on religious fractionalization

contemporaneous religious diversity. Taking a typical estimate, for instance, an additional violent incident between Muslims and Christians is associated with close to 5 percent less religious fractionalization in the country where this incident took place some four hundred years later. The result increases in magnitude as controls are introduced and remains statistically significant. Additionally, the *duration* of Muslim versus Christian conflicts impinges upon fractionalization negatively, decreasing the latter by 6 to 9 percent, depending on the specification. The *frequency* of Jewish pogroms is also associated with increased religious fractionalization, although the magnitude and significance vary by specification. However, the duration of pogroms is associated with decreased fractionalization.

Results such as these invite the question of why Muslim on Christian conflicts had an opposite impact than those between Protestants and Catholics or Jewish pogroms. There is no clear-cut answer to this. A plausible conjecture is that the types of conflict in question also differ from one another in the extent to which the underlying sources of conflict have been mitigated or resolved in the course of time—however superficially or fundamentally that may be.

In particular, the process through which the Protestant and Catholic Christian denominations came to terms with their underlying differences was arduous and prolonged. As described earlier, the seeds of this confrontation lay in centuries past and the "heretical" movements of Lollardy, Huguenots, and Hussites. The confrontation spanned more than 130 years between the start of the Reformation in 1517 and its culmination with the Treaty of Westphalia, signed at the end of the Thirty Years' War in 1648. When this fundamental ecclesiastical disagreement was eventually resolved, religious pluralism started to become the accepted European norm.

By way of contrast, one ought to bear in mind that the era under investigation coincides with a period when both Christianity and Islam had been established long ago, but the competition between them had once again intensified with the Ottomans' domination of eastern Europe in the fifteenth and sixteenth centuries and the Spanish Reconquista in 1492. As I have repeatedly referenced, the One God/One True Religion duality inherent in all three major monotheisms has historically been an important factor in sustaining violent encounters between Muslims and Christians. These differences may well account for why various different types of conflicts and violence influenced modern-day religious fractionalization across countries differently.

The fact that the *duration* of Jewish pogroms depressed religious fractionalization but their *incidence* stimulated it is also puzzling. However, it is important to point out that the impact of duration is conditional on the incidence of pogroms and vice versa. Hence this might be the result of the influence of a history of *sustained* suppression driving religious homogeneity. Moreover, fractionalization measures are based on self-reported data. Thus a country with a history of religious repression might have forced Judaism to go underground by making it unacceptable to report being Jewish, thus leading to increased homogeneity. This was most certainly the case in the Iberian peninsula after 1492 but sporadically even before that.

For instance, starting in the ninth century, the Spanish Reconquista began to take shape with the Christian kingdoms up north pushing the frontiers southward into Muslim-held lands. By the mid-thirteenth century, Christian kingdoms had regained back most of the peninsula. Although the adherents of the three Abrahamic traditions coexisted on the peninsula rather peacefully by medieval standards even after the Reconquista began, there were on occasion flare-ups, such as the movement of the Cordoban martyrs, a group of al-Andalus Christians "who provoked and achieved martyrdom at Muslim hands in the ninth-century Cordoba" (Constable, 2006, p. 307).

Pogroms that lasted longer might have exerted more influence or simply encouraged migration and thus increased homogeneity. As already discussed in chapter 3, a large number of the Sephardim resettled in the Ottoman Empire during the reign of Sultan Beyazıt II (r. 1481–1512), who dispatched the Ottoman navy for their transfer. The number of Sephardic Jews who were resettled in various parts of the still-fledgling Ottoman empire—in particular, in Salonica, Avlona, Palestine, and Istanbul—is estimated to have totaled one hundred thousand (Kumrular, 2008, p. 24). On the flip side, pogroms could have invoked the same sort of mechanism as the conflicts within Christian sects discussed above, magnifying internal differences and subsequently resulting in increased religious fractionalization.

The discussion thus far focused on the impact of the long-term patterns of violence on religious fractionalization across countries today. When Fletcher and I statistically examined whether the long-term patterns of violent confrontation had any meaningful bearing on ethnic or linguistic fractionalization, we found no consistent and meaningful effect. One exception was provided by the statistically significant and negative impact of the *duration* of Muslim on Christian conflicts on ethnic fragmentation and the negative and significant role of pogroms on ethnic fractionalization in some specifications.

An important issue and limitation of the statistical results examined above is that these measures of religious and ethnic fractionalization do not extend back in time to allow control for the dynamics of fractionalization historically. However, there is somewhat of a consensus that religious fractionalization is more responsive to the external environment than either ethnic or linguistic fractionalization (Alesina et al., 2003). In any case, I will next provide some evidence that the geographic areas in the current domain of the fifty-two countries in this study were uniformly more homogenous throughout the sixteenth century—if not until much later—than they are today.

To start with, consider Europe, the Middle East, and North Africa at the turn of the fifteenth century. At the time, Christianity had been split for close to three-and-a-half centuries along its eastern Orthodox and Roman Catholic denominations. And the Nestorian as well as the Coptic churches had already split from Rome close to a millennium prior to 1400 CE. However, there was little if any geographic overlap in the domain of each of these Christian denominations at the turn of the fifteenth century. Moreover, while the precedents for the Protestant Reformation had been set in western, northern, and central Europe with the

Cathar/Albigensian uprisings in 1177 CE as well as the Waldensian movement in the same year, Europe west of the Balkan peninsula was a homogenous ecclesiastical block within the domain—and under the monopoly—of the Roman Catholic Church (Moore, 1994; Rhodes, 2005). In England, it was not until 1534 that fractionalization began in earnest, with the Church of England separating from the Roman Catholic Church during the reign of Henry VIII (MacCulloch, 2003, pp. 193, 194).

In the east, the Ottoman Empire had made significant territorial gains in the late fourteenth century, yielding the geographic areas within what is now Bulgaria, Romania, and most of eastern Greece to Ottoman control. The Ottomans followed the traditional Islamic policy of religious tolerance toward the other "people of the book." Jews, Christians, and other believers of the One True God had the right of protection of their lives, properties, and religious freedoms, provided they accepted Ottoman rule and paid the special head tax, *cizye*. Hence there is not much on record to suggest that a large number of Balkan Christians converted to Islam, with only some small minority groups, such as the Bogomils of Bosnia, who had been persecuted under Christian rule, having chosen to do so (Shaw, 1976, p. 19). Nor was there any significant amount of resettlement by the Ottoman Muslims within the newly acquired eastern European territories. While the Balkans are currently one of the most religiously fractionalized geographic regions covered in this study, there is much to suggest that this fractionalization was fairly low and bounded by contemporary standards throughout the sixteenth and the seventeenth centuries. Along these lines, there is some consensus that the Ottomans' deliberate policies of low taxes and religious toleration generally helped augment the religious and ethnic diversity of the Balkans and eastern Europe (Karpat, 1974; Shaw, 1976; Kafadar, 1996; Faroqhi, 2004, pp. 37, 64).

It is well known that the Ottomans were directly involved in aiding the relocation of Huguenots from France to Moldavia, then an Ottoman territory. The Ottomans also indirectly supported the Serbian Orthodox immigrants against the Hapsburgs in some Balkan protectorates.

At the turn of the sixteenth century, the Iberian Peninsula was a most homogenous Catholic region. Of course, that was on account of the Spanish Inquisition, under which Monarchs Isabella I of Castile and Ferdinand II of Aragon had begun in 1478 to purge the Iberian Peninsula of all religions and Christian denominations except Roman Catholicism. While the inquisition did not officially end until 1834 when Isabel II abolished it, the Muslims and Jews of the peninsula as well as its Christians of rival denominations had relocated out of the peninsula entirely by the early sixteenth century (Landes, 1998, p. 139).

One also needs to bear in mind that fractionalization data are driven, to some significant extent, by the political regimes in effect. In more repressive regimes, the measured fractionalization rates are more likely to be biased downward (Alesina et al., 2003). Hence the fact that the geographic areas Fletcher and I investigated were unambiguously much less democratic and typically much more repressive prior to 1900 and most certainly before 1600 also suggests more homogeneity back in time. Similarly, one ought to also take into account that there is much less denominational diversity within Islam than there is within Christianity. Hence, by construction, geographies that historically experienced more intra-Muslim violence would also correspond to areas that were more religiously homogenous then and even today. Nevertheless, in isolating the impact of various types of conflict in general (and the intra-Muslim confrontations in particular) on contemporaneous religious diversity, one can—as we did in generating the effects discussed above—control for regional differences in overall religious homogeneity as well as whether the majority of people within each country were predominantly adherents of Islam or Christianity.

The fact that fractionalization is shown to evolve over time and that the empirical work below incorporates time lags of anywhere from one to four centuries between the conflict data and fractionalization ought to sufficiently isolate the impact of the former on the latter. But in interpreting empirical work on the relationship between fractionalization and economic outcomes, the inclination is to explore the potential channels of adverse impact via the role of fractionalization in generating conflict. From this perspective, the direction of causality that I advocate here runs counter to such traditional approaches. Be that as it may, it is important to acknowledge that, if historical trends did exist over the very long periods considered here, they were in the direction of generating higher fractionalization, not less. As I will soon elaborate, given the main results—especially those involving the Muslim versus Christian confrontations—such a channel of reverse causality would produce an attenuation bias. This is on account of the fact that the argument of reverse causality establishes a positive effect that runs from higher fractionalization to more frequent conflicts and violence. But in a variety of cases—most notably regarding the impact of Muslim-Christian confrontations—there is a negative impact of violent conflicts on fractionalization. (Direct supporting evidence for the long-term evolution of fractionalization is hard to come by. But for the evolutions of ethnic, religious, and linguistic fractionalization over shorter time horizons following the disintegration of authoritarian socialist regimes, see Campos and Kuzeyev [2007].)

Furthermore, the historical evidence suggests that there were fundamental changes in religious and ethnic fractionalization during the twentieth century in the geographies described here, let alone the five centuries preceding it. In the Middle East, Europe, the Near East, and parts of northern Africa, which are subject to my analysis, medieval history reveals that religious pluralism came mostly on the back of violent confrontations due to either international political and religious rivalries or domestic religious splinters (Iyigun, 2008).

8.4 From Ethno-religious Battles to Huntington and Beyond

From a very long-run perspective, then, it is easy to see how the contemporary levels of fractionalization along the ethnic, linguistic, and religious dimensions are by-products of the patterns of violent confrontations over the course of medieval and post–Industrial Revolution history. Covering 953 violent confrontations that took place in 52 countries in the Middle East, the Near East, Europe, and North Africa more than half a millennium between 1400 CE and 1900 CE, I have, in particular, documented that the frequencies and types of conflict influenced contemporary levels of religious and, to some extent, ethnic and linguistic fractionalization, too.

In the grand scheme of things, these findings are relevant for assessing the ubiquitous "Huntington hypothesis." That is on account of the fact that these results demonstrate that the demographic structure of countries in Europe, the Middle East, and North Africa still bears the traces of a multitude of ecclesiastical and cultural clashes that occurred throughout history. More specifically, those geographies where clashes took place more often and with a longer duration between Muslim and Christian civilizations are likely to be the areas that are more homogenous today whereas the areas with a more frequent history of conflicts within the Judeo-Christian or Muslim civilizations are more likely to be heterogenous and fractionalized now. Accordingly, modern-day fractionalization might simply be a manifestation of ethnic and religious groups that have painfully learned to coexist. In contrast, a fairly homogenized country is likely to be a geography where the reason for that homogeneity is a historically persistent source of conflict that produced attrition and migration. Either way, the likelihood of internal violence and conflict would be lower now, rendering the relationship between fractionalization and the propensity of conflict within countries statistically insignificant.

That ethnic, religious, and linguistic cleavages within countries could be sources of violent conflict and internal strife is by now part and parcel of the Huntington hypothesis: "conflicts occur between groups from different civilizations within a state and between groups which are . . . attempting to create new states out of the wreckage of the old." What is more obscure, however, is that Huntington (1993, pp. 137, 208) himself was cognizant of the attenuating effects of conflicts in the long run: "Many countries are divided in that the [ethnic, racial and religious] differences and conflicts among these groups play an important role in the politics of the country. The depth of this division usually varies over time. Deep divisions within a country can lead to massive violence or threaten the country's existence. This latter threat and movements for autonomy or separation are most likely to arise when cultural differences coincide with differences in geographic location. If culture and geography do not coincide, they may be made to coincide through either genocide or forced migration."

Given that the economics literature has long linked the institutional quality of countries and their sociopolitical as well as economic stability to various forms of fractionalization, a salient issue is whether conflicts and religious confrontations have a direct impact on institutions and the political system or if the impact of violence and religious confrontations solely filters through fractionalization. In addition, today's political borders and country sizes could, to some extent, be manifestations of the long-term historical patterns of conflict, too. These two issues will be explored in the next chapter.

NINE

Conflict, Political Efficacy, and National Borders

The social sciences literature has rather firmly established the adverse impact of fractionalization on measures of institutional quality. Indeed, combining the data set utilized in chapter 8 with measures of polity scores and institutional quality, one can verify that ethnic and linguistic fractionalization, in particular, had detrimental effects on polity scores.

Such findings raise an intriguing question, however: if fractionalization is influenced in part by violent conflicts and religious confrontations, which then have a bearing on the cross-country differences in the quality of polities, do long-term patterns of violent conflict have a *direct* role in the quality and efficacy of political institutions?

This is a question that I will attempt to answer in this chapter, given the data at hand. Specifically, I will first explore the extent to which the long-term history conflicts within country borders came to bear on the existing quality of political institutions. Then I will examine whether the frequency and location of conflicts historically factored in where modern-day political borders are drawn.

9.1 Conflicts and Institutional Quality

The data set used in chapter 8 provides a total of 953 conflicts covering the five centuries between 1400 CE and

1900 CE. The data identify the geographic locations of each of these conflicts and assign them to one of the fifty-two countries that exist today in Europe, the Middle East, the Near East, or North Africa. Also remember that conflicts in this data set are classified according to the religious, ethnic, and linguistic identity of the actors involved and that information on the fractionalization data constructed has been by Alesina et al. (2003).

As a starting point, I'd like to investigate if conflicts alone can help explain differences in institutional quality or if ethnic, religious, or linguistic fractionalizations came to bear on institutional features as well, even when one accounts for the role of the long-term history of conflicts on institutions.

On the basis of this statistical analysis, one can pick up the strong impact of the history of conflicts over the period between 1400 CE to 1900 CE on the quality of polities in 1994. Whereas the incidence of Muslim versus Christian conflicts and intra-Islam confrontations had a dampening effect on religious fractionalization, they are shown to have positive and statistically significant effects on polities. As was the case with religious fractionalization, the incidence of intra-Christianity conflicts had no meaningful bearing on polity scores.

Do violence and religious confrontations have a *direct* long-term impact on polity scores, or do they impact on polities only *indirectly* through fractionalization?

When I statistically explored this particular issue, I found that neither religious nor linguistic fractionalization impacts cross-country differences in institutional quality, as proxied by polity scores. By contrast, ethnic fractionalization turned out to be a strong negative predictor of institutional quality across countries. Interestingly, Christian versus Muslim conflicts and Muslim against Muslim confrontations continued to show significant and positive effects on institutional quality.

As a sidenote, to see if violent conflicts impacted a narrower measure of polity, I explored if violent conflicts affected how democratic countries are today. In doing so, I generally found conflicts to have insignificant effects on democracy.

9.2   Caveats, Qualifications, and Channels of Impact

These estimates suggest that the history of violent confrontations among Muslims and between Christians and Muslims impacted the institutional environment positively by lowering religious fractionalization not only indirectly but also directly. How the latter effect comes to materialize is open to speculation. Perhaps a long history of violent conflict among Muslims and between Christians and Muslims served to make societies aware of the high costs of violent strife and bolster a culture of consensus building.

Nevertheless, there are some not necessarily mutually exclusive observations I can make on this basis. One, the very long-run histories of conflict, in general, and those that are of an ecclesiastical nature, in particular, had some long-lasting and direct effects on cross-country differences in institutional quality. Two, the long-standing standard arguments as well as findings that fractionalization impacts institutions seem to be sensitive to whether the direct effects of the history of violence on institutions are controlled for, although the role of ethnic fractionalization in institutional quality seems to be the most robust. Third, the fact that religious and linguistic fractionalization don't seem to have robust effects on institutions is not tantamount to concluding that they have no impact on the evolution of institutions, although they do suggest that fractionalization is endogenous.

If conflicts and religiously motivated or sustained confrontations do help to explain the cross-country variations in the quality of polities and the extent of fractionalization, then what factors influence the historical patterns of conflict? Besides some of the literature referenced above that puts a premium on cultural differences as a determinant of violent conflicts historically, some other influential contributions, such as Tilly (1992), have at least implicitly emphasized the role of technological change and geography. This is an area of ongoing investigation pursued further in Iyigun, Nunn, and Qian (in progress).

In interpreting these findings, it is also important to bear in mind that the data cover the history of a limited geographic area extending from Europe, the Middle East, and the Near East, to the Arabian peninsula and North Africa; they cover neither sub-Saharan Africa, Far East Asia, nor the Americas. Thus while the geographic coverage pertains to the regions of the world in which major ecclesiastical dynamics and interactions unfolded more frequently historically, one would have to be cautious regarding the validity of these conclusions in different places and at different times.

9.3 Borders Are a Manifestation of Conflict, Too

A potential shortcoming of the analyses I have carried out thus far in the previous chapter and this one stems from the fact that the units of observation are based on countrywide data, although country size and border formations are obviously endogenous (Alesina and Spolaore, 2007; Spolaore, 2009). This would be most relevant for my findings to the extent that causality runs from violent confrontations to country size and formation, to measures of fractionalization.

To account for such effects and channels of causality, Fletcher and I typically controlled for land areas and dates of independence. Neither of these controls had significant effects on fractionalization, although the role of violent conflicts remained robust to the inclusion of the controls. We found this indicative of the fact that the history of conflicts had independent effects on fractionalization that went beyond any role it brought to bear on country size and formation.

One can in fact explore the determinants of conflict and state formation based on the same underlying data employed in the preceding chapter. Based on data from Iyigun, Nunn, and Qian (in progress), the cross-section units of observation for this exercise are 2,500 geographic grid cells of roughly 150 kilometers east-west and 100 kilometers north-south covering Europe, the Middle East, and North Africa. Moreover, conflict and state borders data are organized as a panel covering seven time periods at the top of each century from 1400 CE to 2000 CE.

One can use these data to primarily test the determinants of conflict as well as state formation and consolidation geographically over time. To that end, when one controls for other factors that could impinge upon state formation, it becomes apparent that more intra-Christian conflicts within a cell did make it more likely that it was politically fragmented later on. And Muslim-Christian conflicts had a similar fragmentary effect according to typical estimates.

I interpret this to be evidence consistent with earlier findings: Christian versus Muslim conflicts and Muslim versus Muslim confrontations not only produced more religious homogeneity within country borders but also reshaped them. By producing more political fragmentation, ecclesiastical conflicts might have had an influence on cross-country measures of fractionalization, too.

Recall that the history of conflicts by the religious identity of the parties involved has less statistical power for explaining the extent to which countries were religiously fragmented in 1900.

In culmination, I have established in the last four chapters that religious identities and their differences affected patterns of conflict and political rivalries in the Old World. Based on data from 1400 CE to the late twentieth century, I was able to validate and quantify this claim. Chapters 8 and 9 also showed how those conflicts left observable and measurable sociopolitical imprints, displaying the extent to which modern-day countries in Europe, the Middle East, the Near East, and North Africa are religiously or ethnically homogenous. Equally if not more important, I found that the patterns of religiously motivated conflicts over the very long term came to bear on political borders, country sizes, and their fragmentation as well.

In the final culminating two chapters, I will turn to less subtler—but by no means any less important—social, political, and economic implications of religiously motivated confrontations in the very long run. For epistemological purposes, I will first review European ramifications before wrapping things up with the long-term role of religion as well as religiously motivated conflicts and competition in the Middle East.

TEN

Religious Coexistence, Social Peace, and Prosperity

Modern history of Europe begins under stress of the Ottoman conquest.

LORD ACTON (1834–1902)

10.1   Is There a Link?

If the historiography examined in chapter 5 and the empirical evidence unearthed in the subsequent four chapters are
any guide, one has to take somewhat seriously the importance of rivalries, cooperation, and conflict inherent in the
Abrahamic monotheisms in aiding and abetting the rise of
religious pluralism and diversity in Europe starting around
the mid-sixteenth century. What I hope the arguments and
analyses have done, in particular, is show that monotheisms possessed advantages that enabled them to survive
and spread over the course of history and that, once they
were pitted against one another as a consequence, *differences between* them were strong enough to typically trump
and relegate *disagreements within* them. In the least, such
dynamics were relevant with respect to the confrontation
between the Ottomans and Europeans at the turn of the
sixteenth century.

But how important was de facto religious coexistence for
setting western Europe on a path to sustained prosperity as
early as the seventeenth century—a coexistence and acceptance that, at least in part, involved the Ottomans?

As is well known, the impact of Protestantism on European sociopolitical and economic evolution has intrigued social scientists for centuries. The origins of this debate can be traced back to Weber (1930), who subscribed to the view that Protestantism—particularly its offshoot Calvinism—had "cultivated an intense devotion to one's work or 'calling' in order to assure oneself that one had in fact been selected for salvation" (Rosenberg and Birdzell, 1986, p. 129).

According to Weber, Calvinism had generated this transformation by espousing the view that seeking material pursuits through work was an alternative form of service to God. According to this exceptionalist view of Protestantism, the foundations of the Industrial Revolution were provided by the various unique *cultural* aspects of Protestantism operated through individuals and their morality, work ethic, sense of justice, and fairness. Accordingly, if European institutions evolved to accommodate sustainable economic growth more effectively, it was due to the manifestation of these Protestant values at the social and political levels.

While this is a unique and culturally particularist view and there are some credible doubts about the validity of this hypothesis, it is much less contentious to observe that European religious proliferation, which the Protestant Reformation epitomizes, might have altered the economic incentives of individuals and institutions alike. In recent years, there have been a variety of contributions that focused on these aspects of the Reformation, some of which carrying out empirical analyses of the various implications of this line of thought. I will elaborate further on these below.

In this chapter, I will review the extent to which the existing social sciences literature emphasized religious pluralism as having a role in the European Enlightenment and the Industrial Revolution. And as a matter of taxonomy, I will do so by categorizing the effects of European religious pluralism at the individual and institutional levels.

10.2 Individual Effects

That there is a unique Protestant work ethic and a causal link from this to the rise of European capitalism in the eighteenth century is the cornerstone of Max Weber's ideas in *The Protestant Work Ethic and the Spirit of Capitalism* (1930). And due to the fact that R. H. Tawney further honed and refined Weberian ideas in his *Religion and the Rise of Capitalism* (1926), this hypothesis is labeled the Weber-Tawney thesis.

As MacCulloch (2003, p. 584) details,

[Weber asserted a causal link] between these two phenomena, more particularly between Calvinist Protestantism and modern capitalism—thus adroitly standing on its head the contention of Karl Marx and Friedrich Engels that Protestant ideology was the superstructure of change in economy and society. . . . Tawney pointed out that an urge to accumulate capital and monopolize the means of production can be found in many cultures and civilizations, but he also contended that this instinct found a particular partner in "certain aspects of later Puritanism"—individual self-discipline, frugality, self-denial.

One of the main thrusts of Martin Luther was his emphasis on the laity's responsibility to study and personally examine the scripture for themselves. As such, Protestantism empowered the individual by emphasizing his or her personal responsibility in ecclesiastical matters. Hillerbrand (1968, p. xxiv) makes a culture-centric distinction that differs somewhat from the classic Weber-Tawney thesis when he states,

The point of the Protestant proclamation was that religion was to be personal and creative. It called for personal involvement, not merely the affirmation of the dogma of the church or the external participation of its rites. It also called for the bold scrutiny of theological tradition and the willingness to reject it where it did not seem to be in harmony with the biblical message. . . . All ecclesiastical affirmations were to be examined creatively in light of Scripture. Accordingly, an air of freedom surrounded the Protestant proclamation, for such a personal and creative religion left little room for the regulations and regimentations. The Christian was a free lord over all things, Luther said, and a dutiful servant of all things. The Reformation was hardly the cradle of the modern world—in a variety of ways its questions were medieval questions— Luther's plea at the Worms was hardly a plea for religious tolerance of the autonomy of conscience, and Calvin's economic thought was hardly the paradigm of Adam Smith. This must not obscure the fact, however, that these and many other "modern" notions made their first appearance during the sixteenth century, and the Reformation did its share in stimulating them: Protestantism stressed the centrality of the individual; sought to reduce the intervention of political power in ecclesiastical affairs; cast the glow of "vocation" over formerly menial undertakings; and raised the spirit of free, personal, and creative inquiry. All this could not help but change the face of society.

Needless to mention, such ideas of Protestant cultural superiority have fallen out of favor due to three observations.

First, some historians and area experts contend that the Weber-Tawney thesis has the causal link wrong in that the rise of capitalism gave birth to Protestantism—not the other way around. Regarding this point, Rosenberg and Birdzell (1986, p. 131) stress that "by this, Weber's critics have essentially meant that Protestantism offered a set of beliefs which were highly congenial and flattering to the successful capitalist, who therefore embraced it. Or, less individuously, one might argue that the new merchant and capitalist class felt religious and moral needs not satisfied by the religious institutions of feudalism, thereby creating a vacuum which Protestantism filled."

Second, the notion that Protestantism and its various offshoots such as Zwinglianism, Calvinism, and Anabaptism invest individuals with more tolerance and a higher moral code has been anecdotally and historically challenged. As Mokyr (1990, 2002) aptly observed, the Counter-Reformation era was probably as bigoted and intolerant a period as the pre-Reformation era. And the empirical evidence contradicts the notion that Europe became a tranquil, civil, and peaceful place following the arrival of Protestantism.

Finally, the debate about the cultural virtues of Protestantism has revolved around whether subscribing to Protestantism itself imbues the individual with certain attributes more commensurate with capitalism. As such, most attempts to unearth the impact of Protestantism on capitalism or industrialization have focused on whether capitalist institutions emerged first in places where Protestantism prospered, such as the United Kingdom and Northern Germany, and if their development lagged in other places where Catholicism prevailed, like Italy, parts of southern Germany, and the low countries. The available evidence contradicts this contention, as capitalist institutions developed swiftly and effectively in some Catholic parts of the continent too—either preceding the Industrial Revolution or alongside it as a by-product.

On this, MacCulloch (2003, p. 585) observes that "Protestant England and Protestant Netherlands undoubtedly both became major economic powers in the seventeenth and eighteenth centuries—pioneers in economic production and virtuosos in commerce and the creation of capital and finance systems, while formerly Catholic Italy stagnated. Why? Any simple link between religion and capitalism founders on both objections and counterexamples. . . . Striking counter examples would be the economic backwardness of reformed Protestant Scotland or Transylvania." Along these same lines, Rosenberg and Birdzell (1986, p. 131) note that "the capitalist institutions emerged in many places where Catholicism had prevailed, especially in such places as Italy, portions of Southern Germany, and portions of the Low countries, though perhaps not so rapidly as in Protestant areas." In some of its variant forms, these north versus south investigations attempted to discern the influence of Protestants in the commercial activities of predominantly Catholic areas. For example, in discussing why the Industrial Revolution began in the United Kingdom despite the fact that it is regarded as the least "Protestant" of all Protestant countries, Rosenberg and Birdzell (1986, p. 131) propose that it might have had something to do with the disproportionate representation of the Calvinist Scotch in British business.

At a more fundamental level, though, there is an ongoing debate on the development of institutions and the timing of the Industrial Revolution. According to the "institutions" school espoused by North and Thomas (1973) and North (1990), institutional development precedes economic growth and development. Nonetheless, as some papers such as Shiue and Keller (2007) point out, institutional development may accompany economic development and not precede it.

But save for these cultural characterizations of the uniqueness of Protestantism, economists have come to recognize in recent years that perhaps the most influential aspect of the Reformation was that it involved a strong emphasis on human capital accumulation. A very distinct aspect of the Protestant Reformation was the Lutheran calls for individuals to study and read the Bible for themselves. And there exists a great deal more evidence that Lutherans took heed and that such calls did spur a greater emphasis on literacy as well as various interpretations of the scripture with the translation and the printing of the Bible in the vernacular instead of its original Latin. In this respect, one can argue that Protestantism did to Christianity what the educational reforms between 64 CE and 200 CE did to Judaism, promoting human capital accumulation via the reading and study of the Torah (see Botticini and Eckstein, 2005, 2007, and 2012).

This point is convincingly emphasized by Becker and Woessmann (2009, p. 581), who find empirical support for the idea that the Protestant Reforms spurred human capital accumulation among the followers of the Protestant reformers:

As an unintended side effect of Luther's exhortation that everyone be able to read the Gospel, Protestants acquired literacy skills that functioned as human capital in the economic sphere. This human capital theory of Protestant economic history is consistent with Luther's preaching, with the cross-country pattern in 1900, and with county-level evidence from late nineteenth-century Prussia. Using the roughly concentric dispersion of Protestantism around Luther's city of Wittenberg during the Reformation to obtain exogenous variation in Protestantism, we find that Protestantism led to substantially higher literacy across Prussian counties in the late nineteenth century. Our results are consistent with the hypothesis that this higher literacy in Protestant regions can account for the major part of their edge in economic progressiveness over Catholic regions.

Indeed, as revealing as the findings of Becker and Woessmann are, the idea that the Reformation fostered human-capital accumulation had also been suspected as early as the 1960s. In expounding on this idea, Hillerbrand (1968) notes that about one million copies of Luther's tracts had been published by 1523 and that the literature produced by the Reformation scholarship—led by preeminent figures of the time such as Luther, Zwingli, and Calvin as well as other minor reformers such as Bucer, Melanchthon, and Carlstadt—would not have been published had there not been sufficient demand. But at least as important as the volume of this literature was the vernacular language in which it was published. In fact, this helps to account in some good measure what made all the Reformation literature more accessible and generated the large volume of demand. According to Hillerbrand (1968, pp. xxiv–xxvi),

This religiously lively and exuberant age produced an enormous literature. . . . The number of Protestant publications was legion. By 1523 some thirteen hundred different editions of tracts by Luther alone had been published; assuming that each edition involved between seven hundred and fifty and eight hundred copies, we reach a total of about one million copies. The first truly popular tract from Luther's pen the *Sermon on Indulgence and Grace* written in German and printed in 1518, was reprinted fourteen times in 1518, five times in 1519, and four times in 1520. . . . But more must be said about the literature of the Reformation than its mere quantity . . . their tracts were brief (seldom more than forty pages in length), they could be read quickly, were inexpensive, and were written in the vernacular. This last was, perhaps, their most incisive characteristic. The Protestant reformers made a determined effort to speak to the common people.

10.3   Institutional Effects

While one can debate whether the Reformation involved cultural innovations or generated positive externalities of human capital accumulation, one thing is clear: the acceptance and spread of Protestantism in Europe in the sixteenth and seventeenth centuries ended the millennium-and-a-half long ecclesiastical monopoly of Catholicism in western Europe. And from an economics standpoint, it is hard to overemphasize the market structure and competitive implications of this momentous change for the European ecclesiastical market.

Some historians have argued that the religious competition Protestantism brought to Europe fostered less ecclesiastical involvement in commercial activity. For example, in discussing this issue, Rosenberg and Birdzell

(1986, pp. 128–32) first elaborate on the role of Protestantism in developing a "European" moral code of conduct that is more commensurate with commerce:

Protestantism sanctioned a high degree of individual responsibility for moral conduct and reduced the authority of the clergy; and Protestant merchants were able to free themselves of clerical constraints which they found incompatible with their own experience. Under the circumstances, it would have been too much to expect the Catholic clergy to continue to stress doctrines which could only turn prosperous parishioners toward Protestantism. More and more, the religious world came to concede that what seemed right within the world of commerce was right for that world. . . . Thus, religious authorities, whatever judgments they might pronounce over the conduct of business affairs, gradually abandoned the position that the day-to-day conduct of business ought to be regulated by, or be directly subject to, ecclesiastical authority. In the course of the sixteenth and seventeenth centuries, the business sphere was, in a word, secularized.

In his book *One True God*, Rodney Stark (2001, pp. 221–22) also devotes significant attention to a variant of this argument. To him, it is not secularization that is important but the fact that religious pluralism paves the way for religious freedom, coexistence, and civility:

While religious conflict was often muffled by the Catholic monopoly, the potential for violent outbursts was ever present and often realized. Moreover, even when nonconformity was tolerated, this was done without civility. . . . By its very nature, the diversity of religious demand requires pluralism. Only specialized "firms" can adequately serve each of the niches inherent in any religious "market" because efforts directed toward a lower-tension niche always destroy credibility vis-a-vis higher tension niches. In the absence of pluralism, unserved niches always foster dissent. . . . As with most other kinds of firms, monopoly churches can exist only when backed by the coercive powers of the state, for there can be no limit to the ability to formulate and offer religious culture. Thus, the "natural state" of the economy is for there to exist a large number of suppliers. Where there exists particularistic religions, *norms of religious civility* will develop to the extent that the religious economy achieves a *pluralistic equilibrium*. A pluralistic equilibrium exists when power is sufficiently diffused among a set of competitors that conflict is not in anyone's interest.

The coexistence Stark has in mind emerged only after the brutal Reformation and Counter-Reformation Wars, which provided rounds of killing motives in continental Europe during the sixteenth and seventeenth centuries and, according to the empirical evidence examined earlier, heightened when the Ottoman threat ebbed.

That noted, once the Ottoman threat aided the survival of Protestantism and it became clear after its official recognition in 1555 that the Counter-Reformation Wars would not be able to reclaim the lands lost to Protestantism in central and northern Europe, religious cohabitation became the norm. MacCulloch (2003, p. 652) states, for example,

Here it is possible to argue that the most significant contribution of the two Reformation centuries to Christianity was the theory and practice of toleration, although it would be possible to argue that the contribution was inadvertent and reluctant. Christianity's previous record on toleration, either of Christian deviance or of other religions, might kindly be termed unimpressive. The eastern Churches (the Orthodox, the Copts, and other Churches of Monopyhsite or Nestorian belief) generally have a better record than the Latin West, but that has been forced on them by circumstance: Power was taken out of their hands by the Muslim invasions and they have had much less chance than the steadily more centralized Latin Church of being successfully intolerant. . . . This dismal record began to change in the Reformation, though once more in the first instance through force of circumstances, as the rival bidders for a monopoly on the expression of Christianity found that they could not impose that monopoly.

Such competition generating and sustaining moderation directly derives from Hotelling's spatial competition model, in which more competition yields centrist tendencies. Along these lines, Barro and McCleary (2003, 2005) apply the Hotelling concept to the contemporary religion markets and find that less monopoly power and more secularization (defined strictly to cover states without official religions and less regulation of religious activities) is good for economic progress. Their reasoning is associated with that of Stark, who credits Adam Smith for the original idea: competition reduces monopoly rents and induces the suppliers to meet the needs of the customers, however varied and differentiated those needs are. As with most other markets, monopoly rents are generated and sustained on the back of government involvement and regulation. Thus it follows that when the links between government and ecclesiastical authority can be decoupled, religious diversity will emerge, which, in turn, may or may not manifest itself in the sociopolitical and economic spheres as well.

Generally, economists have been debating the relationship between the Industrial Revolution and European fragmentation and competition not only in ecclesiastical matters but also in all other sociopolitical and economic aspects (see, for example, Rosenberg and Birdzell, 1986, pp. 136–39). According to this view, competition in the religious realm was only one dimension of an unusually fragmented sociopolitical landscape. With a stricter interpretation, in fact, ecclesiastical pluralism was aided by political fragmentation in the first place. As discussed in chapter 6, Europe indeed was unusually fragmented politically at the end of the thirteenth century. And even though the rise of the Ottomans was accompanied by a significant degree of unification, Europe remained fairly fragmented politically in the seventeenth and eighteenth centuries as well. Some scholars have thus attributed the Protestants' survival and rise to this political atmosphere. Accordingly, the causality ran from political competition to religious diversity and to the Industrial Revolution.

Mokyr (2005, pp. 22–23) summarizes these ideas succinctly when he states,

The picture of Europe in the period 1500–1750 is one in which innovative, often radical, intellectuals are able to play one political authority against another: different polities against each other, and when necessary also central vs. local power, the private against the public sphere, and spiritual against secular authority. By moving from one place to another when the environment became too hostile, the members of the intellectual class could remain active in the transnational community of scholars. . . . For the West as a whole, the salutory effects of this pluralism cannot be overestimated.

These arguments noted, there are also volumes of literature on the particular link between theological diversity, the birth of the Enlightenment, and the Industrial Revolution (for more details, see MacCulloch, 2003, pp. 647–55, and Hill, 1967). What renders these views important for the subject matter of this book is that ecclesiastical diversity and competition did have a unique and independent role to play in triggering the Industrial Revolution.

The more fundamental question, of course, is how ecclesiastical pluralism and tolerance became a European norm and political institution.

All three monotheisms are about One True God, and they are all pillared, at least implicitly, on One True Religion, too (Niebuhr, 1932; Armstrong, 1988; Stark, 2001). On this basis, I have documented the sociopolitical and economic benefits of monotheism and shown that societies derived important advantages from beliefs in One True God and One True Religion. Thus an important corollary of these benefits and the historical record is that ecclesiastical pluralism could not have emerged as the outcome of natural sociopolitical or economic processes.

While all monotheisms provided key benefits to societies in their early development, there has always been an element of latent and dormant trigger of confrontation in One True Religion. One has to bear this in mind when analyzing the interactions of the Catholic establishment with various religious reformers and how those interactions responded to the threat of Islam by the Ottoman Empire in the fifteenth and sixteenth centuries. As already established, the origins of religious pluralism in the Judeo-Christian world lies, at least in part, in its confrontation with Islam, and, further, belief in the superiority of one's own brand of monotheism is what historically galvanized the faithful to defend, promote, and expand their own monotheisms. Protestants and Catholics share a lot more in common than they do with Muslims. As unique as Protestantism might be in imbuing individual values of work ethics or devotion to literacy, and however important its competitive effects on the European religious market in the sixteenth century, the historical precedents of European religious pluralism, tolerance, and coexistence lie in defending the One True Religion against Islam.

10.4 A Comparative-Development Coda

As the material reviewed thus far can attest, the history literature on the impact of Ottomans on the Reformation is fairly detailed. Similarly, the various effects of the Protestant Reformation on Europe's sociopolitical and economic history have also been impressively explored. But there is another strand in the economics literature that renders it highly relevant to comprehensively establish the extent to which the Muslim Ottomans might have influenced the predominantly Christian Europe, especially during the sixteenth century.

In particular, there is also a nascent but influential view that European private economic institutions were very dynamic in the centuries preceding the Reformation and that Europe's economic organization contrasted sharply with organizations elsewhere. According to this view, spearheaded by the combined works of Kuran (2004b) and Greif (2006), for example, while the Ottoman state was in many respects dynamic (with its readjustment of its military organization as well as fiscal policies and mechanisms numerous times), its private economy was essentially stagnant (including organizational forms used to pool resources, conduct trade, and carry out production).

In contrast, Europe had put in place certain preconditions of the modern economy but, at the turn of the sixteenth century, it still lacked an environment of relative peace and internal stability, which was essential for its eventual economic takeoff. Had the extent of European conflicts not abated and gone on at their preexisting rates, it might not have been optimal for European organizational forms to modernize. In this regard, for example, Hunt and Murray (1999) have shown that, during the Black Plague, when expected life spans shortened and contracts became harder to enforce, merchants and producers reverted to earlier more primitive organizational forms.

Against this background, it is highly pertinent that the Ottoman Empire peaked in strength, influence, and military might late in the fifteenth century and the Ottomans remained a formidable threat to central and eastern Europe throughout most of the seventeenth century. But the development of individualism in Europe was more than a religious, educational, and intellectual phenomenon. The religious transformation coevolved with the private economy, which was developing institutions conducive to individual initiative. Each of these developments stimulated the other.

ELEVEN

Meanwhile, in the Orient . . .

Gavur icadı!
ANONYMOUS, TURKEY

It is somewhat of a worn-out cliché to state that the early Islamic civilizations were in many ways ahead of premedieval Europe. Many a great breakthrough in mathematics, the arts, and the sciences were made by the Islamic Arab civilizations of Mesopotamia and the Middle East in the early Middle Ages, and throughout the fifteenth century, the Middle East and the Orient remained more advanced than Europe in multiple dimensions. Bernard Lewis has articulated such throughout much of his career (2002, pp. 3–4).

Although there is no specific breakdown of historical income comparisons between the Islamic world and Christian civilizations dating back to that era, Angus Maddison (2001) compiled per capita income estimates for different geographic regions of the world dating back to the first century CE.

Table 11.1 shows some comparisons of interest for these purposes. By the turn of the second millennium CE, geographic domains that were under Muslim control were outperforming Europe, despite how meager the living standards were throughout the world. As shown, while incomes per capita in Islamic geographies during the first millennia hovered around $450 (which is slightly above the subsistence level of the range of $250 to $400 per person), they dropped in

Table 11.1 Population and income estimates for the East and the West

Year (CE)	0		1000		1500	
Region	Population	Income	Population	Income	Population	Income
Western Europe	24.7	450	25.4	400	57.3	701
Eastern Europe	4.8	400	6.5	400	13.5	462
European total	29.5	442	31.9	400	70.8	655
Iran	4	450	4.5	450	4	565
Turkey	6.1	450	7.3	450	6.3	565
Egypt	4	450	5	450	4	565
Iran, Turkey, Egypt total	14.1	450	16.8	450	14.3	565
China	59.6	450	5	450	103	600
India	75	450	75	450	110	550
China and India total	134.6	450	134	450	213	574

Population is given in millions, and income is gross domestic product per capita in 1990 US dollars.

Europe by more than 10 percent over that time span to roughly equal the persistence level. Furthermore, the population levels in Iran, Turkey, and Egypt rose by 20 percent over the same time interval, whereas they grew by about 8 percent in western and eastern Europe. In the next five centuries that followed, there were some early signs of revival in Europe, with its population level doubling and its per capita income rising by more than 60 percent. But the income levels in Islamic domains rose, too, by more than 25 percent between 1000 CE and 1500 CE.

Toynbee (1946) has argued that imperial expansion might not coincide with economic power and that it might well bode signs of sociopolitical decline and decay. However, the geopolitical and military gains Muslim sovereignties made against Christians during this period were quite persistent and unequivocal. Hence, in attempting to gauge the power of Muslim and Christian cultures from a comparative perspective, it is helpful to be cognizant that the economic, military, and technological disparities between the house of Islam and the predominantly Christian West were mostly manifest in imperialistic terms throughout the medieval era (on related but complementary themes, also see Findlay and O'Rourke, 2007).

By the late seventeenth century, the long interreligious rivalry between Europe and the Ottomans gradually morphed from military conflict and confrontation to the economic realm. This was partly on account of the fact that the European powers began to dominate their Islamic foes technologically and militarily around that time. Not only did something start to "go wrong" in the Islamic world starting in the early eighteenth century, if not earlier (Lewis, 2002), but an unprecedented economic takeoff began to unfold in the Anglo-Saxon western European economies with the onset of the Enlightenment and the Industrial Revolution. On this point, see Hoffman (in progress) for an interesting account of how Europe came to dominate the world thanks, in part, due to a competitive political landscape that encouraged inventiveness in military technologies. This "European miracle," in the words of Jones (1981), and the concomitant stagnation of the Middle East under years of Ottoman rule left no doubt that Christian societies were on a strictly superior economic path.

Today, the development gap between the Judeo-Christian world and the Islamic countries remains wide, and despite some recent progress in various socioeconomic and political aspects, there are few encouraging signs that the gulf between the Muslim world and the Judeo-Christian domains could be breached in the foreseeable future.

To put things in perspective, global income inequality is awfully high (Pritchett, 1997) and Muslim countries are relatively poor, and, as a result of this, a significant chunk of the inequality in the world income distribution is associated with the Muslim/Judeo-Christian divide. Figures 11.1 and 11.2 plot the distributions of real per capita GDPs half a century apart, in 1960 and 2010, respectively. The x-axis represents the real per capita incomes in real terms (expressed in 2010 US dollars) and the y-axis shows the frequency of countries at any given level of per capita income. The solid lines show the income distribution among the non-Muslim countries, which averaged slightly under $4,700 in 1960 but tripled in fifty years to reach about $14,000 in 2010. The dashed lines show the same distribution for Muslim countries; it was densely clustered around $1,500 in 1960, increasing nearly eight times in fifty years to reach around $11,600 in 2010. By this account, while the income gap between the Muslim and non-Muslim continues exists, it has considerably shrunk in the last half century.

Nevertheless, most of that narrowing is due to oil exports and the high standards of living attained in a handful of small Muslim countries. A comparison of the changes in median per capita incomes (as opposed to the means) amply highlights this fact: the median income among Muslim societies stood slightly under $1,000 in 1960 in real terms quadrupling in fifty years to reach just under $4,000. However, the median incomes of non-Muslim countries tripled over that time frame, rising from a touch under $3,000 in 1960 to slightly under $9,000 in 2010.

The scorecard on political institutions and constitutional democracy is not much different either. While economists and political scientists

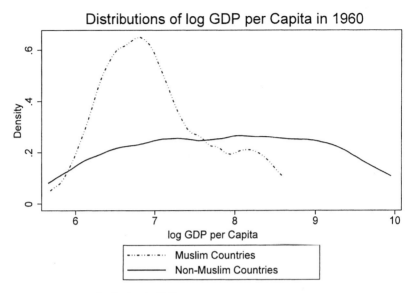

Figure 11.1 Income distributions in 1960

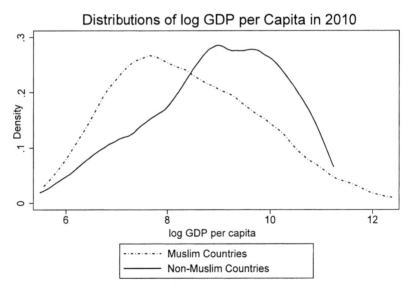

Figure 11.2 Income distributions in 2010

still grapple with whether democracy is an outcome of development, as the Lipset hypothesis (1959) suggests, or a precursor of socioeconomic progress—however complicated and nonmonotonic the relationship between development, incomes, and democracy might be—one thing is clear: Islamic countries are much less democratic and, although there has been a move toward more democracy in much of the rest of the world in the last three decades, there has barely been an improvement in Muslim countries since the 1980s. Moreover, it has been empirically shown that the economic efficiency of governments in heavily Muslim countries is inferior to those of others (La Porta, Lopez-de-Silanes, Shleifer, and Vishny, 1999).

The pro forma accounts of the comparative economic histories of European and Middle Eastern civilizations go just about thus far. More often than not, they leave one with the impression that the seeds of sedentary lifestyles were sown in Mesopotamia and the Middle East; that modern societies owe various fundamental breakthroughs in the sciences and technology to ancient Mediterranean Greek civilizations, medieval Arab states, and Chinese dynasties; and that the "European miracle" is a tale of the Occident first catching up with the Orient and then leaving it in the dust.

But look closer and it becomes fairly evident that the standard economic narratives are, at best, incomplete. One reason for this is that the contemporary era does not mark the first and only time civilizations that populated the currently Muslim geographic domains lagged behind those in western Europe. In fact, the Near East lagged behind Europe prior to the advent of Islam in the seventh century, and Islamization of the Arabian Peninsula, the Middle East, and Anatolia generated a swift social, political, and economic convergence. "In Arabia and throughout the Middle East, the Bedouin tribes lived in fierce competition with one another other for the basic necessities of life . . . it seemed that the Arabs were doomed to perpetual barbarism. . . . There was, therefore, a widespread feeling of spiritual inferiority [vis-à-vis the Jews and Christians]" (Armstrong, 1993, pp. 133–36).

Toynbee (1946, pp. 225, 226) also alludes to what the advent of Islam meant for the Arabian Peninsula politically and institutionally:

There were two features in the social life of the Roman Empire in Muhammad's day that would make a particularly deep impression on the mind of an Arabian observer because, in Arabia, they were both conspicuous by their absence. The first of these features was monotheism in religion. The second was law and order in government. Muhammad's life-work consisted in translating each of these elements in the social fabric of "Rūm" into an Arabian vernacular version and incorporating both his Arabianized monotheism and his Arabianized imperium into a single master-institution—the all-embracing institution of Islam—to which he succeeded imparting such titanic driving-force that the new dispensation, which had been designed by its author to meet the needs of the barbarians of Arabia, bust the bounds of the peninsula and captivated the entire Syriac World from the shores of the Atlantic to the coasts of the Euroasian Steppe.

What is quite striking, therefore, is that the birth, rise, and swift spread of Islam during the seventh and eighth centuries helped polities in the Middle East, North Africa, the Arabian Peninsula, and Anatolia catch up with and overtake their rivals elsewhere, particularly in the West. Indeed, even though there is no explicit data to corroborate or refute this view, the rapid rise of the Arabian Umayyad and Abbasid dynasties within almost a century following the birth of Islam in 622 CE to such a dominant extent that it yielded them control of the Arabian Peninsula, North Africa, and the Iberian Peninsula lends some credible support.

Why Muslim societies now economically and sociopolitically lag behind those in the West and more and more those in the Far East has its own vast literature. Often, part of the focus is on the extent to which faith factored in the seeming inability of the Muslim world and, particularly, the Ottoman Empire to keep up with Western advances.

A focus on Ottoman history in search of answers to such questions is not altogether unwarranted, since the Ottomans were in frequent and direct contact with various European establishments before, during, and after the onset of the Industrial Revolution and they represented the most advanced Islamic culture that medieval and early industrial era Europe had to contend and compete with.

So what, if anything, can we learn from Ottoman history on the role of religion in sustaining or failing to sustain economic growth and development?

11.1   The Cognitive Dissonance of the Sick Man of Europe

Like Judaism and Christianity, Islam too is erected on the fundamental One God/One Religion duality, a concept labeled *particularism*. In the case of Islam, this duality was also augmented by the view that both Judaism and Christianity were superseded by the ultimate Islamic revelation and that, in the words of Bernard Lewis (2002, p. 4), their "power was overcome by the greater, divinely guided power of Islam."

Chronology mattered here but so did the Muslims' early development successes. Both reinforced the Muslim belief that their faith was the final and ultimate revelation of One God. It wasn't that Islam was intolerant of the two earlier monotheisms; Armstrong (2006, p. 462) notes quite the contrary, while also stressing the Qur'anic view of Jews and Christians as "peoples of earlier revelations" who should be engaged with courtesy and respect. Indeed, to an Abbasid Muslim living in Baghdad in the early ninth century or an al-Andalus Berber living in Granada in the eleventh century, there wasn't much to argue about. And, to an Ottoman roaming Constantinople another five centuries later, at the turn of the sixteenth century, time had proven it all.

Nevertheless, as tables began to turn starting in the late seventeenth century, so too began the Muslim cognitive dissonance. Ottomans were in close contact with the West when profound economic changes were beginning to take shape in Europe. It should come as no surprise, then, that they were also the ones who had to deal with the harshest side effects of their increasing dissonance.

To their credit, as early as the first part of the seventeenth century, the Ottomans seem to have caught on rather quickly that the world was changing—and fast at that.

The prototype reformist sultan was Osman II, whose reign lasted from 1618 to 1622. He was followed by Sultan Murad IV (r. 1623–40) and the exceptional era of Grand Vizier Mehmed Köprülü (r. 1656–83), who both followed up with reforms of their own. Not surprisingly, however, their premise was the inferiority of anything Western, and their instincts typically involved a stronger emphasis on the Muslim-Ottoman fundamentals.

Shaw (1976, p. 175) labels this initial wave of reforms as the traditionalistic reform period:

It is erroneous to believe that the Ruling Class faced the internal decline without making any efforts to remedy the situation. There were reformers and reforms at crucial times during the seventeenth and eighteenth centuries. But even the most intelligent and perceptive of Ottoman reformers at this time adhered to the basic premise that the Ottoman system was far superior to anything that the infidel might develop, an attitude that had considerable justification only when first evolved in the sixteenth century. According to this idea, the reason for Ottoman decline was a failure to apply the techniques and forms of organization that had achieved success at the peak of Ottoman power, normally equated with the reign of Süleyman the Magnificent.

Lewis (2002, p. 90) also makes the same point about Islam vis-à-vis Christianity in general but also draws a difference between openness to Western ideas in the fields of medicine and military technology: "The relationship between Christendom and Islam in the sciences was now reversed. Those who had been disciples now became teachers; those who had been masters became pupils, often reluctant and resentful pupils. They were willing enough to accept the products of infidel science in warfare and medicine, where they could make the difference between victory and defeat, between life and death. But the underlying philosophy and the sociopolitical context of these scientific achievements proved more difficult to accept or even to recognize."

Historians date the beginning of the Ottomans' decline to the Peace of Karlowitz signed between the Holy League and the Ottomans in 1699. With that treaty, Ottomans ceded most of Hungary, Transylvania, and Slovenia to Austria; Podolia to Poland; and most of Dalmatia to Venice. According to Shaw (1976, p. 225), Karlowitz also marked the ushering in of the second-generation Ottoman reforms:

The loss of territories long considered integral parts of the empire also shook Ottoman morale to the point where, to many people, any kind of effort to save the empire seemed impossible. For the first time a few Ottomans began to see that reform was possible if only the empire could discover what Europe had done to achieve its new supremacy and incorporate what was best into the Ottoman system. Reformers now began to accept the possibility that Europe might have developed certain specific techniques that might be used to strengthen and preserve the traditional ways, particularly new forms of military organization and weapons. Traditionalistic reform, therefore, became a combination of old and new, creating an amalgam that, while not successful in itself, opened the way for a new style of modern reform during the nineteenth century.

Shaw's astute observation highlights two critical elements that speak volumes about how religion came to bear on Ottoman—and by extension Middle Eastern—economic calcification. First, only when the Ottoman Empire's inferiority became exposed with successive territorial losses against the Hapsburgs was there a painful recognition that perhaps studying the ways of the Christian West—and not discounting them due to long-held beliefs regarding its culture and capabilities—was central to successful reforms.

Second, even then there was an attempt to keep things confined to the military and national defense realms. Unfortunately, the fact that military reforms took precedence over others helped subordinate the hurdles of cultural and religious beliefs, but it did not ensure the successful implementation of even the necessary reforms, as the empire was slow to adapt and it held the view that the fundamentals of its own military organization were superior to the West (Imber, 2002, p. 284).

It is during this era that the empire saw the reforms of Sultan Mahmud I, Halil Hamit Paşa, and the older Janissary Corps. While the main emphasis was mostly on military reforms around this time, it also saw the Tulip Period, named as such due to the tulipomania that swept through the Ottoman upper classes. The legacy of the Tulip Period was the initiation of some public works projects, such as the overhaul of the irrigation and water supply system of Constantinople, a renewal of interest in Ottoman literature, and an emphasis on European-inspired architecture, which manifested itself in the numerous new palaces, gardens, and fountains built around the Ottoman capital.

The first printing press in the Muslim world was also introduced during this era by a Hungarian convert in the name of Ibrahim Mütefferika in 1727, exactly 234 years after its invention in Europe. In its eighteen years of operation, Mütefferika's printing press published a total of sixteen works in twenty volumes about the earth sciences, history, and geography. While the press stopped operating after Mütefferika's death, it marked the birth of the Ottoman intellectual reawakening. It is this awakening that is credited for the Tanzimat Era of the nineteenth century, when the pace of Ottoman reform movement picked up and its scope widened. The pivotal event of the era was the unveiling of the Tanzimat Decree by Sultan Abdul Mecid in 1839, which was the earliest constitutional document in any Islamic country and culminated with the establishment of the first ever House of Parliament in the Muslim world, the *Meclisi Mebusan*, in 1876 (Kinross, 1979, p. 474).

This is all in the way of noting that the combination of differences of faith, the chronology of monotheisms, and the successes of Islamic societies against the Christian West for close to a millennium inculcated the Ottomans with a hesitation—hysteresis, if you will—of sociopolitical and economic transformation in response to Western advances. Nonetheless, this is all about the reaction or lack thereof of the Muslim world to advances in the Judeo-Christian world. It speaks nothing of why the dynamics of monotheisms—to which I attributed at least part of the sociopolitical and economic transformation of Europe staring in the seventeenth century— did not spur a transformation of the Muslim world in the first place.

11.2   External Foes and Islamic (Dis)unity

Given the central theme of this book, there are two related issues I now have to dissect: First, given that Muslim societies faced Christian or Jewish hostilities at various times in their history, has that produced effects that were similar to those in Europe? And if not, why? Second, if there are historical cases of Muslim unity that came about in reaction to external hostilities by civilizations that adhered to other monotheisms, then why did this not produce the equivalent of a Muslim Industrial Revolution?

Recall that, on the basis of the analytical framework advanced in chapter 4, I concluded that, for external threats to produce cooperation and coexistence among otherwise conflicting parties, such threats need to be perceived as grave and existential. In addition, private property rights over the resources or endowments at stake need to be reasonably secure in the absence of any external conflict. On this basis, there are some relevant historical observations I need to make to bear on this topic.

To start, the material in chapter 4 ought to have made it clear that, indeed, when the Muslim civilizations were seriously under the threat of a different monotheism, they did set aside their internal differences. At the time of the first crusade, there were serious divisions among the Muslims of the Middle East during the reigns of the Fatimid and Ayyubid dynasties, but, as Brundage (2006, p. 287) discusses, the Muslim response to the shock of the First Crusade was unification and power consolidation: "No subsequent crusading venture ever equaled, or indeed even approached, the success of the expedition of 1095–99. Modern historians generally agree that the First Crusade succeeded as it did mainly because the Muslim powers of the Middle East at the end of the eleventh century were divided among themselves." The outcome of this unity was not only the elevation of the concept of jihad to a more prominent status in Arabic and Islamic writings but also the countercrusade that enabled the Ayyubid leader Saladin to recapture Jerusalem in 1187 CE (Brundage, 2006, p. 288).

But this brings up a more important counterpoint. Why did these episodes of *external-threat-cum-cohabitation* not leave lasting and effective imprints on sociopolitical and economic institutions in Islamic societies and manifest themselves in economic advancement and sociopolitical progress?

In a most relevant piece, Timur Kuran (2004b) reviews the historical mechanisms of institutional stagnation among the Muslim societies of the Middle East. Like Judaism and Christianity, Islam too had unique institutions, among which one can list individually oriented contract law that stymies corporate development, a financial system without banks and one that forbids interest payments, an arbitrary system of taxation upon which a weak system of private property rights are built, and a highly egalitarian system of inheritance laws that constricts capital accumulation. None of these per se was a hindrance to production in a relatively static socioeconomic environment, but in a world in which technological and economic change began to rule, their interplay inadvertently began to stifle economic advancement. Specifically, Kuran (2004b, p. 72) notes, "If the Middle East failed to develop modern economic institutions on its own and was forced to transplant them from abroad, this was not because Islam expressly blocked economic advancement, but because of unintended interactions among Islamic institutions designed to serve laudable economic objectives, such as efficiency and equity."

These are important contrasts with Europe at the turn of the sixteenth century because Europe did have in place various precursors of economic growth and progress by then. They include a legal system that recognized corporate law (which in turn fostered capital accumulation), no implicit obstacles in the provision of public goods by centralized and local governments (which aided infrastructure development), and better fundamentals in the security of private property rights (which encouraged investment). Together, they suggest that the end of European religious wars—regardless of whether they were a forced outcome—might have generated the sufficient ingredients for the European takeoff, whereas in the case of Islam and the Middle East, various necessary elements were missing.

In this regard, there exists also a thesis articulated by some Arab reformers of the nineteenth century that Ottoman imperialism was an important root cause of Arab economic and sociopolitical stagnation (Armstrong, 1988, p. 513). There are two problems with this argument: First, imperial expansion was a good proxy for the political and economic strength of civilizations historically, and this remained true throughout the middle of the twentieth century. Thus when the vast geographies of the Middle East, North Africa, and the Arabian Peninsula went from Abbasid and Umayyad dynasties' control in the eleventh century to Ottoman control by the end of the sixteenth century, this was a manifestation of the decline in the Arab civilizations and the momentum and strengths of the Ottoman Turks—not the other way round. Second, the decline of the Muslim world vis-à-vis the Christian West was a relative one because Europe went through the Enlightenment and Industrial Revolution. Thus, from this perspective, what needs to be answered is whether the Arab civilizations would have gone through their own economic miracle absent the yoke of the imperialist Ottomans. This brings us squarely back to Kuran's observations.

11.3 The Pending Islamic Reformation?

In light of all this, can one conclude that there is an imminent Islamic economic takeoff on the horizon?

I will wrap things up with the following three observations: First, as Timur Kuran (2011) establishes carefully and in detail, there is nothing inherent in Islam that retards economic development. Given the history of Islamic civilizations, one can only concur with his assessment that "although Islam, like other religions, harbors elements inimical to economic productivity and efficiency, these elements have not formed an absolute barrier to economic growth or creativity. This is easily seen by examining the whole of the Middle East's economic history since the rise of Islam, as opposed to the last quarter-millennium in isolation" (Kuran, 2004b, p. 88).

Second, in order to understand the hysteresis involved in the reluctance of Islamic societies to emulate and borrow ideas from Judeo-Christian civilizations, one needs to keep in mind the chronology of monotheisms in conjunction with the One God/One Religion duality. As discussed earlier, Islam was the final monotheism to arrive on the scene and, in light of the One God/One Religion duality, this produced a considerable impact on how each of the monotheisms viewed one another. Further, the rapid rise of Islamic empires in the Arabian Peninsula, North Africa, and the Middle East subsequent to the birth of Islam and Islam's cultural, political, and scientific dominance of the West for almost a whole millennium thereafter made an objective evaluation of the transformation of the West vis-à-vis the Muslim world hard if not impossible.

Third, it is important to recognize how the role of faith in resistance to adoption of Western ideas slowly morphed into a pragmatic approach to change in the late Ottoman Empire and the young Turkish Republic. As noted earlier in this chapter, the Ottomans fully embraced reforms in the late nineteenth century and, in the early twentieth century, the Turkish Republic took it to levels that had not been seen before in the Islamic world. To that, one can now add the nascent twenty-first-century economic powers of the Islamic city-states of the Gulf region.

As for a full Islamic awakening (that would help Islamic countries close their economic and sociopolitical gap with the rest of the world), one would have to bear in mind the implications of the points just made in conjunction with the chronology of Islam. Institutions that affect the political, social, and economic realms do evolve, but history proves that, when innovations need to be borrowed from abroad and they cut across cultural and especially religious lines, they do so painfully slowly, arduously, and in various mutant transfigurations. Thus the fact that Islam was born over six centuries later than Christianity is relevant in this regard. Culture and faith are two important dimensions through which, in the words of Hausmann and Rodrik (2003), economic development is almost always highly contextual.

Furthermore, as Kuran (2004a, 2004b) has noted, various institutions of Islam came to exist in the seventh and eighth centuries, well after the birth of Islam. Thus while they are not the dictates of the Qur'an and the Hadith in and of themselves, they do reflect the egalitarian principles inherent in the religion itself. Consequently, there is room for some of the various institutions of Islamic economics and politics to evolve, and recent changes in the economic and financial regulatory spheres adopted by the Gulf region states attest to this possibility. But especially when it comes to political and social reforms, the importance of homegrown and religiously compatible initiatives could not be emphasized enough.

Here, too, the case of modern Turkey could be illuminating: After the birth of the Turkish Republic in 1923, various reform initiatives spanning a wide array of economic, political, and social issues were swiftly undertaken, all in top-down fashion by Mustafa Kemal Atatürk, the founder of the modern republic. Included among those were various educational reforms, the granting of women's suffrage, the abolishment of the Islamic caliphate, the adoption of the Latin alphabet, and the closing of the religious madrasas, to name a few.

As can be seen in figures 11.3 and 11.4, the tangible effects of many such reforms in a predominantly Muslim society have been nothing short of revolutionary and long lasting. As shown in the left panel of figure 11.3, for instance, the percentage of adults with no education—although rapidly declining everywhere—has been significantly lower in Turkey than in the rest of the Muslim world. (Note that, in these figures, the comparison group comprises more than twenty predominantly Muslim countries in Africa, the Middle East, Near East, and Far East Asia, including Algeria, Bahrain, Bangladesh, Djibouti, Egypt, Indonesia, Iran, Iraq, Jordan, Kuwait, Libya, Malaysia, Morocco, Oman, Pakistan, Qatar, Saudi Arabia, Syria, Tunisia, United Arab Emirates, and Yemen.) The panel on the right plots the percentage of uneducated women at the top of each decade for the last fifty years. As can be seen through a comparison of the two panels, the percentage of uneducated women is more than ten percentage points higher than that of uneducated men. By this measure, the gender gap in educational attainment is quite large but declining in Muslim societies. Here, too, there is a lot more gender equality in Turkey than in the rest of the Muslim world, as shown in the right panel of figure 11.3.

Be that as it may, of all such social and political reforms in Turkey and elsewhere in the Muslim world, the most reaction, regress, and resistance

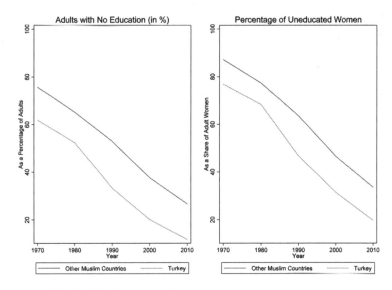

Figure 11.3 Educational attainment over the years

have been reserved for reforms perceived as attempts to Westernize and not necessarily modernize.

The two panels of figure 11.4 respectively plot the average years of schooling among all adults and women who are twenty-five years of age or older in Turkey versus the rest of the Muslim world. As shown, while in the 1970s, Turkish adults and women had close to half-a-year more schooling than their counterparts in the rest of the Muslim world, this gap started to narrow in the following two decades, eventually leading to schooling averages in other Muslim countries that now exceed those in Turkey. (Note that educational attainment rates and schooling outcomes are significantly better in small Muslim countries [such as the Gulf states]. Thus the educational attainment gaps would look somewhat better in favor of Turkey if one considered a population weighted average of outcomes among other Muslim societies instead.)

As a comparison of the two panels can attest, most if not all this reversal in educational attainment can be accounted for by the slowdown in Turkish women's average years of schooling, which began to noticeably take hold in the mid- to late 1980s. That period coincides with the steady rise of political Islam in Turkey, which culminated with more than a decade of political consolidation and sociopolitical as well as economic transformation of the country. In this, there are traces of cultural and religious factors not necessarily standing in the way of socially and economically superior

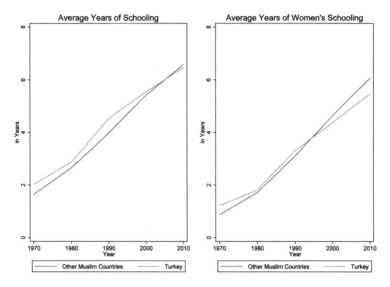

Figure 11.4 Years of schooling over time

developments. But unless those desirable outcomes are the by-products of top-down reforms that hold in check cultural and religious norms as they did in Turkey, the latter give way to social, political, and economic advancement at their own pace.

The Industrial Revolution is, of course, a Western phenomenon, and until only recently when the rise of the Far East started to became a sustained and a wider-reaching reality, it was hard to distinguish between modernization and Westernization (i.e., Christianization). But the paths of various economies in Asia, some of which have been following a perceptibly different course than those taken by the Western economies, offer hope to Islamic countries (Hausmann and Rodrik, 2003; Iyigun and Rodrik, 2005; Rodrik, 2007). In light of everything reviewed thus far, this is due to the fact that it will become increasingly easier to disentangle modernization from Westernization as the paths to socioeconomic development become more varied. And this would be valid, however nuanced and "in the eyes of the beholder" variety differences in those development paths might turn out to be.

In this regard, the current era and wave of globalization offers both a challenge and an opportunity for Islamic countries. Globalization is also a challenge for them due to the same reasons it is also a challenge, say, for France: there are inherent risks involved in the process that, in turn, feed all kinds of insecurities and foster resistance to change. The difference in the case of Islam, of course, is due to the needs of reform in the traditional institutions of Islam that have stagnated for far too long. Globalization is an opportunity for Islamic reforms precisely because, over time, it might help multiply the examples of economic and sociopolitical successes and make the latter less of a Western phenomenon.

In culmination, it would be stating the obvious to note that ecclesiastical organizations are an important component of a society's fabric and its social infrastructure. Religious norms, especially those of the three main monotheist traditions of Judaism, Christianity, and Islam, have often played a prominent role in institutional design, and, in the case of Islam, this is also by doctrine. Religious norms have in many cases dictated how political, social, and economic institutions ought to function. In addition, religious practices, beliefs, and norms are intertwined with "culture" as the latter is broadly defined, and there exists a sizable literature in economics—with roots in anthropology and sociology—that stresses culture matters (see, for example, Banfield, 1967; Huntington, 1996; Putnam, 1993; Iannacone, 1992; Fershtman and Weiss, 1993; Temin, 1997; Landes, 1998, 2000; Guiso et al., 2003, 2006; Greif, 2006; and Fernandez, 2007).

If not for anything else, ideology and religion all involve features that make sociopolitical institutions less malleable and amenable to change. Taken together, such observations suggest that there is a need to account for the role of religion and faith in institutions, economic history, and development as comprehensively as possible.

The history of the world shows that religion played a pivotal role at various junctures. A prevalent fact is that the birth, acceptance, and spread of the three monotheisms of Judaism, Christianity, and Islam have provided important sociopolitical benefits in the form of domestic stability and regional growth to their adherent societies. Nonetheless, the fundamental features of monotheisms, or at least how they were interpreted and evaluated by some monotheism adherents, also caused them to become pitted against one another after the three One God faiths became the dominant faiths. In a painful way, the Holy Crusades, the Islamic jihad, the Gaza ideology, the European Wars of Religion, and the Spanish Inquisition all manifest the success of monotheisms becoming the dominant theistic form.

The divergent economic and political paths taken in Anglo-Saxon countries and continental Europe on the one hand versus the Middle East and the Arab world on the other also involve manifestations of religious affinity and differences and their repercussions in the social, political, and economic institutions. It is with these observations in mind that one has to evaluate and analyze the spectrum of the effects of faith and religious beliefs on socioeconomic and political development.

References

Abu-Lughod, J. L. (1989). *Before the European Hegemony: The World System A.D. 1250–1350* (Oxford: Oxford University Press).

Alesina, A., R. Baqir, and W. Easterly. (1999). "Public Goods and Ethnic Divisions," *Quarterly Journal of Economics*, 114 (4), November: 1243–84.

Alesina, A., A. Devleeschauwer, W. Easterly, S. Kurlat, and R. Wacziarg. (2003). "Fractionalization," *Journal of Economic Growth*, 8: 155–94.

Alesina, A., and E. Spolaore. (2005). "Conflict, Defense Spending, and the Number of Nations," *European Economic Review*, 50 (1), December: 91–120.

———. (2007). "Conflict, Defense, and the Number of Nations," *European Economic Review*, 50 (1), January: 91–120.

Anderson, C. S. (1967). *Augsburg Historical Atlas of Christianity in the Middle Ages and Reformation* (Minneapolis: Augsburg Publishing House).

Anglin, J. P., and W. J. Hamblin. (1993). *World History to 1648* (New York: HarperResource).

Armstrong, K. (1988). *Holy War: Crusades and Their Impact on Today's World* (New York: Anchor Books).

———. (1993). *A History of God: The 4,000 Year Quest of Judaism, Christianity and Islam* (New York: Ballantine Books).

———. (2006). *The Great Transformation: The Beginning of Our Religious Traditions* (New York: Anchor Books).

Atlas of World History, concise edition. (2002). (Oxford: Oxford University Press).

Axelrod, R. (2006). *The Evolution of Cooperation*, rev. ed. (New York: Basic Books).

Banfield, E. C. (1967). *Moral Basis of a Backward Society* (New York: Free Press).

Baring-Gould, S. (1877). *The Mystery of Suffering: Six Lectures* (Piccadilly, UK: W. Skeffington).

Barro, R., and R. McCleary. (2003). "Religion and Economic Growth," *American Sociological Review*, 68 (5), October: 760–81.

———. (2005). "Which Countries Have State Religions?," *Quarterly Journal of Economics*, 120 (4), November: 1331–70.

Becker, O. S., and L. Woessmann. (2009). "Was Weber Wrong?: A Human Capital Theory of Protestant Economic History," *Quarterly Journal of Economics*, 124 (2): 531–96.

Benz, E. (1949). *Vittenberg und Bizanz* (Marburg, Germany).

Berg, M. (2005). *Luxury and Pleasure in Eighteenth-Century Britain* (Oxford: Oxford University Press).

Berman, E. (2000). "Sect, Subsidy and Sacrifice: An Economist's View of Orthodox Jews," *Quarterly Journal of Economics*, 115 (3), August: 905–53.

Berman, E., and D. D. Laitin. (2008). "Religion, Terrorism and Public Goods," *Journal of Public Economics*, 10–11, October: 1942–67.

Bisin, A., and T. Verdier. (2001). "The Economics of Cultural Transmission and the Evolution of Preferences," *Journal of Economic Theory*, 97 (2), April: 298–319.

Botticini, M., and Z. Eckstein. (2005). "Jewish Occupational Selection: Education, Restrictions, or Minorities?," *Journal of Economic History*, 65 (4), December: 922–48.

———. (2007). "From Farmers to Merchants, Voluntary Conversions and Diaspora: A Human Capital Interpretation of Jewish History," *Journal of the European Economic Association*, 5, September: 885–926.

———. (2012). *The Chosen Few: How Education Shaped Jewish History, 70–1492* (Princeton, NJ: Princeton University Press).

Bowles, S. (2006). "Group Competition, Reproductive Leveling and the Evolution of Human Altruism," *Science*, 314: 1569–72.

———. (2009). "Did Warfare among Ancestral Hunter-Gatherer Groups Affect the Evolution of Human Social Behaviors?," *Science*, 324: 1293–98.

Brecke, P. (1999). "Violent Conflicts 1400 A.D. to the Present in Different Regions of the World," presented at the 1999 meeting of the Peace Science Society.

———. (in progress). "The Conflict Dataset: 1400 A.D.–Present," unpublished manuscript, Georgia Institute of Technology.

Brook, K. A. (2006). *The Jews of Khazaria* (New York: Rowman & Littlefield).

Brundage, J. A. (2006). "Latin Christianity, the Crusades and the Islamic Response," in *Religious Foundations of Western Civilization: Judaism, Christianity and Islam*, edited by J. Neusner, 267–304 (Nashville: Abingdon Press).

Campos, N., and V. S. Kuzeyev. (2007). "On the Dynamics of Ethnic Fractionalization," *American Journal of Political Science*, 51 (3), July: 620–39.

Caselli F., and W. J. Coleman II. (2013). "On the Theory of Ethnic Conflict," *Journal of the European Economic Association*, 11: 161–92.

Chandler, T. (1987). *Four Thousand Years of Urban Growth: An Historical Census* (New York: St. David's University Press).

Chaney, E. (2008). "Religious Competition and the Rise and Fall of Muslim Science," unpublished manuscript, Harvard University.

Charriere, E. (1848). *Negociations de la France dans le Levant* (Paris).

Chejne, A. (1974). *Muslim Spain: Its History and Culture* (Minneapolis: University of Minnesota Press).

Choi, Jung-Kyoo, and S. Bowles. (2007). "The Coevolution of Parochial Altruism and War," *Science*, 318: 636–40.

Clingingsmith, D., A. I. Kwaja, and M. Kremer. (2009). "Estimating the Impact of the Hajj: Religion and Tolerance in Islam's Global Gathering," *Quarterly Journal of Economics*, 124 (3), August: 1133–70.

Coles, P. (1968). *The Ottoman Impact on Europe* (New York: Harcourt, Brace & World).

Collier, P., and A. Hoeffler. (2005). "Coup Traps: Why Does Africa Have So Many Coup d'Etat?," unpublished manuscript, Oxford University, Department of Economics.

———. (2007). "Civil War," in *Handbook of Defense Economics*, 2nd ed., edited by Todd Sandler and Keith Hartley, 711–39 (New York: Elsevier).

Constable, O. R. (2006). "Judaism, Christianity and Islam in Spain from the Eighth to the Fifteenth Centuries," in *Religious Foundations of Western Civilization: Judaism, Christianity and Islam*, edited by J. Neusner, 305–47 (Nashville: Abingdon Press).

de Vries, J. (1994). "The Industrial Revolution and the Industrious Revolution," *Journal of Economic History*, 54: 249–70.

Diamond, J. (1997). *Guns, Germs and Steel: The Fate of Human Societies* (New York: W. W. Norton).

Dixit, A. (2004). *Lawlessness and Economics: Alternative Modes of Economic Governance*, Gorman Lectures (Princeton, NJ: Princeton University Press).

Durant, W. (1950). *The Age of Faith: The Story of Civilization* (New York: MJF Books).

Durkheim, E. (1915). *The Elementary Forms of the Religious Life*, translated by Joseph Swain (London: George Allen and Unwin).

Easterly, W., and R. Levine. (1997). "Africa's Growth Tragedy: Policies and Ethnic Divisions," *Quarterly Journal of Economics*, 111 (4), November: 1203–50.

Ekelund, R., R. D. Tollison, G. M. Anderson, R. F. Hebert, and A. B. Davidson. (1996). *Sacred Trust: The Medieval Church as an Economic Firm* (New York: Oxford University Press).

Ekelund, R., R. Hebert, and R. Tollison. (2002). "An Economic Analysis of the Protestant Reformation," *Journal of Political Economy*, 110 (3), June: 646–71.

Ekelund, R., and R. D. Tollison. (2011). *Economic Origins and Monopolization of Christianity* (Chicago: University of Chicago Press).

Encyclopedia Britannica. (n.d.). http://www.britannica.com.

Faroqhi, S. (2004). *The Ottoman Empire and the World around It* (London: I. B. Tauris).

Farrington, K. (2002). *Historical Atlas of Empires* (London: Thalamus).

———. (2006). *Historical Atlas of Religions* (London: Thalamus).

Fearon, J., and D. Laitin. (2003). "Ethnicity, Insurgency, and Civil War," *American Political Science Review*, 97: 75–90.

Fernandez, R. (2007). "Culture and Economics," in *The New Palgrave Dictionary of Economics*, 2nd ed., edited by Steven N. Durlauf and Lawrence E. Blume (New York: Palgrave Macmillan).

Fernandez, R., A. Fogli, and C. Olivetti. (2004). "Mothers and Sons: Preference Formation and Female Labor Force Dynamics," *Quarterly Journal of Economics*, 119 (4): 1249–99.

Fershtman, C., and Y. Weiss. (1993). "Social Status, Culture and Economic Performance," *Economic Journal*, 103 (419): 946–59.

Findlay, R., and K. H. O'Rourke. (2007). *Power and Plenty* (Princeton, NJ: Princeton University Press).

Finke, R., and R. Stark. (1992). *The Churching of America 1776–1990* (East Brunswick, NJ: Rutgers University Press).

Fischer-Galati, S. A. (1959). *Ottoman Imperialism and German Protestantism, 1521–1555* (Cambridge, MA: Harvard University Press).

Fletcher, E., and M. Iyigun. (2009). "Cultures, Clashes and Peace," with Erin Fletcher, IZA working paper no. 4116, April.

Frazee, C. A. (1983). *Catholic and Sultans: The Church and the Ottoman Empire, 1453–1923* (Cambridge: Cambridge University Press).

Geobytes. (n.d.). City Distance Tool. http://www.geobytes.com/CityDistanceTool .htm.

Gibbon, E. (1776). *The History of the Decline and Fall of the Roman Empire*, abridged ed. (New York: Penguin Classics).

Glaeser, E. L. (2005). "The Political Economy of Hatred," *Quarterly Journal of Economics*, 120 (1): 45–86.

Goffman, D. (2002). *The Ottoman Empire and Early Modern Europe* (Cambridge: Cambridge University Press).

Golden, P. B. (1980). *Khazar Studies: An Historio-Philological Inquiry into the Origins of the Khazars* (Budapest: Akademia Kiado).

Goodwin, J. (2000). *Lords of the Horizon: A History of the Ottoman Empire* (New York: Owl Books).

Greif, A. (2006). *Institutions: Theory and History* (Cambridge: Cambridge University Press).

Grossman, H. I. (1994). "Production, Appropriation, and Land Reform," *American Economic Review*, 84 (3), June: 705–12.

Grossman, H. I., and M. Iyigun. (1995). "The Profitability of Colonial Investment," *Economics and Politics*, 7 (3), November: 229–324.

———. (1997). "Population Increase and the End of Colonialism," *Economica*, 64 (3), August: 483–93.

Grossman, H. I., and M. Kim. (1995). "Swords or Plowshares? A Theory of the Security of Claims to Property," *Journal of Political Economy*, 103 (6), December: 1275–88.

Guiso, L., P. Sapienza, and L. Zingales. (2003). "People's Opium? Religion and Economic Attitudes," *Journal of Monetary Economics*, 50 (1): 225–82.

———. (2006). "Does Culture Affect Economic Outcomes?," *Journal of Economic Perspectives*, 20 (2): 23–48.

Haavelmo, T. (1954). *A Study in the Theory of Economic Evolution* (Amsterdam: North-Holland).

Hafer, C. (2006). "On the Origins of Property Rights: Conflict and Production in the State of Nature," *Review of Economic Studies*, 73: 119–43.

Hausmann, R., and D. Rodrik. (2003). "Economic Development as Self-Discovery," *Journal of Development Economics*, 72, December: 603–33.

Haywood, J. (2005). *The Penguin Historical Atlas of Ancient Civilizations* (New York: Penguin).

Hess, G. D., and A. Orphanides. (1995). "War Politics: An Economic, Rational-Voter Framework," *The American Economic Review*, 8 (4): 828–46.

———. (2001). "War and Democracy," *Journal of Political Economy*, 109 (4): 776–810.

Hill, C. (1967). *Reformation to Industrial Revolution: The Making of Modern English Society, Vol. I, 1530–1780* (New York: Random House).

Hillerbrand, H. (1968). *The Protestant Reformation* (New York: Harper Collins).

Hirshleifer, J. (1991). "The Paradox of Power," *Economics and Politics*, 3 (3), November: 177–200.

Hoffman, P. (in progress). "Why Europeans Conquered the World," unpublished manuscript, Cal Tech.

Homerin, E. (2006). "Islam: What It Is and How It Had Interacted with Western Civilization," in *Religious Foundations of Western Civilization: Judaism, Christianity and Islam*, edited by J. Neusner, 105–46 (Nashville: Abingdon Press).

Hotelling, H. (1929). "Stability in Competition," *Economic Journal*, 39 (1), March: 41–57.

Hume, D. (1911). *A Treatise of Human Nature* (London: J. M. Dent and Sons).

Hunt, E. S., and J. M. Murray. (1999). *A History of Business in Medieval Europe, 1200–1550* (Cambridge: Cambridge University Press).

Huntington, S. P. (1993). "The Clash of Civilizations?," *Foreign Affairs*, Summer, 22–49.

———. (1996). *The Clash of Civilizations and the Remaking of World Order* (New York: Simon and Schuster).

Iannaccone, L. R. (1992). "Sacrifices and Stigma: Reducing the Free-Riding in Cults, Communes and Other Collectives," *Journal of Political Economy*, 100 (2), April: 271–91.

———. (1994). "Why Strict Churches Are Strong," *American Journal of Sociology*, March.

Imber, C. (2002). *The Ottoman Empire: 1300–1650* (New York: Palgrave Macmillan).

Inalcik, H. (1973). *The Ottoman Empire: The Classical Age, 1300–1600* (London: Littlehampton Book Services).

———. (1994). *An Economic and Social History of the Ottoman Empire, 1300–1600* (Cambridge: Cambridge University Press).

Inglehart, R., and W. E. Baker. (2000). "Modernization, Cultural Change, and the Persistence of Traditional Values," *American Sociological Review*, 65 (1), February: 19–51.

Iyigun, M. (2008). "Luther and Suleyman," *Quarterly Journal of Economics*, 123 (4), November: 1465–94.

———. (2010). "Monotheism (From a Sociopolitical and Economic Perspective)," IZA working paper no. 3116, November.

———. (2013). "Lessons from the Ottoman Harem: On Ethnicity, Religion and War," *Economic Development and Cultural Change*, 61 (4), July: 693–730.

Iyigun, M., N. Nunn, and N. Qian. (in progress). "Empirics Meet Charles Tilly," unpublished manuscript, University of Colorado.

Iyigun, M., and D. Rodrik. (2005). "On the Efficacy of Reforms: Policy Tinkering, Institutional Change, and Entrepreneurship," in *Institutions and Growth*, edited by T. Eicher and C. G. Penalosa, 159–88 (Cambridge, MA: MIT Press).

Janeba, E. (2007). "International Trade and Consumption Network Externalities," *European Economic Review*, 51 (4): 781–803.

Jaspers, K. (1953). *The Origin and Goal of History*, translated by Michael Bullock (New Haven, CT: Yale University Press).

Jayyusi, S. K. (1992). *The Legacy of Muslim Spain* (New York: E. J. Brill).

Jha, S. (2013). "Trade, Institutions and Religious Tolerance: Evidence from South Asia," *American Political Science Review* 107 (4), November: 806–32.

Jones, E. L. (1981). *The European Miracle: Environments, Economies, and Geopolitics in the History of Europe and Asia* (Cambridge: Cambridge University Press).

Kafadar, C. (1996). *Between Two Worlds: The Construction of the Ottoman State*, reprinted ed. (Berkeley: University of California Press).

Karpat, K. (1974). *The Ottoman State and Its Place in World History* (Leiden, Netherlands: E. J. Brill).

Kennedy, H. (1996). *Muslim Spain and Portugal* (New York: Longman).

Kennedy, P. (1987). *The Rise and Fall of the Great Powers* (New York: Vintage Books).

Kinross, L. (1979). *Ottoman Centuries* (New York: Harper Perennial).

Konrad, K., and S. Skaperdas. (2012). "The Market for Protection and the Origin of the State," *Economic Theory*, 50 (2), June: 417–43.

Kortepeter, C. M. (1972). *Ottoman Imperialism during the Reformation: Europe and the Caucasus* (New York: New York University Press).

Kumrular, Ö. (2008). *Türk Korkusu: Avrupa'da Türk Düşmanliğinin Kökeni* (IStanbul, Turkey: Doğan Kitap).

Kuran, T. (2004a). "The Economic Ascent of the Middle East's Religious Minorities: The Role of Islamic Legal Pluralism," *Journal of Legal Studies*, 33, June: 475–515.

————. (2004b). "Why the Middle East Is Economically Underdeveloped: Historical Mechanisms of Institutional Stagnation," *Journal of Economic Perspectives*, 18, Summer: 71–90.

————. (2011). *The Long Divergence: How Islamic Law Held Back the Middle East* (Princeton, NJ: Princeton University Press).

Lagerlöf, N. (2010). "From Malthusian War to Solovian Peace," *Review of Economic Dynamics*, 13: 616–36.

Landes, D. S. (1998). *The Wealth and Poverty of Nations: Why Some Are Rich and Some So Poor* (New York: W. W. Norton).

————. (2000). "Culture Makes Almost All the Difference," in *Culture Matters: How Values Shape Human Progress*, edited by L. E. Harrison and S. P. Huntington, 2–13 (New York: Basic Books).

La Porta, R. F., Lopez-de-Silanes, A. Shleifer, and R. W. Vishny. (1999). "Law and Finance," *Journal of Political Economy*, 106 (6), December: 1113–55.

Levine, D. K., and S. Modica. (2013). "Conflict, Evolution and the Power of the State," unpublished manuscript, Washington University in Saint Louis.

Levy, J. S. (1983). *War in the Modern Great Power System, 1495–1975* (Lexington, KY: University Press of Kentucky).

Lewis, B. (2002). *What Went Wrong? Western Impact and Middle Eastern Response* (London: Phoenix Press).

Lipset, S. M. (1959). "Some Social Requisites of Democracy: Economic Development and Political Legitimacy," *American Political Science Review*, 53 (1): 69–105.

MacCulloch, D. (2003). *The Reformation: A History* (New York: Viking).

MacMillan, M. (2002). *Paris 1919: Six Months that Changed the World* (New York: Random House).

Maddison, A. (2001). *The World Economy: A Millennial Perspective* (Paris: OECD Publications).

Mauro, P. (1995). "Corruption and Growth," *Quarterly Journal of Economics*, 110 (3), August: 681–712.

McCleary, R. M., and R. J. Barro. (2006). "Religion and Political Economy in an International Panel," *Journal for the Scientific Study of Religion*, 45, June: 149–75.

McEvedy, C., and Jones, R. (1978). *Atlas of World Population History* (New York: Facts on File).

McNeill, W. (1984). *The Pursuit of Power: Technology, Armed Force, and Society since A.D. 1000* (Chicago: University of Chicago Press).

Miguel, E, S. Satyanath, and E. Sergenti. (2004). "Economic Shocks and Civil Conflict: An Instrumental Variables Approach," *Journal of Political Economy*, 112: 725–53.

Mokyr, J. (1990). *The Lever of Riches* (New York: Oxford University Press).

————. (2002). "The Enduring Riddle of the European Miracle: The E and the Industrial Revolution," unpublished manuscript, Northwestern University.

————. (2005). "The Great Synergy: The European E as a Factor in Modern Economic Growth," unpublished manuscript, Northwestern University.

———. (2010). *The Enlightened Economy: An Economic History of Britain 1700–1850* (New Haven, CT: Yale University Press).

Moore, R. I. (1994). *The Origins of European Dissent*, originally published by Allen Lane, 1985 (Toronto, ON: University of Toronto Press).

Neusner, J. (2006). *Religious Foundations of Western Civilization: Judaism, Christianity and Islam* (Nashville: Abingdon Press).

Niebuhr, R. (1932). *Moral Man and Immoral Society: A Study in Ethics and Politics* (Kentucky: Westminster John Knox Press).

North, D. (1990). *Institutions, Institutional Change and Economic Performance (Political Economy of Institutions and Decisions)* (Cambridge: Cambridge University Press).

North, D., and R. P. Thomas. (1973). *The Rise of the Western World: A New Economic History* (Cambridge: Cambridge University Press).

North, D., J. J. Wallis, and B. R. Weingast. (2006). "A Conceptual Framework for Interpreting Recorded History," NBER working paper no. 12795, December.

———. (2008). *Violence and Social Orders: A Conceptual Framework for Interpreting Recorded History* (Cambridge: Cambridge University Press).

Parker, G. (1988). *The Military Revolution: Military Innovation and the Rise of the West, 1500–1800* (Cambridge: Cambridge University Press).

Peirce, L. P. (1993). *The Imperial Harem: Women and Sovereignty in the Ottoman Empire* (Oxford: Oxford University Press).

Pirenne, H. ([1937] 2001). *Mohammed and Charlemange*, reprinted ed. (New York: Dover Publications).

Pommeranz, K. (2000). *The Great Divergence: China, Europe and the Making of the Modern World Economy* (Princeton, NJ: Princeton University Press).

Pritchett, L. (1997). "Divergence, Big Time," *Journal of Economic Perspectives*, 11 (3), Summer: 3–17.

Putnam, R. (1993). *Making Democracy Work: Civic Traditions in Modern Italy*, with R. Leonardi and R. Y. Nanetti (Princeton, NJ: Princeton University Press).

Rand McNally and Co. (2005). *Historical Atlas of the World* (Skokie, IL: Rand McNally).

Ray, D., and J. Esteban. (2007). "Polarization, Fractionalization and Conflict," *Journal of Peace Research*, 45: 163–82.

Rhodes, R. (2005). *The Complete Guide to Christian Denominations: Understanding the History, Beliefs, and Differences* (New York: Harvest House).

Richardson, L. F. (1960). *Statistics of Deadly Quarrels* (Pittsburgh, PA: Boxwood Press).

Rodrik, D. (2007). *One Economics, Many Recipes: Globalization, Institutions, and Economic Growth* (Princeton, NJ: Princeton University Press).

Rosenberg, N., and L. E. Birdzell Jr. (1986). *How the West Grew Rich: The Economic Transformation of the Industrial World* (New York: Basic Books).

Rubin, J. (2008). "The Lender's Curse: A New Look at the Origin and Persistence of Interest Bans throughout History," *Journal of Economic History*, 68 (2): 575–79.

————. (2010). "Bills of Exchange, Interest Bans, and Impersonal Exchange in Islam and Christianity," *Explorations in Economic History*, 47 (2): 213–27.

Saliba, G. (2007). *Islamic Science and the Making of the European Renaissance (Transformations: Studies in the History of Science and Technology)* (Cambridge, MA: MIT Press).

Setton, K. M. (1962). "Lutheranism and the Turkish Peril," *Balkan Studies*, 3 (1): 136–65.

Shaw, S. (1976). *History of the Ottoman Empire and Modern Turkey*, vol. 1 (Cambridge: Cambridge University Press).

Shiue, C. H., and W. Keller. (2007). "Markets in China and Europe on the Eve of the Industrial Revolution," *American Economic Review*, 97 (4), September: 1189–216.

Skaperdas, S. (1992). "Cooperation, Conflict, and Power in the Absence of Property Rights," *American Economic Review*, 82, September: 720–39.

Smith, A. ([1776] 2001). *The Wealth of Nations*, complete and unabridged ed. (New York: Modern Library Classics).

Spolaore, E. (2009). "National Borders, Conflict and Peace," National Bureau of Economic Research working paper no. 15560, December.

Stark, R. (2001). *One True God: Historical Consequences of Monotheism* (Princeton, NJ: Princeton University Press).

Stark, R., and W. S. Bainbridge. (1987). *A Theory of Religion* (Rutgers, NJ: Rutgers University Press, 1987).

Stark, R., and R. Finke. (2000). *Acts of Faith: Explaining the Human Side of Religion* (Berkeley: University of California Press).

Tawney, R. H. (1926). *Religion and the Rise of Capitalism* (London: Mentor).

Temin, P. (1997). "Is it Kosher to Talk about Culture?," *Journal of Economic History*, 57 (2), June: 267–87.

Tilly, C. (1992). *Coercion, Capital and European States: AD 990–1992 (Studies in Social Discontinuity)* (New York: Blackwell Publishers).

Tornell, A., and A. Velasco. (1992). "The Tragedy of the Commons and Economic Growth: Why Does Capital Flow From Poor to Rich Countries?," *Journal of Political Economy*, 100 (6), December: 1208–31.

Toynbee, A. J. (1946). *A Study of History: Abridgement of Volumes I–VI*, edited by D. C. Somervell (New York: Oxford University Press).

————. (1957). *A Study of History: Abridgement of Volumes VII–X*, edited by D. C. Somervell (New York: Oxford University Press).

Ursu, J. (1908). *La Politique Orientale de Francois I, 1515–1547* (Paris).

Weber, M. (1930). *Protestant Ethic and the Spirit of Capitalism*, translated T. Parsons (New York: Scribner and Sons).

Weil, D. N. (2005). *Economic Growth* (Boston: Addison Wesley).

Wilkinson, D. (1980). *Deadly Quarrels: Lewis F. Richardson and the Statistical Study of War* (Berkeley: University of California Press).

Woods, F. A., and A. Baltzly. (1915). *Is War Diminishing? A Study of the Prevalence of War in Europe from 1450 to the Present Day* (Boston: Houghton Mifflin).

The World Factbook. (n.d.). (Washington, DC: Central Intelligence Agency). https://www.cia.gov/library/publications/the-world-factbook.

Wright, R. (2000). *Nonzero: The Logic of Human Destiny* (New York: Vintage Books).

———. (2009). *The Evolution of God* (New York: Little, Brown and Company).

Zinkeisen, J. W. (1854). *Drei Denkschriften uber die Orientalische Frage von Papst Leo X, Konig Franz I von Frankreich und Kaiser Maximilian I aus dem Jahre 1517.* (Gotha, Germany).

Index

The letter *f* following a page number denotes a figure and the letter *t* a table.